Complete
Contracting

D0617465

Other McGraw-Hill Books of Interest

Complete Contracting

A–Z Guide to Controlling Projects

Andrew Civitello, Jr.

RED ROCKS
COMMUNITY COLLEGE LIBRARY

McGraw-Hill

New York   San Francisco   Washington, D.C.   Auckland   Bogotá
Caracas   Lisbon   London   Madrid   Mexico City   Milan
Montreal   New Delhi   San Juan   Singapore
Sydney   Tokyo   Toronto

Library of Congress Cataloging-in-Publication Data

Civitello, Andrew.
    Complete contracting : A-Z guide to controlling projects / Andrew
Civitello, Jr.
        p.   cm.
    ISBN 0-07-011354-8 (acid-free paper)
    1. Building—Sueprintendence—Handbooks, manuals, etc.   I. Title.
TH438.C56   1996
692′.8—dc20   96-39020
                                                                          CIP

McGraw-Hill

*A Division of The **McGraw·Hill** Companies*

Copyright © 1997 by The McGraw-Hill Companies, Inc. All rights
reserved. Printed in the United States of America. Except as permitted
under the United States Copyright Act of 1976, no part of this publica-
tion may be reproduced or distributed in any form or by any means, or
stored in a data base or retrieval system, without the prior written permission of the publisher.

69090

1 2 3 4 5 6 7 8 9 0   DOC/DOC   9 0 1 0 9 8 7 6

#3565786 3   +H
                                                                    438
ISBN 0-07-011354-8
                                                                    . C56
The sponsoring editor for this book was Larry Hager, the editing   1997
supervisor was Peggy Lamb, and the production supervisor was Donald
F. Schmidt. It was set in Century Schoolbook by Estelita F. Green of
McGraw-Hill's Professional Book Group composition unit.

Printed and bound by R. R. Donnelley & Sons Company.

This book is printed on recycled, acid-free paper containing a minimum of 50% recycled, de-inked fiber.

McGraw-Hill books are available at special quantity discounts to use
as premiums and sales promotions, or for use in corporate training programs. For more information, please write to the Director of Special
Sales, McGraw-Hill, 11 West 19th Street, New York, NY 10011. Or contact your local bookstore.

Information contained in this work has been obtained by the
McGraw-Hill Companies, Inc. ("McGraw-Hill"), from sources
believed to be reliable. However, neither McGraw-Hill nor its
authors guarantee the accuracy or completeness of any information published herein and neither McGraw-Hill nor its
authors shall be responsible for any errors, omissions, or
damages arising out of use of this information. This work is
published with the understanding that McGraw-Hill and its
authors are supplying information, but are not attempting to
render engineering or other professional services. If such services are required, the assistance of an appropriate professional should be sought.

About the Author

Andrew Civitello, Jr. has managed construction projects of many sizes and types for clients that include local, state, and federal government agencies and departments, municipalities, banks, service organizations, and private developers.

A graduate of Syracuse University, he has been a project manager for major construction companies, and president of a Connecticut general contracting firm oriented to public projects. He is now an independent consultant for the disciplines of planning and scheduling, changes/claims, and project management for clients that include general contractors, subcontractors, attorneys, design professionals, and owners. He is an university instructor for project management subjects, an arbiter for the American Arbitration Association, and an expert witness for scheduling, estimating, and claims.

He is the author of *Construction Operations Manual of Policies and Procedures* (McGraw-Hill, 1994), *Contractor's Guide to Change Orders* (Prentice-Hall, 1987), *The Builder's and Contractor's Yearbook* (Prentice-Hall, 1987), *The Construction Manager* (Prentice-Hall, 1987 through current issue), *The Construction Operations Manual of Policies and Procedures* (Prentice-Hall, 1982), and co-author of *Construction Scheduling Simplified* (Prentice-Hall, 1985).

RED ROCKS
COMMUNITY COLLEGE LIBRARY

An Important Note

The discussions provided in *Complete Contracting* are not professional advice. Throughout this book are important examples of the way in which the respective issues are considered by the author, and the way that those situations have been handled by construction professionals. Many operations and responses can be handled precisely in the way presented, but many cannot or should not. It is important to be aware that laws vary across state lines and that trade practices differ depending upon the geographic location of your business and/or the jobsites. Beyond that, all operations boil down to your own business decisions regarding appropriate responses to complex situations. Before any action is taken with respect to any of situations treated in the book, the advice of a competent attorney should be sought.

Complete Contracting has been designed for fast reference by busy construction professionals. Your comments, questions, and suggestions regarding *Complete Contracting*, its information, and presentation are most welcome. They can be addressed to:

Complete Contracting
P.O. Box 190
Bethany, CT 06524

To Gail, Dan, Nick, Joe, Baby Girl, & Jac ... not necessarily in that order

Contents

Introduction

A contractor, its been said, is a gambler who never gets to cut, shuffle, or deal. Despite the fact that the building industry is the largest in the nation, we contractors get the least help in managing and developing our businesses. Graduation never seems to come from the school of trial-and-error.

You are the one who's signing off every day to all kinds of crazy terms, conditions, specifications, schedules, bonds, bids, guarantees, promises, commitments, and on and on. By the time Friday (or Saturday) afternoon arrives, the piles of paper on your two or three desks are different, to be sure, but no smaller. The one certainty is that throughout the day, things will routinely happen that will destroy the plans that you've carefully laid out for the next eight hours.

Every minute of each day, owners, architects, engineers, subcontractors, suppliers, and general contractors are all trying to make someone else (you?) responsible for *their* problems. Whoever isn't trying to leave you with the responsibility for their own professional liability think they're lawyers.

The industry has forced a perspective onto all of us that requires every issue to be dealt with on at least two levels:

1. Production efficiency and management effectiveness
2. Control of the tremendous liabilities that seem to increase exponentially each day

The AIA Document A201 General Conditions of the Contract has over *twenty* separate technical "notice" requirements. Its 1984 edition has a change clause that's roughly seven times longer than the one in the 1976 edition, and an arbitration clause combined with the other "dispute resolution" language that is about *twelve times larger*. The significant revisions made in the mid-1980s to the standard AIA documents that dramatically affect the entire industry did not seem to me to make anyone's (including design processionals') lives any easier. It seemed that no one ever said:

Let's identify the *common, recurring problems that continue to affect us all over and over on every project,* and see how we can approach the relationships to ease some of the pressures.

But instead took the approach of:

Let's throw more boilerplate at the same old problems, and try to cover our backs (and our tracks) with a little more confusion—and a lot more legal fees.

So, as we approach our construction business at these different levels, we find many books and seminars that are purportedly designed to help, but only a precious few really seem to be addressing our unique and complex problems with any reality.

On the other extreme are those books detailing "sophisticated" (overly complicated?) procedures that seem to be written more for those companies that are the size where their primary management concerns are more like "what do we do with this bureaucracy?" than "how do we keep our heads above water and everybody's hands out of our pockets?"

If you try to use these approaches without tempering them with a relevance to the way that you conduct *your* business, you risk implementing systems that may wind up existing for their own sake. Massive injections of overhead costs can place you into that distinct group of companies that have developed the dubious ability to lose their shirts under perfect control. Or to put it another way, you can procedure yourself out of business.

The truth is, neither side of the pendulum swing is acceptable:

1. Too simple a structure and not only will you lose profits from ineffective operations, but you will be taken advantage of by too many people who are only too willing to do so.

2. Too complex, and you'll swamp yourself with your own operations.

What we need, then, is a mechanism that takes thorough knowledge as it relates to the contractor, and boil its application down to fast, complete, time saving, and profit-preserving ways to get all the parts in place, while *reducing* the paperwork and follow-up problems that more "sophisticated" (complicted) systems invariably create.

Most important, all this has to be accomplished in a manner that ensures that this "mechanism" (the cure) does not become more difficult to live with than the problem.

Complete Contracting is the first combat guide and survival manual that addresses not only the entire range of critical, special, and rou-

tine issues facing contractors every day, but does so in the way contractors actually work. It will give you the most punch with the least
effort—in the shortest possible time.

It is an A–Z guide to hands-on contracting procedures, strategies,
tactics, techniques, and processes that detail the written and unwritten rules of each issue. Each topic is arranged in alphabetical order,
and is organized in a manner that will allow you to identify the issue
in seconds, and speed to the *relevant* working information in minutes.

The 90–10 Rule of Information

Most people are familiar with the "90–10 Rule" as it relates to purchasing: 90% of the goods and services are typically worth only 10% of
the total price, while 10% of the items are typically worth 90% of the
total price. This realization should give managers some idea of where
they should be spending their time.

Complete Contracting's "90–10 Rule of Information" states that:

- You can deliver 90% of the effectiveness with 10% of the management effort—*if
  you know where to get that information and how to direct that effort.*
- You can get to 90% of the *relevant information*—if you know were to look for it.
- It is likely to require 90% of the effort to get to 10% of the information—which
  may wind up being of marginal use.
- Its quite easy (and quite common) to get only 10% of the effectiveness after having spent 90% of the effort—if you *don't* do it right.

Most books written for contractors are in conventional formats with
large amounts of rambling discussion. Reading through the entire
book represents the 90% effort. Even if you manage to steal enough
time to actually get through the whole thing, a great amount is likely
to be lost by the time you need to use the information. If you need to
research through the book to help solve an immediate need, you'll
have to sift through the whole thing, correlating related topics if such
an effort will be at all possible. Time consuming indeed.

Allowing for normal retention rates, peppered with the distractions
caused by the regular work week, the result is that you might come
away with one or two ideas that might get a shot at implementation—that 10%. If 100% of the information wasn't available in the
first place, the odds of accomplishing even that diminish accordingly.

The other big time waster is that if 150 or 200% of the desired type
of information turns out to be actually there, put there by an author
who is correctly concerned with comprehensive treatment, you'll need
to wade through all the extra material to determine its relevance (or
lack of) to your immediate interest.

Complete Contracting is the first tool of its kind that will give you the ability to get at that 90% of the real information with 10% (or much less) of the effort.

It does so *at the moment of implementation*; thereby preserving the material's original effectiveness.

From that point, if you need or want more, the individual sections contain directories of related topics, and highlights cross referenced topics right in the text. Your additional research will be accomplished within just a few additional minutes.

These advantages won't just "preserve" your profits—they will help you to create *new* profits as well—by helping you to get and keep *control* over the new and the same old problems.

Each method is time tested, and are being used successfully by contractors across the country. Each has survived the acid tests of effectiveness *and* efficiency. Bureaucratic procedures that add overhead but no muscle are squeezed out.

If we contractors won't be able to cut, shuffle, or deal, *Complete Contracting* will become your ace-in-the-hole that will give you the edge in handling every situation as it comes up.

What This Book Will Do for You

Complete Contracting is the first guerrilla warfare guide and survival manual for construction professionals.

Literally an A–Z guide, *Complete Contracting* is a comprehensive manual that details the written—*and unwritten*—rules of every important subject affecting today's contractors. The discussions are direct, frank, and designed to allow time-squeezed contractors to get to the right information, when it is needed—in time to make sure that every advantage is taken of every situation.

Each topic is arranged in alphabetical order, for a fast-tracked approach. Each discussion is a fresh look from a different angle—through a contractor's eyes with a view toward how theories "really" work.

The format is designed for:

- Immediate identification
- Fast research
- Quick correllation to related information

Features of the Format

Each section begins with a short Contents or Topic Outline.

- It takes only a few seconds to skim through the outline to get the complete overview of the subject and its treatment. You will instantly be able to determine for yourself the applicability of the material to your immediate problem.

Immediately adjacent to the Contents is the "Related Topics" list.

- If the *Contents* confirms to you that the material is on target (the 90%), the *"Related Topics* list will direct you immediately to the supplemental information if you wish to pursue that material.

- If the *Contents* confirms that the particular section is for whatever reason not what you're really looking for, the "Related Topics" list will get you to where you need to go in the shortest possible time.

The subject is described in concise, but comprehensive detail.

- Almost in outline format, you'll be able to speed through the material to grasp all the important points fast.

- The most important points are emphasized, and where appropriate, examples are given for clarity.

Key words appearing in the text that apply to related sections are highlighted in boldface directly in the text.

- Seeing the related information used in the context of the current section will immediately and intuitively clarify its relationship with the current material.

- Seeing the boldface word is immediate indication that a related section exists. Simply flip to the alphabetical section to get right into progressive detail—as *you* determine your need.

If additional material is desired after reviewing any complete section, simply follow the cross references identified in the "Related Topics" list and highlighted in boldface directly in the text. Within seconds, you will have steered yourself directly to the most high powered material available, and have tailored it to your specific requirements—and you will have done all this while steering yourself around inappropriate articles, saving valuable time and energy.

The opening *Contents* will remain to provide a summary for quick future reference, complete review, and on-the-spot refresher in recurring circumstances, such as job meetings, change order proposal submission, and so on.

Complete Contracting Offers:

√ *An Accelerated Management Development Program*

- Consistently thought provoking, the book gives hundreds of field-tested and proven ideas, methods, strategies, tactics, and techniques that will contribute fundamentally to your personal success and to the success of your company now and for years to come.

- Every important topic is included, and every significant issue within those topics is exposed. The book will become your personalized professional development program, tailored to the areas of the contracting business that you are most concerned with now. It will grow with you, increasing in value to you by continuing to provide important guidance as your own experiences and responsibilities broaden.

√ *Step-by-Step Instruction*

- Short, readable, to-the-point outlines and discussions are laid out in a reference format to guarantee that you'll be able to locate any subject and all related components within a few seconds. Procedure and direct attention are described in explicit, instantly useful detail to take you cleanly and logically through the subject's applications—the first time.
- You'll read all the important points and their implementation within just a few minutes. Explanations are illustrated with real life examples that contractors will readily identify with.

√ *A Fresh, Unique Perspective*

- The information is provided authoritatively, but also from a perspective that is often different from those of most writers on the subject. A recognized expert in the areas of contracting project management, contracts, scheduling, claims, negotiation, and changes, the author's perspective is based on how situations *really* work in real-world contracting and business situations.

√ *On-the-Spot Reference Guide*

- Reading the book cover to cover will expose new ideas as well as present new perspectives for more familiar concepts. But don't stop there. Designed for fast reference at the point of need, you'll be able to find what you need in seconds, and assimilate the complete material within minutes.
- Do *not* put the book on shelf. Keep it with you at all times, and immediately refer to it *before* beginning anything that you were just about to tackle. Before stepping into the field office for the next job meeting, read the section on "job meetings." Before completing that next change order proposal, or even writing your next letter, refer to those pertinent sections. And so on. Keep it with you in the office, and take it with you on the road. Have copies available for your key managers and supervisors, and watch your company immediately benefit through the consistent and professional treatment of all contracting business situations.

Consistent use of the material in this book will help you to develop that rare ability to detach one's self from the obvious constructs of a problem, and, like a chess master, view the entire game board so each decision is made in full consideration of all variables and possible scenarios. Your actions will be made from a superior perspective—in complete anticipation of the next move or sequence of moves. It will put your future (and not your past) into the driver's seat.

Complete Contracting is unique in its ability to be implemented.

It will give you the fastest way to increase productivity, job satisfaction, personal achievement, and profits. This is not just "theory." It is a compilation of powerful management methods that are already producing very real results. Use them because they work.

Andrew Civitello, Jr.

Complete
Contracting

Acceleration

Concept

"Acceleration" is a condition in which, through circumstances beyond your control, you are forced to speed up at least certain portions of the work at the expense of efficiency and cost control. Reasons often include an owner's refusal to accept a proposed extension of time, or a practical time constraint otherwise required by the progress schedule.

Acceleration can take the forms of overstaffing activity to the point where workers are stepping over each other, adding too much equipment in a confined area, using available (but not the most efficient) equipment, working overtime and/or additional shifts, or some combination of all these things.

In the manufacturing world, there are often generally accepted efficiency losses and extra costs associated with additional shifts. In a particular industry, for example, it may be commonly accepted that an identically staffed and equipped second shift produces half or two-thirds (or whatever) of the production of the first shift. In these cases, it becomes much easier to establish the extra costs associated with the reduced efficiency of such additional shifts.

Maintain Records

But contracting and its trades don't fit such rules very neatly and without challenge. It is therefore absolutely essential that accurate records be maintained throughout every period of definite or even possible acceleration. Such records can include:

- **Daily field report**
- **Time and material (T&M)** tickets
- Payroll records
- Labor distribution records
- **Photographs (preconstruction, progress,** and **special); Video, preconstruction**
- **Scheduling** progress reports

Action Steps

When you feel for whatever reason that you are being forced into an acceleration:

1. Review the contract for applicable provisions and technical requirements, and adhere to them as closely as possible. Pay particular attention to **notice** requirements.

2. Notify the responsible party (presumably the Owner) by certified mail/return receipt requested and by fax that you:
   - Are being forced (or directed) into acceleration
   - Will experience additional costs as a result
   - Will keep track of all added costs
   - Will submit such added costs for reimbursement
   - Reserve all rights to claim damages resulting from these and any other effects that are unforeseen at this time

3. Keep complete, accurate, and detailed records *as the work progresses*. Take photos and videos. Be sure that the **daily field report** and applicable **time and material** tickets are current and complete.

4. Include the details of all effects in the progress schedule update and its analysis/report.

5. When all costs are known, submit the invoice for the documented added costs as you had notified. Do not let time go by unnecessarily. Finish the issue while it is fresh.

Acceptance Time

Concept

It takes time to get used to new ideas. People like to think they're smart. Simply allowing time gives people a chance to rationalize a decision—to come up with their own reasons why it's not such a bad deal.

Time:

- Enhances the impression that your position is legitimate. (See **concessions.**) Positions given in on too easily will have greatly diminished value in the mind of your opponent. People simply do not appreciate anything that they get too easily.

- Allows people to "soak" on a previous real or tentative concession. Dropping $5000 on a price to the "bottom line," for example, will *be* the bottom line if the deal is finalized now—but it may not be the bottom line next week, after the concept soaked for a while.

- Allows new facts, ideas, and viewpoints to surface.

- Gives room to allow others to convince the rest of their organization that the deal isn't so bad.

- Allows others to come up with their own face-saving mechanisms.

- Can add credibility to the idea that you're spending time shopping and/or negotiating with others. After time has passed, for example, you're only able to "confirm" the legitimacy of your original position to your opponent.

Action

1. Unless there is an extremely pressing reason, try to allow as much time as possible in your negotiation for acceptance time. Later is better than now.

2. Use the time to "lobby" your opponent. Try to find as many subtle ways as possible to spread information that will help various members of your opponent's organization to rationalize *your* position.

Adhesion Contracts

Description

An adhesion contract is a take-it-or-leave-it proposition. It is a contract that has been prepared completely by one party and presented for complete acceptance by the other, and gives no opportunity to negotiate. All public bids and contracts are adhesion, and the concept can also apply to specific clauses within other contracts that are simply not available to any negotiation. It is the adhesion nature of a contract which will make both **ambiguities** and right-to-choose apply cleanly.

The law provides that if a contract term is ambiguous or otherwise unclear, then the clause in question will be construed against the party who drafted the provision. In addition, if a contract term or provision is subject to more than one "reasonable" **interpretation,** the party who did not draft the contract has the "right" to choose the interpretation. In such a case, the interpretation need not be the *most* reasonable, but simply be *reasonable.*

The reasons for these provisions include the idea that those who draft contracts have (or should have) a clear idea of their intent and have had every opportunity to make their intentions clear. Therefore, if a provision is not clear, the party who did not draft the contract or provision should not be penalized.

The reason that these provisions apply only in the case of adhesion contracts is that any negotiated term is essentially drafted by both parties. In **negotiation**, both have had an opportunity to provide for their intent and to clarify the description, and so neither party should have an advantage over the other in the interpretation of the provision.

Advantages and Disadvantages

There is nothing inherently "wrong" with an adhesion contract. Although "negotiable" contracts may give opportunity to reach more even-handed provisions between parties who genuinely wish to arrive at an equitable contract, a serious problem with most negotiable contracts is that too often one party has a significant upper hand as a practical matter over the other during the contract negotiation phase. In such a case, one party may wind up begrudgingly agreeing to certain terms and conditions strictly so that a deal is not lost entirely.

The serious risk in these situations is that such a contract has in fact been "negotiated." As such, **ambiguities** will no longer be resolved against the drafter, because both parties together are the drafter. Similarly, the right to choose the **interpretation** will not automatically be given to one party or the other.

Accordingly, it may ironically turn out that an adhesion contract or provision may be preferable to one that has been unacceptingly negotiated. In such a case, at least the rules regarding ambiguities and interpretation would sift out more squarely in the hands of the party who did not draft the deal. This fact alone can often put hope back into the equitable resolution of an otherwise formidable problem.

Agenda

Concept

Agendas are very often underestimated and overlooked in terms of their importance in negotiations. If you formulate and control the agenda, you will *control the timing and content* of all discussions. You will also control what will, and perhaps more important, will not be said.

Agendas can:

- Clarify or hide real objectives
- Force quick decisions
- Restrict discussions or permit digressions
- Establish firm timetables or allow open ends
- Directly guide actions toward problem resolution in the shortest possible time or procrastinate actions and decisions

Regular **job meetings** should have prearranged agendas in the form of "old business" and a fairly standard format for new items. Even there, however, the agendas of the individual items can still be controlled. The agendas of special meetings are subject to even more manipulation.

Action Rules

The action rules that follow can be conducted as clear, distinct steps as they appear in the case of larger or special issues. Each step, however, is still a part of the process of approaching every issue at every regular or special meeting, however formally or informally applied.

1. *Confirm attendance prior to any meeting.* If specific individuals are required to resolve any issue, make sure that they are present.
2. *Think through the entire problem resolution process.* List each step, along with the corresponding people necessary to settle it. Catalog the specific actions necessary by each individual, along

with the earliest and latest acceptable dates for their actions. This catalog will become your agenda.

3. Be sure that you are thoroughly prepared to discuss every issue and subissue.
   - Have complete information.
   - Have your presentation package finalized.
   - List every conceivable objection, along with its corresponding answer.
   - Practice; know all the bases, and be able to cover them spontaneously.

4. If you cannot be completely prepared for any reason, use whatever means possible to adjust your agenda accordingly. Put resolution of the issue off until you *can* be prepared.

5. Prior to the meeting, notify all expected participants of *your* specific agenda. This removes excuses on their parts that they do not have the appropriate people available, have not secured required information, or are not otherwise prepared to discuss and *resolve* the issue.

6. Include the expectation of problem *resolution* in your agenda notification.

7. Be aware of other people's efforts to control or divert your agenda. Be prepared to force corrections.

8. Have good reasons for forcing compliance at the meeting with the prearranged agenda. Know and be believable with your own excuses for *not* discussing items that are not on the planned list:
   - Key or affected people are not available.
   - There's limited time available to cover the prearranged items; the new items must be tabled for another time.
   - Use "I don't know" if you need to. Nobody can insist that you *must* "know."
   - You have every right to be unprepared for "surprises" (whether you're prepared or not).
   - Never discuss any item unless you're fully prepared to do so.

Agent Construction Management (ACM)

Contract Relationships

Construction management (CM) means many different things to many different people. In terms of function, every contractor has been a "construction manager" at least to a degree, largely through the performance of the administrative aspects of the contracting. As the term is being used here, functions and services performed on a specific assignment can vary as defined in the particular construction management agreement. By design, they will be carried out by the CM firm on behalf of the owner.

The agent construction manager is said to be "not at risk." This is because the agent CM does not contract directly with any members of the construction force, which operates essentially as the owner's staff. The owner contracts directly with the Agent Construction Management (ACM) firm in order to provide the distinct services in a consultant capacity. There is direct *contact* between the ACM and the trade contractors of the construction force in much the same way as a general contractor would interact with its subcontractors; but there is no direct *contract* between the ACM and those trade contractors. Refer to **contract versus contact** for important related discussion.

In this arrangement, there is no direct liability borne by the ACM for the performance or nonperformance of those trade contractors. Each of the individual trade contractors is in effect a separate general contractor, contracting directly with the owner.

Communications

Communications in the ACM arrangement operate essentially identically to those of the **general contracting** arrangement. Trade contractors communicate directly with the ACM, who interfaces with the design professionals just as a general contractor would. Communication between the ACM and the owner is again very similar to that between general contractor and the owner on construction-related matters, but because the ACM is often also involved in design coordination, the ACM will be privy to that process as well.

Advantages and Disadvantages

The ACM project delivery method is usually selected because the owner values the input of construction experience as early as possible in the concept stage in order to improve the construction efficiency of the ultimate design. If this aspect of the ACM is performed effectively, the owner might ultimately obtain the same function while actually reducing the facility costs because *constructibility* is a primary consideration during the design development process. Better knowledge of local construction sequences, for instance, may reduce time, thereby saving everyone money. An owner may benefit from a contractor's superior working knowledge of sensible ways to format bid packages as well. This kind of assistance can make it easier to deal with trades not only during construction, but through callbacks and guarantee work.

Another reason for the selection of the ACM method is to provide a capability for "fast-tracking" the construction sequence without losing control over the individual trade contact structures. In a fast-track environment, certain portions of the work can be bid, awarded, and begun at the site well before the entire facility design is complete. The foundation work can start while the structural steel and the curtain wall designs are being finalized, or interior partitions can begin before the final wall finishes are selected in total. These individual bid packages are managed and policed by the construction manager as their respective designs become finalized.

With ACM on a fee basis, additional cost borne by the trade contractors as a result of subsequent changes to previously completed designs are passed back to the owner through the ACM.

The primary reason why the owner would consider agent construction management as opposed to **construction management with a guaranteed maximum price** is to remove any possibility of conflict of interest between the construction manager's management responsibilities and construction profit motives. With the right ACM, the professional fee paid for the service can be a significant bargain for the owner.

Refer to **construction management with guaranteed maximum price** for important related discussion.

Agreements versus Understandings

Handshake Deals

It is almost impossible to have a conversation of any length about construction without someone lamenting over the idea that handshake deals at one time were sufficient to do business, whereas now long, excruciating contract negotiations are necessary even for the simplest deal. The idea is usually regarded as a slur on the integrity of the individuals involved in the contemporary deal.

To put things in proper perspective, however, assume at the outset absolute integrity on the part of both parties to the deal. The problem actually begins because, in the handshake deal, effort has not been put into a precise description of the actual work product, including expected levels of quality. The first point of departure can therefore be nothing more than an idea. Your idea of doing a good job may not be the same as my idea of doing a good job. We both intend to be dealing with a good job, but we are dealing from two fundamentally different positions.

The problem is compounded when we both hand our handshake deal to two other individuals to implement it—your designer and my superintendent. Just like you and me, both of these individuals genuinely intend to do a good job. The difficulty, however, is that those two individuals have two (more) distinct ideas of what a good job actually is.

And so even before the first shovel hits the ground, we begin the project essentially with a minimum of four ideas of what a good job is going to look like. We all genuinely intend to do one, but there is really little hope of getting there from here—even when all parties to the deal have absolute integrity and honest intentions. Add to the mix some combination of mistakes, face-saving, and even questionable intent, and it becomes easier to see how a deal that has not been very clearly defined in writing has a plummeting possibility of making anyone happy.

Gentlemen's Agreements

Gentlemen's agreements are versions of the handshake deal. In addition to the concerns described above, consider adding the possibility that one or both parties to the original deal may at some point be removed from this scene before the deal has a chance to be completed. People get shifted to other areas of their organizations, get promoted, get fired, go back on a deal, and even genuinely remember things very clearly—but very differently than you very clearly remember them. Again, get it in writing.

Ambiguities

Related Topics

Adhesion Contracts

Coordination

Duty to Inquire

Interpretation—Right to Choose

Latent Defects

Patent Errors

Trade Practice

Concept

An ambiguity is anything that is unclear. It can be a conflict, inconsistency, error, omitted information, or confusing redundancy.

- An item may be placed into two specification sections, or into none at all.
- A plan reference may have no specification counterpart (or vice versa).
- The specification for a complete component of work may be divided among multiple bid packages or specification sections.
- The specific manner or procedure to physically complete the details is left out.
- The manner specifically indicated may be in conflict with established **trade practice.**

In order for there to be an ambiguity, there must be more than one way to complete the item contemplated or more than one way to reasonably interpret a contract provision. The specifier may interpret a provision in a way that embellishes the contract, while the competitive bidder may have anticipated completing the item in a way that satisfies the technical requirement only.

Resolved against the Drafter

It is understood that the persons or parties who draft contracts have (*should* have) a clear idea of their own intent. The law considers that such parties have had every opportunity to be certain that those intentions are defined clearly enough to allow reasonable people, competent in their profession, to understand those intentions.

The law (and common sense) further assumes that those people responsible for drafting contracts provide for their own interest, and will have reason to be aware of uncertainties. The owner and architect, for example, many have had a year or more to be sure that the contract documents are clear and complete. If they, through all that time and effort, were not able to produce a clear set of instructions that are subject to only one interpretation, it is not reasonable to expect a contractor (or any other person) to find flaws in the typically short time prior to bid.

The rules for resolving ambiguities are very similar to those for **interpretation** of other contract matters. In the case of **adhesion contracts**—those contracts presented in a take-it-or-leave-it manner—ambiguities are *resolved against the party who drafted the document.*

The only requirement for this outcome is that your interpretation of the situation be reasonable. It does not even need to be the most reasonable—or even more reasonable than other interpretations. Finally, once it can be demonstrated that such a reasonable solution is available, there is no duty on the part of the contractor to continue to search for other reasonable solutions that may or may not exist. After all, the contractor's duty is **coordination** of the requirements of the contract, not routinely performing a complete search of documents.

"Approved" versus "No Exceptions Taken"

Description

In most construction contracts, the contractor is required to receive submittals from its subcontractors, review and *approve* them, and submit the item to the design professionals for their "approval" before the item can be incorporated into the work. Furthermore, the design agreement between the owner and design professional may also specifically provide that the designer "review and approve or take other such appropriate action on contractor's submittals."

Throughout all of this, the word *approved* has been consistently defined throughout the industry as a clear indication that the design professional is authorizing the use of the subject item for incorporation into the work.

The Problem

The problem begins when the contractor who follows the correct procedure receives back from the design professional a stamp bearing language other than the word *approved.* Phrases like *no exceptions taken, reviewed,* and, my favorite, *not rejected* have done much more than simply crept their way into construction language.

The problem seems to have started when professional liability insurance companies realized that there was too much legal precedence surrounding the word *approved.* These insurance companies one by one began to require that a designer remove the word *approved* from the shop drawing stamps as a condition of the professional liability insurance. Since that point, the contracting environment has developed so much concern over so many types of liabilities that the word or anything like it has long since completely disappeared from designers' vocabulary.

What all this means is that after performing due diligence regarding submittal and approval, the contractor goes ahead, orders material, and installs work without having any documents that bear the contractually specified language actually authorizing incorporation of the item into the work. Accordingly, it has been interpreted in too many cases that the contractor has never actually received authorization to proceed. Bizarre, but true.

Resolution

At the outset, understand that because of the involvement of the professional liability insurance companies, design professionals may actually risk losing their professional liability coverage if they alter the language on their stamps—even if they have executed an agreement with the owner to do so. Because of this, any efforts that you put forth genuinely expecting the language to be modified are likely, as a practical matter, to be futile—like beating your head against the proverbial rock.

Instead, focus your energy on displaying the several contract requirements between the contractor and the owner that provide that the design professional will *approve* your submittals. When the debate ensues, simply point out that all you are after is a clear confirmation from the owner/design professional of the language required on a submittal *to expressly authorize the contractor to incorporate the respective item into the work.*

Having so confirmed the understanding, you will have adequately addressed the issue without trying to force the design professional to have a contest with his or her own professional liability insurance carrier.

Arbitration

Description

Arbitration is a **dispute resolution** procedure common to the construction industry. It is the voluntary submission of a dispute to an impartial third party for decision. The decision by an arbitrator (or arbiter) is referred to as an *award.* Depending on the size and complexity of the case, there may be a single arbiter, a three-member panel (a "tribunal"), or some other special arrangement. The arbiter or arbiters may be attorneys, retired judges, or other professionals engaged in the industry.

Originally intended to be quicker, easier, less formal, more direct, and more responsive to the details of an industry-specific dispute than litigation, the arbitration process has undergone developments throughout the recent years that are important to understand before it is ultimately selected as your dispute-resolution mechanism.

A fundamental basis for arbitration is the idea that the arbiter is a person with relevant knowledge and experience in the specific field. He or she is therefore more likely to quickly understand the nature of the dispute and determine its significance. In contrast, a naive jury would otherwise need to be instructed in the basics and background of even the simplest issues within a case. This is also the major premise for the more relaxed rules of evidence, as discussed below.

Arbitration can be agreed to and conducted in accordance with the standards and rules of an official managing body such as the American Arbitration Association or can be determined according to whatever set of completely prescribed rules the parties mutually agree to.

Arbitration is most often referred to as *binding arbitration,* because the agreement to arbitrate will normally provide that the arbitration award will be final and binding on the parties and entirely enforceable in a court of law.

Agreement to Arbitrate

The first requirement of arbitration is that there be an *agreement to arbitrate*. This agreement can be in the form of a preexisting clause in your contract or can be agreed to between the disputing parties at virtually any time—before commencing with the dispute resolution or even after a more conventional litigation has started.

An example of such an agreement is as follows:

> Any dispute arising out of the performance of the work of this contract shall be subject to arbitration in accordance with the Construction Industry Rules of the American Arbitration Association currently in effect.

The agreement can go on to specify the location of the arbitration, can narrow the types of disputes that will be subject to arbitration, and can even describe special conditions or provisions that must be satisfied before arbitration can proceed. As a practical matter, however, the odds of achieving an agreement to arbitrate after the original contract is executed—and after a dispute has reared its head—is very low. This is because the differences between arbitration and litigation will likely be significant, depending on the facts of the particular case.

For example, if the dispute is over payment, the payee might prefer arbitration because the case can be presented relatively quickly; whereas the payer may prefer litigation because the court calendar may push the date off literally for years.

If the case is heavily supported by **trade practice,** that party may prefer arbitration in front of a professional panel. If a case is based on a strict, literal interpretation of the legal word, litigation may be the venue of choice.

What all this means is simply that every case will be better for one party than the other in either arbitration or litigation. It logically follows, then, that if one party decides that it would prefer arbitration, the other would not.

For these reasons, if you do not already have an agreement to arbitrate in place in your agreement, don't get your hopes up for one later.

Arbitrators and Arbitrator Selection

Arbitrators in a construction dispute are usually professionals actively engaged in the field. They can be lawyers or retired judges, but are also likely to be selected from among contractors, subcontractors, design professionals, and special consultants.

The idea is simply that these individuals have specialized knowledge and expertise in the field, and are therefore more quick to understand the nature of the dispute and the significance of the specific claim than would a naive jury that would otherwise need to be instructed and "trained" in the basics and background of even the simplest issues and definitions of common terms within a case. The arbitrators presumably have enough skill and *relevant* experience that would allow them to determine the significance of issues (or lack thereof), the credibility of "facts," and the weight that should be given to certain evidence.

As an example: In an arbitration being heard by construction professionals, the word *retainage* will probably be used in context in a sentence leading to a point. It will be intuitive, direct, and wastes no time. In a litigation, however, it is more likely that the concept of retainage will need to be described, evidence put on, and testimony presented in order to describe how it works, and even to convince the jury that it is a legitimate concept.

The logical development of whatever point you were trying to lead to gets temporarily derailed, time gets wasted dealing with the most mundane of details, and the jury's attention gets repeatedly distracted—you haven't even gotten to the point yet.

The arbitrator selection process should be prescribed in the agreement to arbitrate. If the case is placed under the jurisdiction of some authority such as the American Arbitration Association, the selection process is detailed in their set of rules placed into effect. In agreements providing for some other system, the procedure must be spelled out in detail. For example, an agreement might specify that each party select an arbitrator and that those two arbitrators agree on a third arbitrator.

There are a great many practical, technical, and strategic considerations that can go into your determination of the best arbitrators for your case. The selections should accordingly be made under the advice of those experienced in the process.

Treatment of Evidence

Because of the assumption that the arbitrators have a certain amount of sophistication about construction agreements, rules of evidence are greatly relaxed. In court, the jury is considered naive, and it is "protected" from considering evidence that it "should not" consider.

In arbitration, the arbitrators are assumed to have enough relevant knowledge—indeed, that is presumably the reason they were selected as arbitrators in the first place—so they have the ability to give appropriate weight to any potential evidence.

"Binding" Arbitration

Generally, arbitration decisions are upheld by the courts in those cases where there was a proper agreement to arbitrate, and correct procedure has been followed. An arbitration award may, however, be subject to appeal under certain circumstances. Generally, these circumstances might include those instances where it can be demonstrated and proved that one or more arbitrators:

1. Has some undisclosed relationship with either party or its attorney
2. Is biased
3. Refuses to accept or consider relevant evidence

As-Built Documents

Related Topics

Contract Documents

Documentation

"Equals" and "Substitutions"

Definition

If defined by an attorney or claims consultant, as-built documents embody the record of all contemporaneous project information as it occurred. It would include such things as field reports, time sheets, diaries, correspondence, photographs, and all other types of project **documentation.**

As-built documents, as we refer to them here, however, specifically refer to a record copy of the contract documents—primarily the plans and specifications—which will be used as the medium to record all physical changes to the work.

Contract requirements vary greatly in their specified as-built criteria, but almost every contract will have some kind of as-built requirement. In the past, owners and design professionals were not as insistent on maintaining significant levels of detail on the as-builts, but that has all changed. It is now common for an as-built requirement to provide that the contractor must update all as-built information such as changes, modifications, and actual dimensions of field-installed items. Beyond the absolute requirement, contracts are specifying that contractors must complete as-built information on some periodic basis as an express condition of payment. Such time periods might be monthly, but may be weekly or even daily.

New Importance

As-built documents have assumed a new prominence in their level of importance to design professionals and owners. You will be wise to assume at the onset that you will be held to the letter of the requirement. It will be correspondingly wise to require such identical compliance as an express condition of payment in your respective subcontracts. Refer to the **pass-through clause** for important related discussion.

Subcontract Requirements

Your subcontract requirements should include at a minimum that the subcontractor update on a daily basis in a form acceptable to you all as-built information at least as specifically required by your contract with the owner. In order to provide for those conditions where your owner-contractor may be vague with respect to as-built requirements, your standard subcontract should provide at a minimum that the subcontractor as-builts include accurate engineered dimensions to be transposed on the contractor's field and as-built sets of documents and that the subcontractor certify such information when requested to do so by you. The information should include all connection points, alignments, dimensions, horizontal and vertical control information, **"equals" and "substitutions,"** deviations, and changes of any kind whatsoever.

Enforce the discipline of maintenance of your as-built **documentation** by your subcontractors by emphasizing that the as-builts really *are* an express condition of payment. Use your first payment as your opportunity to clarify to all your subvendors that you take the requirement seriously. You might, for example, advise them that their check is ready, waiting to be picked up, if they bring their completed, acceptable as-builts with them.

Get your subvendors into the routine early, and you might be surprised at the quality of information you will have at your disposal at the end of the project.

As Indicated

Contents

Design Coordination

Corrective Measures

Related Topics

Coordination

Cut-and-Paste

Defective Specifications

"Intent" versus "Indication"

Match Lines

Old Age (Specifications)

RFI (Request for Information)

Strange Specifications

Design Coordination

The "as-indicated" or "see specs" types of notes found on a set of contract drawings might be an early warning that comprehensive attention had not necessarily been given to the coordination of the design documents during their development. They might more accurately be an indicator of one design professional's *assumption* that some other member of the design team—or another design office—had completed the coordination and actually accounted for the detail that the note anticipates. The supporting details might have been assumed to be completed only because they were *supposed* to be completed. Other telltale phrases similarly point to a possible lack of design follow-up. Examples include: *as shown, see structural, see architectural,* and *see plans.* Ultimately, the problem may be one of degree. One or a few such remarks may not be cause for concern; however, if such an approach appears to be more the method than the exception, it might be wise to approach those documents with the idea that there is a strong possibility that the designers did not properly and methodically coordinate the completion of design details. In other words, the plans may be in much worse shape than they might initially appear.

In contrast, an indication that the design coordination process has been done more completely is the regular presence of precise references. Examples include remarks such as "see 3/S-5" instead of "see structural," or "see section 04220" instead of "see specs." The presence of these kinds of remarks is a sign that someone did cross-check the documents to be sure that the respective completing details actually do exist.

Corrective Measures

The presence of vague or specific remarks should be a very clear indication of the overall level of care that has gone into the preparation of your documents. Develop the habit of identifying the situation early, and of taking proactive steps to tighten up on the specific questionable notes and identifying resulting problems before they impact your project.

Review each plan included in the **contract documents.** First identify every vague cross-reference that exists. Mark each with a highlighter. Look for notes such as "as indicated," "as shown," "see plans," or "see specs." Rather than allow them to impact your job one at a time as those respective details become needed, take the time to research each one of them. It's really a very straightforward matter that can easily be handled by **delegation.** Follow up on each note, and either find the completing detail that confirms that it really does exist, or confirm now that it does not.

Catalogue each incomplete, conflicting, or missing reference. Arrange each one on a priority basis. Consider each missing detail as a potential change to be either addressed individually or grouped together. Use your **RFI (request for information)** form to refer to your catalogue of missing or questionable information, and request specific direction for each item.

Attorneys

The Right Stuff

Fifty percent of all attorneys are in the bottom half of their classes. A dilemma faced by construction professionals each day begins with the idea that our construction contracts are complicated, confusing, cryptic, corroborated constructions of contract clauses that are designed to shift the risk from one party (typically the owner) to another party (typically the contractor). As businesspeople, we still try to approach our construction agreements almost naively with the idea that we will just be able to build a project, make a profit, and move on. But while we try to remain focused on the business, the business environment is forcing us more and more to get our business advice from attorneys. Therein lies the fundamental flaw of the construction industry.

Over the last 20 years, it seems that no one has said "Let's look at the same relationships that have perpetuated essentially intact project after project and design our interactions so that we can all collectively achieve the genuine project objectives." Instead we take the approach of "Let's use all our creativity and experience to come up with more complicated, cryptic, and confusing statements that will throw more **boilerplate** between us and the problem. Let's cover the issue with as much smoke as we can in order to confuse the process."

And so the fact of life is that attorneys have become a conventional part of the construction process. Our new challenge in this regard is no longer how to keep attorneys out of the process, but how to control the input of attorneys along a narrowly defined set of responsibilities, and to keep the attorneys from turning a possible problem into a self-fulfilling prophecy. Refer to **experts** for important related discussion.

Types of Attorneys

Attorneys fall into several categories. The first distinction is made between litigating and nonlitigating attorneys. Nonlitigating attorneys are not fighters. They are will writers, estate arrangers, real estate researchers, form filers, and audit managers. They make sure I's are dotted, and T's are crossed, that the paperwork is researched and that the documents are completed properly. They fulfill important functions, and their roles in many aspects of our business transactions are critical.

The litigating attorney may, however, be the one who is more interested in working with you and developing strategy, conducting tough negotiations, and ultimately preparing and presenting a case in court or arbitration. These are the attorneys who, if they are any good, have an instinct for the kill and a love of the fight.

Litigating attorneys fall into two categories: lions and fat cats. Both types have their best use, advantages, and disadvantages, depending on who you are and how you intend to use their services.

The Lions

The lions are generally young (but not too young) and extremely aggressive. They enjoy the fight for the fight's sake and will work incessantly to find the new angle, discover the different approach, and find the key (but often overlooked) information that will sway a decision. They think they're smart enough and mean enough to kill anything in the jungle. They're not overly preoccupied with muscle-bound opponents and can, therefore, confine their attention to guerilla-warfare tactics necessary to work around even the most formidable opponent. The lions will generally be found in a small law firm, or practicing alone. This is not only because partners in a large firm know that they would have to keep an eye on them too, but also because their own drive, initiative, and need for power lead them to control their own situation. They're in control of themselves and don't need the security of a large organization.

The lions have at least a few battle scars, but probably much more battle experience than you would otherwise expect of persons of that age. They know the ropes; they're not just out of law school. Their successful track records have resulted in a string of good contacts, from powerful clients to other professionals and consultants of similar high caliber.

The Fat Cats

The fat cats are generally senior partners in well-known firms who know everyone. They have arrived. They may have power and influence and be able to steer you to contacts. If you are big yourself, the fat cats can be powerful associates who can place a wealth of resources at your disposal. If, however, you are small and the fat cat's law firm "accepts" your business, you'll end up dealing with a junior partner. Your work will be done by paralegals and clerks. The lion hired by your opponent will eat you alive.

Finding Your Lion

Finding your lion may not be easy, but the time and effort (and even expense) may very well be the best long-term investment that you'll make for yourself and your company.

- *Ask respected professionals and consultants.* If you've ever been to court or arbitration you may have seen impressive witnesses, experts, and consultants. Their experiences along the way have probably exposed them to competent and incompetent attorneys. Their suggestions may become an important starting point.

- *Ask nonlitigating attorneys.* If you're pleased with your existing relationship with your present attorney—perhaps one who incorporated your business or has done other legal services for you—and that person has been honest enough to acknowledge that construction law is a specialty that demands a specialist, consider that person's suggestions.

- *Find business associates who have had successful experiences.* Their experiences may or may not have relevance to the particular kind of dispute that you are facing, but a fighter is a fighter. Get some names.

- *Watch local elections.* If any attorneys are running for office, they are lions. It might be smart to give one a hand. If the candidate loses, you end up with a good attorney. If the candidate wins, you have a powerful ally, plus a source of excellent recommendations for good attorneys.

- *Observe performances.* If possible, find out when a few of the attorneys whom you follow will be operating in actual court cases. Go sit in the courtroom for a while and watch them in action. Observe how they conduct themselves, how they lead the team, and how well they seem to be prepared. Observe how well their actions are received and responded to by the court. Go with your feelings.

- *Do not "ask around."* Do not casually ask around and expect to get what you're looking for. You are more likely to get relatives, friends, and their friends recommended.

The time you spend finding the right person to represent you will return benefits of value proportionate to it. Make sure that you've got the winning hand *before* the game begins.

Authority

Contents

Related Topics

Description

There are two types of authority—formal and informal. Of either type, there are, of course, varying degrees or levels. This is where the art of applied authority lies.

Formal Authority

In construction, the first rule is to know the general conditions, working procedure, and any other significant document and be aware of the formal definitions to the limits of each party's authority. The construction supervisor (owner's on-site representative), for example, however benign or power-hungry he or she might be, normally does not have the (formal) authority to alter *any* part of the contract. Know these things to be sure that you deal from a position of knowledge when the construction supervisor is issuing instructions that sound more to you like **constructive changes.**

Often on public projects, it is not a **surprise** to receive **correspondence** from the design professionals directing action, interpreting the contract, or something similar. When this happens, it means that the design professionals may have forgotten (or have failed to realize) that their role in this type of contract may only be as advisor to the owner. It is the appropriate owner's agent who usually has the authority to deal directly with the contractor at various levels—not the design professional directly. Accordingly, on receipt of such a letter, a management decision is required to either:

1. Advise the owner that you've received it, but are holding it without action until directed otherwise by the owner.

2. If it's to your advantage, use it to force a favorable issue by advising the owner of your intention to take action based on it. Leave it to the owner to tell you if it is appropriate or not.

As another example, most contracts include some type of provision that (except in cases of imminent physical danger) the contractor is not to proceed with any proposed change without a completed and properly executed **change order.** So you innocently submit your change order proposal, complete with required acceptance date (the date beyond which the job will be further affected/delayed and the price will go up). But somewhere around the required date you don't get a change order—you may get something called a *proceed order,* or something similar, which is something dreamed up by the owner that says, "We agree the change is required, but we need more time to evaluate your proposal; get started so you don't delay the job, we'll finalize the paperwork later." The catch, however, is that the proceed order is probably also "subject to cost review." Or to put it another way, 4 months after you performed the work, the owner will tell you he thinks half the price was more reasonable.

Because your strongest negotiating position is *before* you've started, when you receive something like a proceed order instead of a change order, call their bluff. Advise them that the contract does not give you the *authority* to perform any changed work without the signed change order. Hold your position and get your price approved.

As a last note on formal authority: Even if the contract documents authorize a consultant to make changes to the contract if they do not affect cost or time, get the change authorized in writing by the owner.

Informal Authority

The key to pinpointing where the informal authority lies is to ask yourself "Who is making the real decision here?" While it may be true with respect to the contract's written word, for example, that "only the chief, construction section has the authority to approve change orders over $1000," when the chief receives your letter notifying of a change, he or she is going to ask the field staff (clerk-of-the-works, construction supervisor, etc.) or possibly someone at a middle level for reasons to justify or reject the change. If the right "pump" (person with the informal authority) has been primed, your item may get greased through. If you've left it up to such persons to draw their own conclusions, you may as well just go play the lottery.

Other people who often have significant informal authority are all technical types—lawyers, engineers, experts, etc. Even though they have no formal authority to make decisions, their input may be con-tractual or procedural. (The request for **change order proposals** must come from the owner, but the change itself must be designed by the architect and bear his or her stamp.) Beyond simple procedure, the opinion of an expert with 100 years' experience and a 10-page resume tends to carry more weight than that of the average human. Refer also to **consultants** for important related information.

Always take special actions and do the best that you can to deal and negotiate only with the parties who have the authority to make the deal or decide the issue. Try to avoid, to whatever degree possible, dealing with front line types who lack informal authority and who are nothing more than fact finders for others. They may have been deliberately placed there to delay, divert, and discourage you.

Averages

Description

Whether you are on the seeking or buying side in a contract or **change order,** or if you're resolving some problem, it is important to know how "averages" work, how they don't work, and how to make them work for you.

Averages are always negotiable. They, like statistics, can be made to justify or disprove just about anything. This is because they are true and untrue at the same time.

It's been said that the average American has one breast and one testicle. It's true and untrue at the same time. The average family has 2.4 children. A price on any manufacturer's standard list reflects the average product, shipped to an average location, to an average buyer, for average use.

If, for example, the "average" cost for concrete in place on the approved Schedule of Values is $550 per cubic yard for the entire job, or some portion of it, consider using that number to substantiate your price on an add or deduct change order, if it will enhance your position. If, however, circumstances require that your cost of a change puts the new concrete placement on the high side, go the direct-cost-plus-markup pricing approach. Even if you are working under a **unit price contract,** there may be a clear way of demonstrating that the conditions anticipated in the preparation of the original unit price are now changed, or are otherwise now different than those of the change currently being considered. *Unit price* does not always mean *locked up.*

Will a 15 percent "average" overhead figure compensate you for the paperwork that you have to process for a $500 change? That $500 change will actually cost you as much to process—and manage—as a $5000 one.

Meaningless Numbers

Don't get hypnotized by meaningless numbers that look right. For whatever "average" you're dealing with now, understand the basis behind its determination. Know how to use it completely to your own advantage.

You are you. You are not average. Take it from there.

Backcharges

Description

A *backcharge* is a charge against a subcontractor's or supplier's account to reimburse the contractor for performing work or supplying materials that should have been accomplished as a part of the respective subvendor agreement. Completing the work of another is usually done to achieve some level of project completion, to move the job logically along to the next step, or to bring some important subvendor compliance back into line (such as cleanup or some safety compliance).

Components

Each contract has a certain cycle that it must follow. In order for a contractor to be justified in its performing of backcharge work and then expecting reimbursement from the subvendor, certain things need to be taken care of every time. The backcharge components are

1. The event giving rise to the issue.

2. Giving notice to the subvendor to correct or be corrected.

3. Securing the backcharge agreement with related written acknowledgement, or confirming disagreement and finalizing notice.

4. Keeping all appropriate **documentation.**

5. Processing the backcharge as a change order (contract modification, amendment, or other mechanism in your accounting system) against the subvendor's account, thereby establishing proper external and internal accounting control.

Right

The concept of backcharges is ingrained in our industry. It's surprising, however, how often our written agreements are silent with respect to this routine procedure. Don't leave your right to backcharge implicit. Include explicit standard language in your subcontract and purchase order forms clearly giving you a right to backcharge when the subvendor has failed to comply with some term of the subcontract and fails to respond to appropriate notice to do so.

Consider the sample clause of the next section in order to address the issues and the backcharge. If you decide to use such a clause in your agreements, review it carefully with your **attorney** before proceeding.

Sample Backcharge Clause

"In the event that (subvendor) fails to comply with the terms of this agreement or fails to perform any portion of its work to the satisfaction of the owner, design professionals, or contractor, contractor may upon 24 hours' notice to (subvendor) have the right to declare this agreement to be breached by (subvendor) and make arrangements that it shall deem necessary to correct and/or complete the work by whatever means reasonable and most expedient means available. In such event, contractor may retain other payments otherwise due (subvendor) under this agreement or any other agreement in effect between contractor and (subvendor), an amount which in the opinion of contractor is sufficient to cover all costs and damages. The cost to be offset against (subvendor's) account(s) will include those relating to coordination, procurement of replacement materials and/or subcontracts, supervision, idle time, actual costs to perform the work, and all administrative expenses required throughout the notification, administrative, and documentation processes. These costs are distinct from and in addition to those costs associated with interference and delay which may also be charged. If any deductions result in a current negative balance of the (subvendor) account, (subvendor) shall reimburse contractor the full amount of the negative balance within 48 hours of notification to (subvendor). Failure to reimburse contractor as required shall result in an interest charge against (subvendor) account(s) in either the amount of: (a) 18% per annum; or (b) the maximum allowable legal rate, whichever is greater."

Components of the Sample Clause

Important components of the above sample backcharge clause include the ideas that it:

1. Clearly provides for the right of the contractor to perform the work of a subvendor when necessary.

2. Defines a reasonable but minimum **notice.**

3. Clarifies that although some effort will be made to ensure that the costs expended to complete the work are reasonable, *expediency* is a priority as well. The contractor will accordingly not, for example, be required to get three bids to perform an item, or otherwise be held to a standard of the least-cost principle, but be allowed to extend reasonable money if it achieves speed. It is further recognized that the major reason for the backcharge presumably is that the subject work is interfering with the current progress. Expediency will go for a minimized total delay in cost to the project.

4. Gives the right to the contractor to recover the cost otherwise due to the subvendor, but allows the *contractor* the right to determine those costs. It further extends this right to definable damages.

5. Defines the costs that will be included in the total backcharge calculation. It clearly describes the backcharge as an issue which causes much more than simple direct cost. It costs the contractor's organization to have to coordinate, order materials, and apply administration and overhead to degrees probably exceeding the contractor's effort on its own work. The entire process must be documented in order for the contractor to justify its position and to follow through on the invoicing. All these items are costs which the contractor would not have to experience if the backcharge item did not exist and should accordingly be entitled to recover from the offending party.

6. Calls attention to the fact that these costs to resolve the particular item are distinct from and in addition to any costs associated with delay. Presumably, other portions of your subvendor agreement also address delay and how you will be handling that issue. The rights of this backcharge clause should therefore not limit any other rights of recovery for other issues.

7. Not only requires reimbursement of a negative balance to the subvendor's account, but subtly allows the contractor to apply such negative balances to *any other agreement* that may be in effect between the subvendor and the contractor at any time. In its strict application, and without consideration for any other components of the contractor-subvendor relationship, it is technically possible for the subvendors to enter into an agreement *subsequent* to the backcharge, against which these respective backcharge costs can be applied.

8. Clearly subjects any negative balance to a maximum allowable interest rate.

Notice

Perhaps the greatest failure on the part of contractors in the application of a backcharge is not providing adequate **notice,** along with an opportunity to correct the defect before actually proceeding with the work of a backcharge.

As a practical matter, there is often regular and continuing communication regarding the particular problem issue, to which the subvendor is not adequately responding. And so the offending party may have "constructive" notice; but it is much better to have *written* notice.

Begin as in the example above with a contract agreement that provides for a minimum written notice. From that point, in these days of fax machines, there is really no excuse for not having adequate written notice. The notice need only include the facts that:

1. You have been requesting the subvendor to take care of the respective issue for some time (reference those back dates in your notice.)

2. You require the work to be complete by a particular day and time.

3. If the work is not complete as directed, you will mobilize to complete the work of subvendor for it, and invoke all applicable provisions of the subcontract with respect to recovery of all costs and damages.

4. You request an immediate *written* confirmation (by return fax) that the subvendor will be complying with your notice, or refuses to comply with your notice. Note here that failure to receive a return fax (or other written communication) by a certain time of day will be considered by you as the subvendor's constructive notice, or "notice by default," that the subcontractor refuses to respond to your directive, and accordingly authorizes you to perform the work of the subject backcharge.

Billing and Payment

For some reason, many contractors somehow consider the backcharges separate and distinct from other formal changes to a subvendor's account. Although we have complied with the **notice,** and performed backcharge work on behalf of a subvendor, many of us stop there and leave the **documentation** of a backcharge at the level of letters and faxes. The accounting department may or may not be coincidentally aware, and the internal purchase order system (or however the internal accounting is effected) is left to deal with the backcharge by chance—often only through the memory of the person arranging the backcharge.

Correct the problem by requiring that every backcharge be immediately processed as a formal change order to the subvendor's account. Be sure the backcharge enters your internal accounting system in the same way any other change order would, and guarantee that the cost issue once having been so confirmed won't be lost in final billing or subvendor account reconciliation process.

Bar Charts

Schedule Considerations

Schedule types vary greatly in their complexity, detail, ability to display information, and documentation ability. See **scheduling** for important discussion in this regard.

Bar Chart Description

A bar chart is perhaps the most common scheduling method used. It is a simplified representation—usually in summary—of when major components of the work are expected to occur in time. The bars themselves are usually placed in their locations because of "implicit" dependencies, without having their relationships to the other components of the work displayed.

It is the simplest of all methods. Activity descriptions are placed in a column on the left, along with other desired relevant information (such as budget costs, early start and completion dates, etc.). A calendar is placed along the top of the chart, extending through the duration of the job. A line or bar is placed alongside each activity's description in the time area to correspond with the calendar above.

Advantages

A bar chart has several advantages:

1. It is simple to prepare and easy to understand.

2. It displays the anticipated time frames of major activities visually.

3. Because it is easy to understand, it can be a good "communicator" to large groups such as building committees.

4. It is historically accepted. It has been used by most site superintendents and project personnel since the beginning of time, and accepted by many design professionals, owners, and financing institutions.

5. Activities are normally listed in order of specification sequence. It is relatively easy to correlate the activity list with the **schedule of values** and other payment records.

Disadvantages

A bar chart has several disadvantages too:

1. It is most often oversimplified in its approach, not providing enough detail to use as an actual management tool.
2. It does not display the activity relationships. The schedule preparer intuitively considered these, but the actual logic demonstration is lost. The problem is emphasized because the activities are normally listed in order of specification sequence, as opposed to any logical sequence. This results in two logically dependent items being physically displayed widely apart without any mechanism for their dependency made clear.
3. It is seldom updated or corrected.
4. "Updating" can record only a greatly simplified version of history—when an activity has actually started and ended. It cannot display cause and effect, forecast events of current (good or bad) activity status, or accommodate changes in any way.
5. Any efforts by project people to reschedule or to accommodate any changes at all from the original program are completely left to the memories of those conducting the change. See **changes—the six deadly sins.**
6. You have no ability at all to communicate changes and their effects—not just to the owner or design professionals, but to your own people.

Conclusion

A bar chart can be a quick, convenient *preliminary* planning tool that can give a good idea of the general project perimeters at the onset of a project, and can serve as a first guide to a more useful scheduling method. It is also a good presentation vehicle that can place complex relationships into understandable form for large groups. It is not, however, an acceptable tool to manage a project by itself.

Refer to **CPM/PDM schedules** and **logic diagrams** for important related discussion.

Bid Openings

Related Topics

Bid Protests

The Bid Opening

A bid opening has been defined as a poker game in which the losing hand wins, and the low bidder as the contractor who's wondering what it left out.

The rules are normally more relaxed for private bidding, but when you are submitting your bid for public work, be sure to know the bid documents completely—particularly if they are unusually complex and requesting what some bidders might consider uncomfortable information—and then make sure that yours is filled out completely and correctly.

The Late Bid

No matter how long your subcontractors have had to submit their proposals, if the bid is set for Wednesday at 1:00 p.m., you'll still be receiving subbids at 2:00 p.m. Your competitors are going to be running into the bid opening within minutes or seconds of the prescribed time in a frantic attempt to include the most up-to-date information. Despite all the odds, you've managed to get the bid form completely filled out and got it there within 2 minutes of the time **deadline.** Then some bidder walks in at 1:02 and hands the clerk its envelope. Many agencies will actually accept it. Some may accept it, but not open it. Some will want to open it anyway.

If such a thing should happen in front of you, don't stand for it. No matter what the agency response, *immediately* protest the receipt of the late bid. You should quickly have even the rest of your competition in the room rallying with you to that cause. Normally that will be the end of it.

If, however, the receiving authority is still insistent on receiving the late bid, don't fear making a little speech to the roomful of your competitors. Point out that you've all managed to comply with the requirements of the bid documents and get your bids all there on time, whereas the late competitor did not. Under these circumstances, why should the roomful of bidders allow a defective bid to reduce the chances of any complying, *legitimate* bid from being awarded the project. Note additionally that this is not a technicality to be waived, but goes to the essence of the **integrity** of the public bidding system.

With such a statement, you might find yourself leading a small rally that will conclude with a clear rejection of the late bid.

The Second Bidder's Second Chance

If after all legitimate bids are opened you're the apparent second bidder, demand to see the low bidder's entire bid. Review it in detail, noting every discrepancy, no matter how apparently slight. Take down *all* the information and note missing data. Review the bidder's bond. If there is an obvious mistake (which are more common than you might think)—if the bid isn't signed, or a price is in the wrong place, or whatever—don't be afraid to make a big deal about it.

Upon returning to your office, immediately draft a confirming letter highlighting your objection to the apparent low bid. If you've managed to comply with the letter of all bid requirements, take the attitude that you've got the right to expect the same effort on the part of all other bidders. Take a stand (on public bids) and you might be surprised with the results. Refer to **bid protests** for important related discussion.

Bid Protests

Public and Private Arenas

In the private arena, where projects are entirely privately funded, owners have great flexibility in dealing with their bid-opening procedures. Public entities however, are required to follow precise rules as established by the funding entity. A primary responsibility of the public entity accordingly is to preserve the integrity of the public bidding system.

If a public bidder meets all of the stated requirements of the bid—including complete preparation of the required proposal form, attachment of required bonds or other approved security, *absence of any modification of the form whatsoever,* and submission of its proposal by the date and time specified—then that contractor must certainly have the right to expect that all other contractors who have been given the same opportunity in the same set of conditions and circumstances would also meet the same requirements. Refer to **bid openings** for important related discussion. When an "unresponsive" bid is considered by the public entity, it creates an extreme disadvantage for all of those bidders who have taken the time, the trouble, and the initiative to comply with all the stated requirements. It's simply unfair.

Defective Bids

I am often surprised when, in a roomful of legitimate bidders, a respective bidder shows up at the public bid opening 5 minutes after the stated time. At first, I'm angered when the public agency will actually receive the late bid. Then I am regularly surprised that bidders who have taken the time and trouble to be responsive in their bid sit quietly and allow the bid to be received. That surprise then turns to amazement when this roomful of competent bidders allows the patently unresponsive proposal to be opened and read.

Protest Response

When faced with a bid that is apparently unresponsive—late, incomplete, marked with exceptions, etc.—protest immediately to the bidding authority. If it is a late bid, draw the attention of the legitimate bidders to the unresponsiveness. Point out that if the group allows the bid to be read, it allows the late bidder an unfair advantage over the entire group. If, however, the issue is a technicality that becomes apparent only after the bids are open, again declare immediately to the public authority that you consider it to be a material defect in the bid and you expect that bid to be rejected.

If contractors as a group show consistent intolerance to any apparent abuse of the public bidding rules, those agencies that might be guilty of perpetuating these types of violations will begin to get the message and improve their conduct accordingly.

Boilerplate

Description

"Boilerplate" is a collection of standard contract language and technical specification sections that are intended to apply to essentially all projects. Whether manual or electronic, most project specifications begin with some general standard format. This might be an existing specification that a design professional has used for a past project, or it might be a commercially prepared standard general format. It's all but guaranteed that the specification did not start out from the ground up with just this project in mind. Much too often, the final result winds up being a collection of long-winded, cryptic, confusing, and even "creative" phrases, paragraphs, contract clauses, and specification sections. The specification writers use a shotgun approach to problem resolution in a blatant attempt to create a catchall net.

Problem

Once boilerplate is included in the specification, it is probably stuck there, and once included it may be modified. As a specification "writing" technique, inclusion of boilerplate may sometimes be sound and sometimes not. A **cut-and-paste** process is often applied to customize the specification to a particular project. If done manually, the process is quite literally to cut out those paragraphs and phrases that do not apply to the current project and paste in those additions that provide specific attention to this unique situation. If done electronically, the process is neater, but essentially the same.

During this time-saving process, there is a strong probability that:

- Language that does not apply will remain.
- Important inclusions necessary for comprehensive treatment may be overlooked or compromised.

As the cut-and-paste process continues, the risk that confusing or inappropriate language will remain increases. It is almost guaranteed that the entire specification will become less integrated and coordinated.

This whole process is applied in order to provide the design professional or owner with catchall phrases in attempts to cover those situations that were not specifically treated in the first place—the ones that fell through the cracks or for some other reason were just not addressed directly and responsibly.

Action

Boilerplate is effective as substantiation of your opponent's position on a matter only if you allow it to be. The diluted, wave-of-the-hand language is generally put there to cover for the rest of the contract where it fails to accommodate a particular condition. In interesting contrast, it is likely that the design professionals, in the same contract, can display their ability to include very specific language in each of those cases to which they had actually given their direct attention.

When your opponent presents you with boilerplate as justification by your opponent for an unreasonable position that would otherwise be considered to be beyond the requirements of the contract, protest loudly. Study your own situation very carefully and determine why the particular condition is the exception to the intention of the catchall phrases of the boilerplate. Be firm in your position. Be unyielding. Do not accept that wave of the hand, for those instances where a pointed finger is more appropriate.

Breach of Contract

Related Topics

Backcharges

Claims Awareness

Punchlist

Remedies

Termination by Contractor

Termination by Owner

Breach and Material Breach

With the best of intentions, we work closely with our attorneys in drafting our own standard-form agreements which methodically indicate all the risks and responsibilities assumed by the other contracting party. Our attorneys then dutifully include (somewhere near the end of the agreement) some provision or collection of provisions that provide that any breach is grounds for termination, that any breach unremedied for some time after notification will be considered to be a "material breach," and that other penalties are associated with such material breaches as a contract equivalent to Armageddon.

The Practical Reality

And so our subcontracts require that the subcontractor provide submittals within 10 days, provide payroll reports with each invoice, hold tailgate safety meetings, and complete its punchlist work within 5 days of notification. If the subcontractor delivers its submittals in 15 days, does not conduct tailgate safety meetings, is deficient in payroll reports, or takes 7 days to complete its punchlist, the contract invariably provides that the contractor must: (1) notify the subcontractor of a breach; (2) within some number of days convert the breach to a material breach; (3) terminate the contract as one of the contractor's **remedies.**

Building Codes

Design and Construction Responsibilities

In general, it is the design professional's responsibility to ensure that the project *design* meets all building code requirements of all governmental and quasi-governmental organizations having jurisdiction over it. Contractors, on the other hand, are normally responsible for *performing* their work in a code-approved manner. This criterion applies to workmanship, installation, and similar considerations. The designer remains responsible for the *design's* compliance with all applicable codes—whether its drainage, provisions for the handicapped, number and location of exits, air exchange rates, and so on are in compliance. The design is up to the designer.

Electrical, mechanical, and certain specialty trades may be specifically given additional responsibilities in this regard, by way of a clearly described *design* requirement in their respective specifications. In such cases, at least those portions of the specifications essentially become a **design-build** contract component, and in such cases, the contractor becomes the designer as well. The two entities become one.

Unless the specific design responsibilities have been clearly included as part of the agreement that you are working under, no one should make a remark to the effect that the contractor "should have known better" that:

- The elevator shaft needs a vent at the top.
- There is insufficient (legal) clearance.
- There are not enough exit lights.
- There are not enough parking spaces.
- Something is the wrong height.
- That wall or door should be of a different fire rating.

Regaining Control

An early warning of a design professional's failure to meet building code design requirements most often comes from a contractor's *construction* experience. It can range from a contractor's extensive expertise in completing a particular item of work in a certain way, down to the idea that something just may not look right. A construction detail, for example, may be completely contrary to the way you have always seen it.

A contractor who has worked in a design-build capacity (and who may possess a related design license) may actually be qualified to code design compliances. Even in this case, however, it is important to realize that:

1. It is still not that contractor's *responsibility* to determine the code-complying design.

2. The "qualified" contractor neither was part of the original design development process nor is privy to any design variances or other considerations that the designer may have used elsewhere in the overall design that may have produced the particular design result—some optional treatment.

Once a possible code violation has been observed, the steps that should be followed may not only be a good idea, but also may be a specific obligation on the part of the contractor. **Contract documents** include wide ranges of treatments in their descriptions of a contractor's "express" responsibilities. The relative ease by which you ultimately might be able to pursue these steps will vary, depending upon the owners' and design professionals' dispositions. The procedure boils down to:

1. Advise (or "question") the engineer or architect of the possible violation. It is possible that the design might have accommodated the code in some other way, or a variance from the specific requirement might have also been achieved at some point during the design development process.

2. Confirm from the project's design professionals that the design component in question does indeed violate a code.

3. On such confirmation, be sure that the owner is advised through some procedure agreed on with the design professionals. Refer to **notice** for important related discussion. You might confirm with the design professional that he or she will serve the notice. If there are any questions as to the timing or content of such notice, simply do it yourself. Waste no time.

4. Take the initiative in leading the design professionals to alternative solutions. If you do "suggest" any solution, be clear that you are not offering any specific design—and that the final solution will ultimately be the *designer's*. Waste no time, and move the issue toward resolution as soon as possible—by urging the designer, not by creating the design.

5. Emphasize (and then follow through) that the finalized corrective action is completely detailed by the *design professionals*. The level and detail of the documentation will be determined by the size and the complexity of the correction. Leave no gray areas. Refer to **RFI (request for information)** for confirming designer response where appropriate. Insist on clarifying sketches or drawings whenever you feel necessary to clarify and document, or to be sure that your instruction is complete. Be sure that the design is "done right the second time."

6. Upon receipt, immediately analyze the completed redesign. Determine if and how the scope of your contract has changed. If it has, prepare an appropriate complete **change order proposal** in the accordance with the requirements of your contract and proper procedure. Refer to **changes—the six deadly sins** and **claims awareness** for related information.

Change Clause

Contents

Related Topics

Description

The change clause authorizes the owner to alter the work, if the change falls within the general scope of the original agreement. Without this provision, there is no inherent right on the part of the owner to make changes that a contractor will be obligated to perform. The clause should provide both the means by which the owner may adjust the plans and specifications, and mechanism by which the contractor may incorporate suggestions.

The change clause should be closely coordinated with a **dispute clause** that should set forth a procedure for dealing with problems that could not be resolved by way of a **change order.**

Basic Elements

Although language varies among contract forms, typical requirements of most change clauses will include the ideas that:

1. Adjustments to the contract may be effected only by a change order.

2. A change order must be in writing, signed by both parties.

3. It must specify adjustment in both contract price and on the project time.

4. It should be for work within the scope of the original contract.

5. No changed work should be performed without a properly executed *written* order (this idea is most often modified to allow the contractor to act in emergencies to prevent injury or damage to property without a written order).

Beyond these basic elements, the change clause may elaborate on some specific administrative procedure. Be sure you know precisely what that procedure is before you submit your first change proposal.

Application Issues

Common issues that arise in the application of change clauses are

1. Does the change fall "within the general scope of the project"? This issue is not significant to most changes as they are being made. However, changes that are large, complex, and significantly delay the completion of the project will cause some other problem for the contractor that is so significant that it could not have been contemplated within the original scope of the agreement, and actually provides the contractor with the ability to refuse the change.

2. Does it really need to be in writing? Even if there is no disagreement as to the written requirement, at what point in the change order's life must it finally be committed to paper? Is there some written or **constructive change** procedure in the contract that can allow changed work to proceed, with paperwork as a follow-up? Who has the *real* authority to authorize the change? Is the written, *express* authority modified by some **authority** implicit in another individual? Beyond *implicit* or *informal* authority, has there been any precedent set by specific action of the parties that spells out the real authority?

3. Have there been any constructive actions on the part of the parties that have modified their written requirement with respect to preparing, executing, approving, and obtaining a change order?

4. Is the consent of your surety required for all changes or changes above a certain dollar value?

5. Is there a mechanism in the clause that describes the procedure for resolving pricing and other agreement problems? Does the contractor proceed under protest? Can a contractor bill for items of work not in dispute, while disputed items are being resolved? Does the work stop? Is the additional **time** addressed in the change order—both total time required for the change (considering all the administrative activities necessary before you can get to the field work) and the *net* effect of the change on the project completion date?

6. Do overhead and profit (OH&P) markups apply to net price changes, or can each item be separated? If OH&P applies to add changes, but not to deduct changes, can each be dealt with as a separate item, in order to avoid combining the deduct changes in a way that will lower the overall OH&P?

7. Does the change really accommodate all the contractor's **consequential costs (damages)?** Does the change delay completion in significant amount of original contract work? Will multiple changes significantly delay release of retainage on the original contract value? Do these kinds of things need to be addressed at the change order proposal stage?

Change Order

A Normal Part of the Construction Process

The business of construction contracting is one of the most intensely competitive environments ever to evolve. If competitive "responsible" bids are to in fact represent the lowest bona fide price to perform the work required by the **contract documents,** the proposal process absolutely requires that a bidder base its pricing on that which is specifically represented or *reasonably inferred* from the information contained in the bid document set. Only the most naive would not expect that a bidder that provides for extreme contingencies and/or "comfortable" profit margins so as to absorb the unforeseen would find itself on the very end of a very long line of competitors arranged by price. It wouldn't be long before that type of bidder has absolutely no further opportunity to demonstrate to any owner its ability to actually build something, because its prices are too high to be considered.

Accordingly, a bidder must price what is *indicated* in the documents. This is not at all to say that bidders must be calculating or opportunistic, or in any way pervert the intent of the design/construction process. It is, however, an acknowledgment of and an acquiescence to the laws of nature. We can complain about the situation and wish it were not so, or we can understand the dynamics and deal with it as best we can as responsible businesspeople.

Contingencies cannot realistically be allowed for in a competitive bid, nor can they be absorbed to any significant degree, and the parade of extra work, interruptions, resequences, and so on cannot be absorbed, either. For the contractor, **time** really is of the essence, and what you see *is* what you get.

"Change" or "Claim"?

Being "change conscious" is not necessarily being "claim conscious." An unresolved change can quickly become a claim, but if the change process is managed properly, the identification, **notice, documentation,** and pricing step can package the change event in a way that will make it clear to everyone involved that the most expedient, cost-effective approach is to resolve change and pay the bill. Refer to **claims awareness** section for related discussion.

Simply put: Keep all your actions, documentation, etc., focused on the idea that the change may at any point turn into a claim, and bear in mind that at any time you may need to quickly organize and present your case. Unfortunately, this may eventually become the reality in too many cases, and so you may always be prepared. As you develop your own procedures, systems, and record-keeping methods, remember that the primary goal of any **documentation** effort is to be able to research and organize the information quickly and clearly. If you conscientiously conduct your business along these lines, ironically, because the organization *is* documented so well, the effort itself will increase regular awareness of all project people of all project issues. It will actually work to *minimize* effects of a change order on the project. You will find that your project people will now know more about their jobs than they ever knew.

Beyond this, if the effort is done properly, the client, other contractors, and any other party involved with the project will see very clearly that you are the one who has documentation and who knows what to do with it. They will accordingly make intuitive decisions that it is in their own best interest to simply resolve things with you, rather than negotiate with you, since you have resources and information so clearly organized at your disposal.

Change Order Components

The Three Costs

This section is very closely related to **change order proposals.** Before a change order proposal can be designed and constructed, an understanding of its components must be clear. These basic elements—the three cost categories of *every* change that will sum up to the maximum amount of compensation justified—are *direct costs, indirect costs,* and *consequential costs.*

As discussed in **equitable adjustment,** the application of these cost categories is a matter of degree. Consequential costs on a very small change, for example, may be so small as to not justify lengthy consideration. On another change, however, the **consequential costs** may dwarf the actual direct cost portions because of extensive interference, delays, and disruptions. The application of each cost category must therefore routinely be considered individually for *every* change proposal. If you then decide to omit or to water down a particular cost category, you should do so directly, after having specifically considered the issue. Even in this case, however, the deleted category should be treated in some way that leaves open the possibility of reintroduction should circumstances of your original consideration of the change become different.

In other words, it may be a legitimate business decision to consider an issue and decide that it does not apply. It is not, however, responsible management to fail to even consider an issue or component.

Direct and Indirect Costs

Direct costs are usually thought of as "hard" costs of the change; they include those items that are specifically and uniquely attributable to the modified work. Although direct costs are often thought of as on-site expenses, in reality they can be much more.

Direct costs share the common characteristic of being clearly assignable to an event, and can be relatively easily documented. By their nature, they also lend themselves to clear accounting. Because of their clear cause-effect relationships, they are readily justifiable as change order cost items, and include such items as labor, material, shipping costs, restocking charges, specific temporary protection, etc. These are the costs that most people (particularly your client) initially and intuitively attribute to a change only.

Indirect costs—most commonly thought of as the "soft" costs—are those items that, although precipitated by a change, may be less obviously related to it. They may be more difficult to recognize for what they are and, if recognized, are harder to apportion to a specific event. They can be difficult to identify and assign. Many can be demonstrated to apply in principle, although the actual values are subject to extreme disagreement. Such differences in opinion generally revolve around whether a particular item can be treated as a specifically attributable cost or whether it should simply be lumped into "overhead."

Indirect cost items can include things such as **home office overhead,** off-site supervision, change order preparation, research, **negotiation,** associated expenses, the effects of project interferences and disruptions, time delays, and any other effect on any other project condition (such as release of retainage on original contract work).

The key to keeping an indirect cost item clearly identified as a specific change order expense, in both principle and absolute value, is again clear **documentation** and accurate, verifiable records. Essentially, documentation, if done correctly, will transform the indirect nature of such a cost item into something much closer to a direct nature. This is the essence of the idea; if this conversion in perception from indirect to direct is not accomplished in the minds of those who are reviewing your analysis, you might find yourself having these cost items ultimately dumped into overhead, despite your objections.

Consequential Costs (Damages)

The third cost category of every change—consequential costs—is often the most difficult of all categories to secure recognition for as legitimate items attributable to a change. The things that most often fall into the consequential costs category are most often thought of as "damages"—the stuff that lawsuits are made of.

Simply put, a consequential cost is any cost that the contractor would not have to deal with had the change not existed. Note that this is very closely related to the concept of **equitable adjustment.** Consequential costs are too often heavily masked by the aura of basic contractor responsibility. To regain clarity and perspective, however, keep in mind that if the change did not exist, the contractor would not have to deal with its effects on the project time, cost, and profitability.

A clarifying example is freezing temperatures. Why, for example, should winter conditions—snow, ice, cold—be anybody's fault? Why should dealing with it not be part of the contractor's responsibility if that contractor has signed an agreement that expressly states that the contractor is to be responsible for all effect of weather?

As it turns out, a common condition that could make such freezing temperatures actually compensable to the contractor might simply be the fact that the winter work would have been avoided entirely—at least during the construction of the critically exposed work—if the change had not been made. The freezing temperatures then are forced on the contractor as a consequence of the change. It is not a **force majeure** item; it is no longer a circumstance that is the fault of neither party; it is now clearly a circumstance that is caused by the owner and forced on the contractor. Accordingly, it should be transferred from a "noncompensable extension of time" into a legitimate cost item as part of the change.

Another example of the consequential cost of a change is a delay in the release of retainage on the primary contract because a late-breaking change has delayed substantial completion of the project. In such a case, it is the existence of the change that has delayed the release of a sizable sum of money to the contractor, thereby significantly impeding the contractor's cash flow. Accordingly, a legitimate approach in a change proposal would be either to include the release of (or significant reduction in) retainage on the primary contract amount as a condition of the **change order proposal** or, if such is not possible, to provide an alternative "add" item to the change order proposal that will increase the change order cost to cover the carrying cost of the retainage for the duration of the changed work.

Again, keep looking for all of those things that would not be on your plate if the particular change did not exist.

Time

Time is probably the most inappropriately treated category by contractors who are faced with change order interruptions. Those responsible for determining the effects of a change to the project are usually competent to determine the duration of the direct work of the **change order**. The problem, however, is that the time of a change includes many more activities.

Beginning with the date of identification of the issue, a particular item of work on the project is usually stopped or otherwise interfered with to some significant degree. From that point, the change procedure needs to run its specified course, tempered by any **constructive change** procedure defined by the real actions of the parties. Direction may be required from the engineer, a drawing may need to be produced, subcontractor pricing needs to be assembled, the change order proposal needs to be prepared, the proposal needs to be reviewed and approved, submittals on the change work may need to be processed, material might have to be ordered after approval of the change change sub-mittals—and *then* the actual work of the change order can proceed.

Clearly analyzing these conditions for what they actually are, you may find that the total duration of the change is actually 2 to 3 times longer than the initial intuitive evaluation of the simple direct-work portion. This fact needs to be brought home clearly, swiftly, and dra-matically to those responsible for dealing with the change on the other side (design professionals and owner). Be sure to know these total effects on your *schedule,* and deal with them openly, specifically, and directly. Don't give away your time.

The second area in which contractors regularly hurt themselves is by executing change orders, after having negotiated the price, that *explicitly state on their face* that *no time* will be added as a result of the change. Contractors may execute such documents believing that at some point they may revisit the issue of time, but such contractors may not fully understand that they may instead be actually executing an express confirmation that no further time will be attributable to the change. In such cases, the contractor will have thereby totally written off any further opportunity to revisit the issue, unless it can be demonstrated that the conditions existing at the time of the execu-tion of such document have themselves materially changed.

Related to this problem are those changes that are executed *with* time extensions confirmed, but include no additional cost to the con-tractor for the additional time that the contractor will be forced to remain on the site. Again, if the contractor thinks that it can revisit the issue as a cost item later, it is setting itself up to be badly disap-pointed. The contractor would be entitled to a time extension, but the owner will not be required to compensate the contractor for any costs or damages associated with the extended time. Both parties must accept the delay and neither party is to bear the cost of the other party.

If instead, however, the contractor has clear records and the ability to display cause-effect, it may become apparent that, were it not for the delay occasioned by a major problem several weeks before, the masonry work *would* have been completed prior to the cold season. In this situation, the contractor might be able to demonstrate that with-out the prior interference, the masonry would have been completed and the current effect of the cold temperatures on the project would have been avoided altogether.

To the extent that this relationship can be convincingly displayed, the cold weather may no longer be force majeure. It may clearly become a cost that is experienced specifically as a *consequence* of the delay caused by the earlier problem. As such, it is a consequential cost, or consequential damage, for which the owner may indeed become liable to pay.

Don't give up too quickly or too easily on cost items that under first impression may appear to be **force majeure,** or another noncompensable problem. Step back. Look at the big picture. Try to determine all of those costs you are now experiencing that you would not have had to deal with if certain problems or issues were not in existence. Learn to draw your cause-effect line, and recover the costs for the consequences of your earlier problems.

Be aware of the document that you are executing. If you do not intend to write off an amount of time, and/or the cost to the company associated with added time, don't. If the face of the change order document requiring your signature addresses time in a way that is not comfortable to you—to the level of your clear agreement and acceptance—look for a way to modify the language so you can revisit the issue at a later date. At the very least, try to leave the change order with the reservation that its effect on the construction schedule will be determined at a later date. Don't give time away unnecessarily.

Change Order Files

Contents

Related Topics

Organizational Requirements

The underlying reasons and objectives for your particular filing system depend on your type of organization. A subcontractor's requirements are different from those of a general contractor, and both are different from those of a construction manager. A subcontractor typically deals with fewer of its own subcontractors and suppliers than the typical general contractor, and a construction manager's objectives may also include many types of formal summaries and analysis.

A subcontractor is likely to have many projects very similar in nature, with very closely related requirements and processes. Every project essentially looks like every other project, with the exception of the client, the dates, and the dollar values. A general contractor, however, rarely builds the same project twice. The general contractor is further bound by the need to manage armies of other companies—its subvendors. Its communication, coordination, and **documentation** requirements are entirely different from those of a subcontractor.

If you clearly understand what the needs of your organization are, you will be in the best position to make your determinations regarding the real objectives to be satisfied in the ultimate design of your filing system. In your ultimate determinations, consider the need for clear identification, ease of preparation, ease of reference, cross-correlation of information, data assembly, and record security.

Filing Efficiency—Paper versus Research Ability

An efficient filing system design begins with the idea that when *any* item is researched, either *all* required pieces of information should be physically present in a file, or clear references to related information (and its file location) should be provided. There should be no need to mentally recall circumstances in an effort to identify related issues in files. If this kind of input becomes necessary, it will be difficult or impossible to recreate it with any degree of effectiveness, and it will surely be compromised in even simple situations. The difficulty increases exponentially, even for those who have been intimately involved with an issue, if the research is required after an appreciable amount of time has passed.

The first half of the tradeoff involves a generally increased amount of paper to be filed. This is weighed against the potential for lost opportunity resulting from overlooked documents that have been filed in not-so-obviously related locations (or lost altogether). The other difficulty might be a little more surprising but nonetheless true; that is, a large number of professionals—both in and out of the contracting business—are concerned that if they don't actually file important documents *themselves,* they won't find them when they need them. This might be a legitimate concern if filing is handled inefficiently, as it is in too many cases, but if you are one of these individuals, take some consolation in the fact that the problem transcends contracting. With the proper system of file identification, however, this important function can be given back to your secretary or administrative assistant, where it belongs.

The content and style of your correspondence itself will have a great impact on its understandability—and its "filability." Its ability to be filed in several related areas without confusing those files with unnecessary (unrelated) information is also a key result of a properly formatted document.

Rules of Good Records

A few rules will contribute greatly to effective **correspondence** and good records. They include:

1. *Confine the subject of any particular correspondence to a single issue, or small group of closely related issues.* If you have two or more unrelated items, keep them in separate letters. Separate items allow quick understanding and focused responses. The clear, individual attention also facilitates the ability to file the particular document where it should be. Research of the issue is sped up because your attention is focused to a clear outline of the record.

2. *Clearly identify the individual project on each correspondence.* As simple as it sounds, combining multiple projects to save paper creates a level of confusion (however implicit) that actually costs much more than the extra piece of paper would have.

3. *Include appropriate file designation numbers in the "Subject."* If the subject involves a prospective change, bulletin, field file, or other established file designation (your own or someone else's), use those numbers to begin the subject description. The simple, rou-

tine treatment can make research of all correspondence related to any issue unbelievably quick.

4. *Confine letters to a single page, whenever possible.* When it first does not seem to be possible, reconsider the letter. Except in the most rare circumstances, all correspondence should be confined to a single document. Make the points in your letter clear and fast, and reach a conclusion. If the issue really is a complicated one, make the main points in a cover letter referencing attached backup. The immediate result for your opponent will be quick understanding of your contentions. Your support for your contentions can be reviewed only by those individuals who need to in order to get your opinion to those higher up the ladder who must make the ultimate decision. Don't confuse those at the top of the ladder. Keep the logic of your position very clear, with your support attached.

5. *Use outline form, if possible.* If you must send a long, complicated letter, do your best to break it down into manageable (understandable) parts. This idea applies equally well to short letters that contain multiple items. Clearly identify each individual item. If you are confirming several facts, separate them out of the body copy and number them. If you are drawing several conclusions, requiring two or more specific actions, or if you are making any statement combining more than one issue, reconsider your correspondence very closely. Try to break it into its individual components, listing each item on its own line and numbering the items in sequence. This procedure will first clarify your thought process. From there, your representation of the facts will be more understandable for everyone up the organizational ladder of your opponent who must ingest the information and make progressive determinations. Finally, your own research at a later date will be speeded up because your attention will be quickly directed to the main points.

6. *Include your own specific file instruction in the copies of your own document.* If your correspondence affects, or potentially affects, two or more issues, file that correspondence in *both* locations. The extra paper, again, is a small price to pay for a guarantee that the document will not be overlooked when each item is being considered or negotiated. As an additional note when filing incoming correspondence, write on the document the locations where you can later find your own response to it. Be sure to include all appropriate file references and their dates. A note such as "See (your company name) response dated (_____)" will do. This effort will later confirm first that the item has, in fact, been responded to. Beyond that, it will speed your own later research again in locating all important documents relevant to a particular situation.

Change Order Proposals

Related Topics

Change Clause

Consequential Costs (Damages)

Constructive Changes

Detail

Equitable Adjustment

Notice

Time

Unit Price Contracts

Standard Form

There are a number of contractual, practical, and desirable issues that a contractor should regularly incorporate into each change order proposal. Once a contractor is aware of every principle involved, a mechanism should be developed within the organization that will provide a regular, routine evaluation of each of these components every time a change order is considered.

Project identification, giving **notice,** treatment of each cost item, dealing with **time,** and adding terms and conditions as a basis of the change should follow a routine procedure to ensure that none of these categories is overlooked while the momentum of a change is stealing time from the project participants.

Once you determine how you like to deal with these situations in your own business, standardize the procedure. Train your people to be aware of each of the ideas, and provide them with a mechanism—a standard approach—to be used every time the change issue rears its head.

Change Order Proposal Components

Consider the following outline as a checklist for developing such a standard procedure.

1. *Project identification.* All of your project correspondence should follow a routine format for easy identification. Begin with the project reference that identifies the project and your company project number, and provide a separate line as a "subject," which will identify the particular issue and correlate it to your change order record keeping system.

2. *Notice.* Undoubtedly, your contract will require very specific notice requirements if you are to preserve your rights to recover extra costs associated with a change. Use the introduction of your letter to

highlight the fact that you are complying with the notice provisions of the contract. Consider starting your letter with "Confirming the discussion at the job meeting of (date)" or "In accordance with general conditions section _____, please be advised...." If your **constructive change** notice was earlier than your written proposal, refer *back* to that date in the introduction of your proposal. Pin it down to its earliest possible date. Make it clear to all concerned that you are reading your contract and have complied with it in every respect.

3. *Direct costs.*   Identify and itemize all those costs directly caused by the performance of the work. Labor, material, and equipment are the obvious ones, but consider restocking charges, expedited delivery charges, equipment transport, and every other cost item directly attributed to the work.

4. *Indirect costs.*   Do your best to identify cost items that *appear* to be of the overhead variety. Administrative time spent in the preparation, identification, and resolution of the change, for example, is *not* time that will actually be recovered under the allowed overhead part of the change. That overhead is for general and administrative expenses *during* the construction of the change. The allowed overhead and profit values really have nothing to do with the preparation and resolution stages of a change.

5. *Consequential costs.*   Consider the change order **time** very carefully. Accommodate the entire time for identification, resolution, development, and completion of the change. Don't cut yourself short. From there, consider every cost that your company will now have, but would not have were it not for the existence of this change. Identify these issues, and decide directly how you will deal with them, given the particular client and your relationship with that client. Refer to **equitable adjustment** for important related discussion.

6. *Standard terms and conditions.*   Every change order proposal should include certain standard terms and conditions which clearly limit your liability with respect to the particular proposal. Included in this category might be remarks such as "This change is for work expressly described herein only," or "Your response is required by (date) in order to avoid additional delay to the project not represented above," or something similar. These types of remarks should be represented the same way for every proposal. Don't forget them, and get your client used to seeing them.

7. *Special terms and conditions.*   There was, whether you realize it or not, a series of particular circumstances that you considered that were a condition of your pricing as it is represented in the change order proposal. Think about what those circumstances were. They include things like your expected approval of the change order by a particular date and time, because it is that specific expectation that

will allow you to complete the change order within the time frame that the proposal anticipated. Accordingly, if action by your client goes beyond that date, so does your analysis of the time included in the change order proposal. Make it a condition. Include every significant item that was considered in your proposal preparation, and consider including optional cost items if your client delays or takes other action. A remark such as "This change order proposal anticipates your release of retainage on the original contract amount by (date). If this is not agreed to, the additional cost of ($_____) will be added to the above price as carrying costs for the retainage for the period of the change, if this change order is approved by the date indicated above."

8. *Response date.*   Above all, require a specific response by a particular date. Indicate clearly that incomplete or inappropriate or late response will cause conditions of the change to be different, and the price and time will be subject to adjustment.

Change Orders, Handling Rejections

Process

This section offers some insight as to the reasons why, despite all obvious logic and support, change proposals can get returned in such a condition that they can hardly be recognized—or worse get flatly rejected.

The process of handling change order rejections is closely related to the rules of good salesmanship and good **negotiation** techniques. They can be boiled down to the following:

1. *Understand the personal and professional motivations of your opponent.* Do your best to think through the *subtle* motivations that can drive the obvious motivations. Know "what's in it for them" at every professional—and personal—level that you can imagine.

2. *Determine those actions that you can take affirmatively in order to satisfy the motivations identified in step 1.* Give special attention to the *personal* motivators. The degree to which personal motivators take precedence over professional motivators is different from organization to organization, person to person, and with level and structure of the particular bureaucracy, if any.

3. *Strategize the entire scenario.* Use the first, most basic tenet of good salesmanship: Think through every conceivable objection to each component of your change order proposal. Determine acceptable answers to each objection in advance. Consider how you might format, phrase, or represent the change order proposal in ways that answer as many of these questions as possible. Weigh each possible action identified in step 2 against the actual benefit to be realized. Assess the probability of the occurrence of each possible action.

4. *Know your contract better than anyone.* Depending on your client, there may be a very good chance that if you do little more than just take the time to read your own contract, you may find yourself knowing much more about the required formal procedure than even

the party who drafted it. *Comply* with the procedure, and let it be clear to everyone that you are reading your contract and you know how to operate within it. The implicit message will be that you correspondingly expect your opponent to be operating within the contract procedure as well.

5. *Be prepared to move forward quickly into the next step in the dispute resolution process.* Know in advance the next step and all those that follow. Understand your power position (or lack thereof). Be courteous and professional, but demonstrate your commitment and resolve. Be clear about your complete intentions to follow through. If it becomes necessary, *follow through.*

"Good" and "Bad" Faith

This can be an uncomfortable concept for some, but the reality of certain business situations unfortunately requires contracting professionals to consider it.

An early question to consider on receipt of a change order rejection is simply whether or not the rejection was made in good faith or bad faith. In other words if you put yourself in the other person's perspective (a devil's advocate) ask yourself if there genuinely appears to be at least the appearance of a legitimate contractual basis for the rejection. Temper this evaluation with an honest effort to empathize with your opponent's personal and professional position within his or her organization. Try and get that person's entire perspective. Put yourself in that person's shoes. Understand the experience that person is (or is not) applying in his or her exercise of judgment.

If after all this consideration it appears that the rejection (whether *reasonable* or not) was made in good faith, it would therefore be based at least on an attempt on your client's part to responsibly evaluate the contract before issuing the response. Your own response to the rejection can likewise be based on a clear application of those provisions of the **contract documents** that support your position. You will be able to move to convince your opponent that your **interpretation** is the right one. You will also need to devote less energy to trying to guess about how to deal with ulterior motives.

If, on the other hand, your complete, and emphatic evaluation from the other party's perspective reveals no reasonable contractual basis for this rejection, it really may be the result of any number of other effects and motivations. An incompetent or incomplete or coerced response might be the cause, but there may unfortunately be other reasons that have nothing to do with your opponent's efforts to apply the contract with any level of **integrity.** The rejection might actually turn out to be nothing more than your opponent's assessment of the odds of your pursuing your remedy or the cost of an argument versus the cost of paying you now.

"Nothing to Lose"

Imagine yourself as a budget-bound bureaucrat working in a bureaucracy in which your operating costs for a project come out of your own budget, but litigation expense (both the effort and cost) is the responsibility of the legal (or some other) department. A contractor presents you with a large, complex change order, including elaborate delay analysis. In addition, to help you protect your position in the bureaucracy, there may even be a statute in existence (if the client is a public entity) that provides that delay costs, and other costs, related to project extension are beyond the authority of the particular department, so you have your out.

Being a good bureaucrat, you know your options are (1) pay the change order now; (2) pay the easy-to-justify portions of the change now, and reject the more marginal or questionable portions; or (3) flatly reject the entire change order.

In the first option, all of the money comes out of your project budget—right now. In the second option, you know that the denied cost may total up to a value just under what it would cost the contractor to fight it in litigation or **arbitration.** You have pushed the contractor into a no-win situation in terms of cost, and you, the bureaucrat, know that there is a very good chance that you will wind up with a bargain. The third option may not appear at first to be a really viable one if the contractor is genuinely entitled to the payment, but the key is the actual structure of the bureaucracy and your own (bureaucratic) disposition. If you don't necessarily find acting in bad faith distasteful, there's really nothing to lose. If you can fabricate any "supportable" reason for rejecting the proposal you will start the dispute resolution procedure provided in the contract. What makes this gross injustice even worse is the idea that every case that goes to arbitration or litigation, no matter how well-founded, carries with it some degree of risk that the contractor will lose (at least a portion of) the claim. If this should happen, not only will the contractor be out significant expense, but the bureaucrat who made it happen might even become a hero in his or her own organization. The next time a similar situation comes up, the bureaucrat might even be able to repeat the procedure with the complete support of the bureaucracy.

Admittedly the scenario described above may be extreme (and definitely cynical), but it is an effect that you should nonetheless be very sensitive to. It can occur in degrees. Continually size up your opponent's situation and disposition. Do what you can to circumvent the possibility of such bad faith maneuvers before they have a chance to start.

Settle or Fight?

This idea is very closely related to the "nothing to lose" attitude just described. If a change is relatively small, or if part of a change that is difficult to resolve is proportionately small, a flat unfounded rejection may again become a possibility. On analysis, it may become apparent that the cost of fighting the unwarranted action will meet or exceed the amount of the unfounded rejection. This situation is much more common than we would all prefer. The ultimate way that it is handled is the result of a decision weighing the effects of a strict individual cost-benefit relationship of the immediate problem against the long-term implications with respect to your relationship with the client. It is only you who will be able to determine whether it is more advisable to go ahead with the expense in the interest of demonstrating your resolve or to acquiesce to the demands of your client in the interest of maintaining your relationship. If you are leaning toward the latter, however, I caution you to very carefully consider what your relationship really is all about. Don't naively give away the store if you are genuinely not being appreciated for your **concessions.**

The Best of Intentions

With the best of intentions, we contractors continually push our way through our construction contracts performing additional work and assuming additional liabilities that were not part of the original bargain. In the interest of performing a service, satisfying the client, minimizing our own downtime, or any combination of these, we find ourselves over and over again putting ourselves in the position of assuming design liability and pushing ourselves further away from recovering an equitable value for the added work.

The Six Deadly Sins

In order of increasing probable damage to ourselves, the sins that we commit either by ourselves or through our employees are (in order of increasing probable damage) as follows:

1. Design a solution.
   - Secure a change order of additional work authorization.
   - Perform the changed work.
   - Submit application for payment.
2. Design the solution.
   - Perform the work.
   - Attempt to secure change order approval.
   - Settle for some change order cost after the fact.
   - Submit for payment.
3. Design the solution.
   - Perform the work.

- Allow some time to pass before attempting to secure change order approval.
- Settle for some percentage on the original dollar of the change order price.
- Submit for payment.

4. Design the solution.

- Perform the work.
- Do not bring to the attention of the owner until the end of the job, combined with numerous other changes.
- Anger the owner, settle for some small percentage on the original dollar.
- Submit for reduced payment at a very late date.

5. Design the solution.

- Perform the work.
- Never ask for payment.

6. Design the solution.

- Have a subvendor perform the work.
- Pay the subvendor.
- Never request payment from the owner.

You may not believe that these kinds of problems are occurring to any significant degree, but I assure you that they are going as you read this line—possibly on one or all of *your* job sites.

Train your people to understand this effect; tell them that you recognize its occurrences and that your company is determined to correct the problem. Be sure that your employees understand that securing approval of changed work prior to its performance is not only your own *contract requirement,* but is your own company's *firm policy.* Be sure every one of your employees knows that their performance with respect to this issue will be a significant yardstick during employee evaluation.

The Six Magic Words

Teach your employees that it is not the position of the contractor to design a solution and thereby assume liability for the revised design. Even with the best of intentions, an irony is that if you design the solution and submit a price, you risk being branded as a "change artist." Every time you open your mouth, you are perceived to have "change" dollars come out.

Instead, work to change the *nature* of the issue's discovery and resolution. Positively and helpfully bring the issue to the attention of the design professionals and the owner's representative, call attention to the specific activities that are immediately experiencing the resulting interference, and ask the owner's representative (or design professional) these six magic words **"What Do You Want to Do"** Once the question has been presented, *stop*. Ask nothing further, and patiently wait for a response. See **RFI (request for information)** for important related discussion.

Step back, and out of the discussion. You might be amazed at how often the job interruption will be appreciated so that the solutions can be explored, and you will be *asked* to provide additional pricing—a subtle difference, but an important one. You stand a greater chance of being looked at as the party who just won't proceed without resolving a problem, instead of as an opportunist who is always looking for an extra buck. Turn the entire relationship around with **"What do you want to do?"**

Claims Awareness

Description

"Claims awareness" (sometimes called "claim consciousness," or something similar) is actually a *perspective,* but not a *practice.* Claims awareness is an understanding whereby a contractor appreciates the fact that a smooth-running construction project at any time may turn into one with a problem. The numerous players, pressures, contract structures, personalities, and so on can transform an otherwise profitable job into one plagued with arguments, bruised egos, multiple changes, disruptions, delays, and even **termination by contractor** or **by owner.** Late projects create huge ripple effects of all kinds of problems for all kinds of people in all kinds of companies. It is not a surprise, for anyone experienced in our industry, for example, that a $1 million project can leave in its wake a $1 million problem.

Because of this reality, one approach contractors have taken in dealing with the volumes of required documentation and the industry risks is to conduct themselves with an attitude of "claims awareness." This is not to say that such contractors actually intend to proceed with claims, but that they are aware that they may become the target of a claim or may have to recover costs for items that are beyond the scope of their responsibility. These contractors are determined to be prepared at all times.

Most important, schedules are prepared, changes are reviewed, records of meetings are kept, and other activities are conducted with the proactive objectives of timely completion and adequate profitably. Almost as important, a focused eye is kept on the intense liabilities associated with our industry. Expect a claim and regularly conduct yourself as if you are about to be involved in a claim, and you may find yourself in the best position to ensure that such a claim *never happens.*

If an opponent perceives you as weak, disorganized, undocumented, and unsure, he or she might not perceive you as a resource that would help resolve a problem when a job is late and over budget. Instead, such an opponent might perceive you as an easy target and therefore might pursue a legal issue against you that would otherwise be disregarded. In the simplest situation, for example, payment might be withheld at least partly, with the anticipation of your questionable ability to bring and maintain a battle. The areas in which you are *perceived* to be weak will be the ones where you can regularly expect problems and attacks.

In contrast, if your opponent perceives you as one who is knowledgeable, timely, prepared, skillful at presentation, and ready to do what needs to be done, you will be just the kind of opponent that that party will not want to deal with on any antagonistic level. In these circumstances, such opponents are likely to determine that it is in their best interest not to pursue available legal actions.

The Final Irony

And so the final irony becomes simply that, if you conduct yourself with the expectation of a legal issue, you may actually improve your chances of *avoiding* legal issues. The art in this approach is to do this while remaining courteous and considerate and without becoming openly antagonistic or appearing intensely opportunistic. If all of these challenging features can be achieved, you have a winning formula that will keep a successful job successful for all parties.

Computers

Price/Performance

If automobiles had undergone the same price/performance improvements as computers have over the last 10 years or so, we would be
able to buy a Rolls Royce for $1.76, and drive 9 million miles on 1 gal-
lon of gas. Most businesses have had their introduction to computers
either through their job cost and accounting or through their word
processing. Having achieved these beginning levels of computer
sophistication, and having been duly impressed with the power and
efficiency of these continually improving systems, we all continue to
look for more areas where computers might apply in our businesses.

Good and Bad Uses

Computers, however, should be used to calculate or develop, not just
to log in or to simply catalog summaries (with the exception of legitimate word-processing uses). For example, what I consider to be legitimate uses for computers include job cost and accounting systems,
word processing, progress schedules, spreadsheets, drafting and
design, and graphics/presentations—items that require *calculation.*

Questionable uses would include things like shop drawing logs,
change order logs, or similar applications where the information itself
does not require changing—just supplementing and adding to.

Consider a shop drawing log, for example. If you are using a computer-generated log, the project engineer must have a physical copy of
the log at his or her fingertips in some form. When new submittal
information is generated, the project engineer must make a physical
note on the computer log form. At that moment, the log itself is merely a notepad. Simultaneously, the actual computer log, in the computer and on the diskette, is immediately out-of-date, whereas the manual noted log happens to be immediately up-to-date.

For this application, there is no computation or presentation; therefore no time-saving function is performed by the computer. To the contrary, by keeping the log in the computer, it is almost certain that the
log itself will *regularly* be out-of-date. In contrast, a simple, clear, and
easy-to-use *manual* log form used in the same way described above
would always and immediately be precisely current with the exact

state of affairs. It requires no transposition, and no supplementary (computer-literate) personnel. It will probably reduce the sheer volume of paper handled, as well.

"Legitimacy" of Information

"If it comes off a computer, it's got to be right...."

Undeniably, there continues to be a perception (at least subliminally) that computer-generated information is somehow more legitimate than that generated manually. The irony in this perception is that computer-generated information stands a much greater chance of not being as carefully reviewed, coordinated, and considered in its detail as manually generated information, and so certain types of computer-generated information might actually be more prone to error than manually generated information. This principle does not apply in all cases (such as estimating unit price databases), but its effect is real in certain situations, and should not be overlooked.

Computer printouts in various forms—spreadsheets, schedules, design forms—have the *aura* of sophistication; they *look* right. The fact remains, however, that people using those computer programs have varying degrees of proficiency and effectiveness with the software, have applied different amounts of time in confirming the accuracy of the information, and may not even have participated personally in the underlying data.

Just because one document is computer-generated and another is manually generated, do not be hypnotized into believing that the computer document is more accurate, usable, or otherwise more legitimate. Be skeptical. A particular document may not even be the result of a sophisticated program. The same old human error will be present.

If, on the other hand, it is *you* who are making the presentation, use this power to your own benefit. If you have a manually prepared document, consider reproducing the document so that it is obviously output from a computer (whether it's been recalculated or not). If *appearance* of having been computer-generated will add any amount of "legitimacy" to your own work product (whether or not it deserves it), don't deny the effect. Use it if you think that it is appropriate to do so.

Concessions

The Obvious

This section is not intended to rehash what we all should know by now regarding concessions. People regularly begin their careers in positions where they learn how to give room for tangible concessions. Pricing, for example, has become an art form in itself for the presentation of a first price that looks reasonable while allowing for a hard-dollar **negotiation.**

We all know what tangible concessions are, and have a tendency to focus our negotiation skills and efforts directly on those tangible items.

Often, however, if we give more specific attention to the *intangible* components of a negotiation, we may uncover alternative (direct and subliminal) methods of getting to our target from other directions.

Understand that these effects are at play, that they are being used against you, and that you should be using them in dealing with your opponent.

Intangible Concessions

If a negotiator regularly adheres to certain guidelines, we can look for all kinds of opportunities to provide "concessions" that in a sense do give something to your opponent, but in actuality will bring you closer, not farther, from your real objectives. Consider lists of "concessions" that really don't give anything away. Create value, however, implicitly or subliminally in the mind of your opponent, and use these intangibles as real bargaining chips. A simple list of intangible concessions might include:

1. *Always give the best explanation possible.* Have reasons for doing everything you do, and make sure that it all makes sense. Often,

all your opponents need is to be able to give a good explanation to their own organization.

2. *Be courteous.* Obviously respect the professionalism of your opponents. Communicate that you understand their position, that there is nothing personal, and you consider them to be performing a fine job under the circumstances.

3. *Give knowledge of the product, price, or other information.* Communicate that you are in command of such information, and have used it in the specific consideration of your own position. Training your opponents in these details might give them the information they need to explain to their own organization why the deal is actually very reasonable.

4. *Listen attentively to what the other person has to say.* Demonstrate very obviously that you value the communication, that you respect your opponents' position, and that you appreciate their effort to educate you. Your efforts in this regard may make your opponents feel obligated to listen attentively to what it is that *you* have to say.

5. *Organize your information in ways that make it easy for your opponents to check information for themselves.* If possible, look for opportunities to steer your opponents toward components of a negotiation that are easily verifiable and will calibrate the accuracy of your statements and positions.

6. *Employ the above suggestions, and look for other ways to contribute to the overall satisfaction of your opponents.* Very often, all your opponents need is a mechanism for demonstrating to their own organization or client that they are performing their own jobs professionally, that your position is in fact reasonable, and that they have taken every appropriate measure to verify the case.

Dos and Don'ts

Don't just "make concessions." There is a right way and a wrong way to give up a real or intangible component. Follow the guidelines below to get the most mileage out of every concession made:

1. *Give yourself room to make concessions.*   Start high (or low), but always have very good, explainable reasons for your starting position. Refer to **detail** for related discussion.

2. *Make the other party* work *for everything.*   No one appreciates anything that has been gotten too easily. If you agree too quickly, or jump too far without serious discussion, it is a guarantee that you will reduce the other person's satisfaction with the outcome. Suppose, for example, you have already made up your mind that you are willing to drop $1000 on an issue, and your opponent suggests that you

drop only $500; if you rush to acceptance, you will leave your opponent with the feeling that he or she did not go far enough. If, on the other hand, you stop, consider, discuss, and put forth arguments why the $500 may not be initially acceptable—make the other party *work* for the $500—by the time you conclude the issue, the other party will be very satisfied that the $500 was the maximum attainable figure and feel that *you* were convinced; not that he or she has been taken advantage of.

3. *Whenever possible, get the other party to open up first.* It seems that history repeats itself over and over again: The first party to make a statement stands the greater chance of losing more. For no other reason, this law of nature seems to be rooted in the idea that your first position may be based at least in part on the *assumption* of the other party's position. To the extent that this is the case, you may be beginning your position already having made a major concession without ever realizing it.

4. *Conserve concessions.* Refer to **acceptance time** for related discussion. Later is better than now. The longer an opponent must wait—and work—for a concession, the more that concession is likely to be appreciated.

5. *Train yourself to get something for every concession that you make.* Such an approach is intuitively reasonable. Peanuts are filling. Teach yourself never to leave an issue having given something away without getting *something* in return.

6. *Avoid "splitting the difference."* When you reach a point in your discussions where your opponent suggests that you split the difference, consider these magic words: "I can't afford to." Splitting the difference may appear reasonable, so when faced with it, don't necessarily object too soon; look for ways to turn it to your advantage. Before you split, try, for example, to add back in previous concessions in order to maximize the *total* value that you will split. You might be surprised at how many times you wind up with more than half.

7. *Learn to say "no" with a smile.* It may sound a bit trite, but a positive, upbeat attitude can actually mean the difference between moving through your agenda in a methodical manner and getting bogged down in deadlock after **deadlock.**

8. *Be persistent.* It has been said that a good salesperson leaves after hearing "no" six to eight times, whereas the great salesperson leaves after hearing "no" ten to *twelve* times. Persistence can demonstrate your resolve, or just plain wear down your opponent.

9. *Keep a written list of all concessions.* Keep track. If your negotiation is trending in the wrong direction, feel free to revisit prior concessions. Be aware at every moment of the total balance of concessions.

10. *Be willing to revisit earlier "concessions."*   If your opponent goes back on a previous concession, or if further developments in the negotiation trend in the wrong direction, there is nothing wrong with revisiting a previous *tentative* agreement. The only deal that counts is the final deal. If the implicit understanding is not sufficient, be sure to qualify each concession with some understanding that the particular concession is contingent on an acceptable *final* deal.

11. *Do not set initial demands too near your final objectives.* Assume that your opponent has started with his or her maximum position, and has not disclosed his or her minimum position in any way.

12. *Do not accept the first offer.*   Even if the first offer is beyond whatever you had hoped for, by virtue of the fact that it is the first offer, there is room for **negotiation.** Beyond this, accepting the first offer will at the very least make your opponent feel foolish. He or she will be made to believe (correctly so) that they started in the wrong place, and that you have won without any effort at all.

Conduit Theory

Description

Conduit theory is an idea whereby one party is very careful to clearly understand all contract rights and responsibilities of *all* parties and to avoid unnecessarily and/or unintentionally getting between two other parties. Conduit theory tells when it is appropriate to step out of the line of direct fire—when it is "contractually correct" to channel a transaction from one party directly to another (through the "conduit").

As an example: A subcontractor notifies you that an item of work usually done as part of that trade is not being provided *this* contract, because it is specified in another section. At first look, it does appear very unusual for that item to be specified in the other specification section. Too often the tendency for the general contractor might be to read the specification, *make an interpretation,* and direct the subcontractor how to proceed. In such a case, what the general contractor will have done is clearly assume the *design professional's* responsibility and *liability* for the specification interpretation, and the owner's responsibility and liability for the subsequent direction.

Instead of unnecessarily assuming these problems, preserve the conduit. Proceed more correctly by evaluating the subcontractor's issue, stepping out of the conduit, and transmitting the issue back to the design professionals for proper interpretation—as your owner/contractor agreement requires. Preserve the conduit of responsibility between the design professionals and the specification section in question—even if the design professionals argue that they do not deal with your subcontractors.

Keep Contract Responsibilities Intact

Your contract is almost certain to provide for two clear situations:

1. The architect (or engineer) will *interpret* the contract documents.
2. The owner will *direct* action.

Don't let either of these entities out of its responsibilities. Know what *all* the responsibilities are for every party to and around your construction agreements. Know how your construction contracts work. Do not unnecessarily step into the line of fire, and thereby directly assume responsibilities and liabilities that are not correctly yours.

Consequential Costs (Damages)

Contents

Description
Problem
Resolution

Related Topics

Acceleration
Change Order Components
Constructive Changes
Documentation
Home Office Overhead

Description

Consequential costs are those costs which are experienced as a consequence of some other action, inaction, interference, disruption, or delay. They are distinct and in addition to direct, indirect, and overhead costs of every type. In fact, many of these types of costs often considered as overhead may actually be considered as consequential costs—separate and distinct areas of entitlement that should be defined as such *before* overhead is applied.

Problem

The biggest problem with consequential costs is that they are most often simply overlooked. Related to this is the common difficulty among many contractors to show the cause-effect relationships that demonstrate the true and total effect that certain problems have on completing construction contracts. When impacted with a change or interference, contractors will correctly identify the direct and sometimes indirect components of the issue, but can fail to even become aware of (much less prepare a price for) the ripple effect problems—those that continue to impact the project as a *consequence* of the original issue.

Resolution

Refer to the concept of **equitable adjustment** for important related discussion. Simply put, equitable adjustment is the idea that a contractor should be made "whole" for all the effects of an interference or problem. In order to do this, the contractor must step back from the issue, clearly look at the entire project, and determine all of those things to be dealt with *that would not exist if it were not for the issue at hand.*

For example, a very large change occurs at the end of a project. There is a sizable amount of retainage concurrently being withheld by the owner until substantial completion of the work. Incorporating the new major change strictly by the terms of the original contract would require the substantial completion date for the entire project to be significantly extended. Under these conditions, the retainage on the original contract which would otherwise be imminently released will now be withheld until the extended substantial completion date caused by the new major change.

The delay in the release of the retainage on the original contract can therefore be considered a consequence of the new change. It may be entirely reasonable, therefore, to either negotiate release or reduction in the original contract retainage as part of the change order, or to include the carrying cost of that retainage for the period of time that the change order will delay its release. Either situation may return the equity of the situation, and leave the contractor closer to being "whole" at the end of the change.

See also **force majeure** for related discussion. Basically, force majeure is the impact on the project that is beyond the control of either party. Rain, cold temperatures, storms, strikes, floods, etc., are often placed in this category; at least at first look. Too often, however, because one type of problem begins by fitting into one of these basic descriptions, it is labeled as force majeure, without further consideration for the conditions that actually placed the contractor into the position of being exposed to the "force majeure."

Again, if you step back from a specific issue and observe the forest despite the trees, a decidedly different picture may evolve.

As an additional example, consider a contract that provides that masonry cannot be placed when the temperatures are 40°F and falling. For legitimate reasons, it is not possible or practical to protect the area so that work can continue, and so any day with these temperature conditions is a day that stops the masonry work. In certain circumstances, the delay caused to the masonry work by cold temperatures might be considered to be force majeure—the "fault" of no one. As such, the contractor would be entitled to a time extension, but the owner will not be required to compensate the contractor any costs or damages associated with the extended time. Both parties must accept the delay and neither party is to bear the cost of the other party.

If instead, however, the contractor has clear records and the ability to display cause-effect, it may become apparent that, were it not for the delay occasioned by a major problem several weeks before, the masonry work *would* have been completed prior to the season of cold temperature. In this situation, the contractor might be able to demonstrate that without the prior interference, the masonry would have been completed and the current effect of the cold temperatures on the project would have been avoided altogether.

To the extent that this relationship can be convincingly displayed, the cold weather may no longer be force majeure. It may clearly become a cost that is experienced specifically as a *consequence* of the delay caused by the earlier problem. As such, it is a consequential cost, or consequential damage, for which the owner may indeed become liable to pay.

Don't give up too quickly or too easily on cost items that under first impression may appear to be force majeure or another noncompensable problem. Step back. Look at the big picture. Try to determine all of those costs you are now experiencing that you would not have had to deal with if certain problems or issues were not in existence. Learn to draw your cause-effect line, and recover the costs for the consequences of your earlier problems.

Consolidation Agreement—Arbitration

Description

Disputes in construction often involve multiple issues affecting many different companies. If there are separate **arbitration** agreements between the contractor and each subcontractor, the contractor and the supplier, the owner and contractor, and the owner and architect, it is somewhere between difficult to impossible to bring all the different affected parties into the same proceeding if a dispute arises involving them all.

Beyond sheer logistics, separate arbitrations will inevitably lead to different results over the same issue—all this despite completely redundant efforts in separate proceedings. This fact underscores the huge advantage of deciding cases involving owners, contractors, and subcontractors in the same proceedings and by the *same* arbitrator or panel, wherever possible.

An appropriate means to accomplish this is to consolidate the separate arbitration proceedings.

Agreement to Consolidate

In many instances, arbitration proceedings can be consolidated only through judicial proceedings in which the court has jurisdiction over all of the parties to the dispute. In other cases, courts have held that in the absence of a specific judicial authority, or a contractual agreement permitting consolidation, they are without any power to compel the parties to participate in any consolidating proceedings. The way around the issue appears then to be to include a simple but complete *agreement to consolidate* in each of the respective owner-contractor, contractor-subcontractor, subcontractor-supplier, and owner–design professional agreements.

Pass-Through Relationships

In most cases, where a subcontract does not contain an agreement to arbitrate but refers to and incorporates a document that does include an agreement to arbitrate (such as the owner-contractor agreement), the contract will be considered to include an agreement to arbitrate. Technically, subcontractor agreements that incorporate a **pass-**

through clause that incorporates by reference the general contract, including its general and supplementary conditions, and every other document referred to in the **contract documents.** If that general contract includes an arbitration agreement, then even if the subcontract is silent, a dispute between the general contractor and the subcontractor should be arbitrable because of the incorporated terms.

This relationship by itself, however, may do nothing to require a subcontractor to agree to consolidate its dispute with any other dispute the general contractor may have with another subcontractor or another party. If, however, the general contract or any other document incorporated by reference *does* contain a consolidation agreement, and the particular subcontract or other document being considered includes a pass-through clause, the chances are very good that the subcontract will include a consolidation agreement. Refer to **pass-through clause** for important related discussion.

"Conspicuous" Contracts

A Disturbing Trend

There seems to be a disturbing trend in construction agreements. On the one hand, general contractors more and more are assumed to be sophisticated enough to be held unequivocally to the precise language of the agreement—whatever reasonable, unreasonable, or **exculpatory clauses** it might contain or however "creative" it might be. Whether large or small, the general contractor is consistently dealt with by the courts and the rest of the world with the simple attitude that it should "know better."

On the other hand, subcontractors and suppliers more and more tend to be treated as if they are nothing more than well-meaning, unsophisticated, unknowing, and naive parties to a contract, and therefore subject to calculated abuses on the part of the general contractor through cryptic contract clauses that lurk in the **boilerplate.**

As a result of all this, the application of a particular clause of a contract varies extremely widely. We must now concern ourselves not only with the idea of a clause, but also if and how it will be *enforceable.*

It is no longer sufficient to simply be clear in contract language. Further, it is no longer sufficient to clarify your agreement with an "understanding." (Refer to **agreements versus understandings** for important related discussion.) Now that you have clear language, and you have defined the understanding of the clear language, you must go ahead and confirm that the subcontracting party really has read it, has received advice from its attorney (or has had the opportunity to do so), *understands* that the contract shifts the risk, and so on, and so on, and so on. It may be ridiculous, but it's reality.

Redirect Attention

In order to counteract this disturbing trend, it unfortunately seems to be necessary for you to make the effort to clearly position yourself outside the scenario.

In order to achieve this, consider including in your own subcontract a position that provides that each party to your agreement clearly *represents* that:

- It has in fact read the entire agreement, is fully informed, understands, and has full notice and knowledge of the terms, conditions, and effects of the agreement.

- It has been represented by an independent legal counsel of its own choice throughout any negotiations prior to the agreement's execution, and has received the advice of its counsel in entering into the agreement, or has had the opportunity to seek and receive this advice.

- It understands that certain terms of the agreement result in one party assuming the liability inherent in some aspects of the transactions, and relieving the other party of its responsibility for such liability.

- It agrees that it will not contest the validity or enforceability of any indemnity, release, or **exculpatory clause** provision of the agreement on the basis that the party had no **knowledge** of such provision, or that the provision is not "conspicuous."

Review this entire section with your attorney before proceeding. The issue has become very important and should not be overlooked.

Construction Management with Guaranteed Maximum Price (GMP)

Contents

Contract Relationships
Advantages and Disadvantages

Contract Relationships

In the construction management with guaranteed maximum price (CMw/GMP) format, the relationships are essentially as described in **agent construction management (ACM)**. Refer there for detail. The difference in a CMw/GMP arrangement is that the construction manager *is* responsible for completing the project for a total sum equal to or less than the guaranteed maximum price. What is more, the CM may be required to sign off to the original GMP with only 80, 70, or even 60 percent of the **contract documents** complete.

Because the construction manager is now considered to be "at risk," it operates essentially as a general contractor with incomplete documentation; the CM contracts directly and individually with the army of trade contractors just as a general contractor would contract with subcontractors.

The originally quoted GMP is highly subject to changes in scope of work because the design professional may complete the conceptual design detail in a way that—as far as the CM is concerned—embellishes the contract. It is therefore extremely important to contract with a construction manager who is skilled and has a long history of successful projects. For a construction manager with less than the most upstanding motives, there are many opportunities for abuse of the relationship.

Advantages and Disadvantages

The CMw/GMP is becoming increasingly popular in large and/or complex projects. The "at-risk" feature of the CMw/GMP is what has drawn many owners to this form of project delivery, after being attracted to the advantages of the more pure **agent construction**

management form. In believing that the at-risk feature provides an equity that was missing in the agent form of construction management, an owner can easily get a false sense of security. Given all these apparent advantages, the owner must still be very careful that it doesn't wind up with a fox watching the hen house.

Constructive Changes

Contents

Theory

Examples

Resolution and Payment

Related Topics

Acceleration

Change Clause

Change Order Components

Defective Specifications

Design Duplications

Equitable Adjustment

Implied Warranty

Impossibility and Impracticability

Unforeseen Conditions

Theory

Constructive change arises not through the stated change procedure in a contract, but through the conduct of the parties. Both standard contract forms and custom-drafted contracts usually provide for some provision that requires that all changes be directed in writing. The owner, however, cannot hide behind this requirement if it either orally directs the contractor to perform changed or extra work, while refusing to issue a written document, or fails to act in some way, forcing the contractor into a changed circumstance.

Actions or inactions by authorized owner representatives may change the scope of work and increase the cost of performance. Because such actions or inactions are not necessarily memorialized by written directive, they are "constructive" by their nature. Refer to **equitable adjustment** for important related discussion.

Examples

Actions or inactions by the owner that require responses from the contractor different from those required by the original contract may constitute a constructive change. (The expected response does not have to be specifically mentioned in the contract; it may also be reasonably inferred from it.) For example, if a contractor provides that a directed change would increase the contract time, but the owner refuses to approve the justifiable time increase, the owner may be constructively directing the contractor to accelerate by requiring that the additional work be completed within the original contract **time.** This "constructive **acceleration**" might be considered to be caused by the owner's failure to act (to grant the time extension).

Additional examples of constructive changes may include cases where:

- The owner knows extra work is required and does not object to it.

- The owner or its representative orders extra work, either orally or in writing, causing other effects on the contract not included in the original order.

- An approved change results in additional work not anticipated by the original change order.

- The parties consistently disregard the requirement or other specified procedure for written change orders as a regular course of conduct of business. The "constructive action" of the parties with respect to this particular contract defines the real manner in which the contract is being applied.

Resolution and Payment

The key to effective resolution and payment for a constructive change is the immediate recognition of the item for what it is. The contractor who simply proceeds with the work of constructive change without prior confirmation of the condition does so with enormous risk.

The **change clause** of a contract entitles the owner to order changes in the work. Therefore, there is a risk to any contractor who refuses to perform the work of even a constructive change. If written confirmation of a constructive change cannot be secured by the owner by the time the work must be done, it may be effective at the very least to notify the owner that you are proceeding with the constructive change under protest, or under some other condition that will definitely allow you to revisit the issue with respect to both price and **time.** If the item is significant, however, any number of actions might actually be appropriate. Be sure your **documentation** is complete, know your contract and possibly consult with your **attorney.**

Types

Consultants come in all sizes and types. Architects, engineers, attorneys, soil scientists, schedulers, management experts, computer gurus, personnel experts, and safety advisors are all consultants in one capacity or another. "Conceptual" consultants include professionals such as planning consultants, **attorneys,** management consultants, and claims consultants. "Specific" consultants include categories such as architects, engineers, cost analysts, and soils specialists.

The problem that we all get into with consultants is that we are too quick to explicitly or implicitly place too much responsibility under consultants' care. An attorney, for example, is likely to highlight that the advice you are about to receive is "legal" advice, and not "business" advice. Having said that, the attorney will then promptly go on to give you all the business advice that you'll stand for. On the other hand, when a consultant is hired to do a specific technical task, we too often directly exert our own opinions or influence on that consultant.

In either case, we have set ourselves up to be disappointed with the performance of the consultant. We go to a consultant with a narrow range of abilities, and depend on that individual for advice on a much broader range of issues. Conversely, we find the technically competent consultant, and hamstring that individual with opinion that lacks technical relevance but comes from authority (those who are paying the consultant).

Improve Satisfaction

The probability of satisfaction with the work product of a consultant is directly related to our ability to:

1. Clearly define the specific project that the consultant is to address.

2. Keep the assignment narrow and focused on specific issues.

3. Include some measure by which we can evaluate the consultant's performance with a minimum of subjectivity.

The more narrowly we can define the *specific* scope of work desired from the consultant, the greater the likelihood that we'll be satisfied with the results. Ideally, we should list specific expectations with *measurable performance standards,* to the degree that such an approach is possible. If we can conceptually break a task into its components, we are in a better position to determine which consultants are better suited to attack *components* of the overall project. Identify those narrow, specific assignments.

Contract Documents

Everything under All Conditions

From the perspective of the party issuing the contract, contract documents should be broad in their description and refer to every item that could conceivably be related in any way to the work being contemplated.

Broad descriptions help to avoid the risk of giving limited direction to the other party. If, for example, your statement includes something to the effect that the contract documents include the "general conditions and supplementary general conditions," you may find that what you thought was part of the supplementary general conditions (because that's the way such a document has always been referred to in your experience) is actually entitled "special condition no. 1." Suddenly, you are faced with the argument that the entire document was never incorporated into your contract. To avoid this, consider a statement to the effect that the contract documents include "all conditions of the contract, including general conditions, supplementary conditions, special conditions, etc." This way, you will not even need to address the issue.

Similarly, a statement that the contract documents include "all addenda issued prior to bid" instead of "addenda 1, 2, and 3," reduces the risk that your failure to include an "addendum 4" may leave your contract with a major gap.

What You See Is What You Get

If you are on the contracting side, look for the ways to broaden your descriptions of the components of the contract documents so you do not unnecessarily risk a specific omission.

If, on the other hand, you are the party who will execute the agreement, you need to take the opposite approach. Consider each such broad statement made by the party who prepared the contract and look for ways to remove any subjectivity and narrow the description.

Do not accept descriptions like "all plans and specifications." Instead, insist upon an **enumeration of contract documents** in which each document that was specifically considered by you in

preparation of your bid is listed, along with its corresponding numerical identification and latest revision date. Do not lose this opportunity
at this initial stage to specify the basis of your price with such precision.

Refer to **enumeration of contract documents** for important
related discussion.

Contract versus Contact

An Important Distinction

An important distinction must be made between the ideas of *contract* and *contact*. It's almost too simple, but the truth is that contact (communication) much too often leads to actions, inactions, assumptions of responsibilities, and other kinds of "wheel spinning"—all because of misunderstanding the specific contract relationships and authority and mistaken assumptions about the actual project operating procedures for *this* particular circumstance.

Contract forms begin with one of several standard formats. General contracting, design-build, agent construction management, and construction management with a guaranteed maximum price (GMP) are the general major forms of agreement between a contractor and an owner. From there, numerous special circumstances are developed over a short or long period of time by inexperienced and experienced owners to customize the **boilerplate.** All of this accumulates to create innumerable "standard" forms of agreement throughout each level of the contracting business. Add to all this the inclusion of specific considerations, the addition of special conditions, the modification of boilerplate, and so on in a customizing routine that has become common practice, and it becomes clear that in fact no two construction agreements are ever the same. Refer to the **power of the standard form** for important related discussion.

Compounded Problem

The fact that all of these contract agreements are different in subtle or obvious ways is *not* the problem. The fact that they all generally *appear* nearly the same *is*. The potential for numerous misunderstandings begins immediately. At the site where all the activity is, the job "feels" like every other job. The traditional owner-architect-general contractor relationship and the tendency of all parties to simply deal with each other in the way they have in the past, create an atmosphere that is difficult to dissolve if some other specific contractual relationships are specified. It can sound almost trite, but even such simple acts as referring to the construction manager as the "contractor," are the essence of many basic—almost subliminal—misconceptions.

Resolution

Understand that every contract *is* different. Know what the specific deal is—right down to the particular language—for *this* deal. Be sure that all of the parties to the deal have the same understanding—the project manager, superintendent, etc. From now on, conduct every business interaction with the awareness that *this* deal is like no other, and the resolution of every issue can begin.

Refer to **power of the standard form** for important related discussion.

Coordination

Contents

Related Topics

Get the Concept Straight

If Daniel Webster ever knew what some owners and design professionals have done to the definition of coordination, he'd come back to life. Webster's defines the verb *coordinate* essentially as "to arrange in proper relative position; to harmonize in a common action or effort." Other dictionaries define the verb as "to arrange in order." In as many dictionaries as I have searched through, I have never been able to locate the definition "search out the mistakes made by others and correct at no additional cost." This is one word that is used to abuse.

As a contractor or construction manager, your primary responsibility is to coordinate the *work*. Coordination does not mean inventing the information. It means:

- Determining relevant information from those parties responsible for generating it.

- Correlating that information with the respective project requirements.

- Distributing information to those responsible for approving and/or using the information.

- Doing all of these things in direct sequence and in sufficient time to allow the work to proceed in an uninterrupted manner.

The operative words in the above description are "coordination of the *work*." It has nothing to do with coordination of *design* as a contractor.

If a contractor locates a design detail that describes how a component of the work is to be constructed, the contractor has *coordinated the work*. Having so coordinated the work, there is no further obligation on the part of the contractor to hunt through the remaining contract documents to confirm that other details confirm or conflict with the initial detail. That process involves coordination of the *design*. While it is true that the process of coordinating the work may actually disclose problems with design coordination, it is by no means the *responsibility* of the contractor to actually perform any of these design coordination activities. Those are plainly the design professional's responsibility.

When a manufacturer's recommendation contradicts whatever is specified, the general contractor is supposed to know this and to "coordinate" the work. Not so. The general contractor's responsibility to coordinate amounts to processing timely and complete submissions and distributing all relevant information to the various subcontractors and suppliers in time to "arrange [their work] in proper relative position." It does not mean anticipating design problems and correcting them in the process.

Shifting Responsibility

When a designer or owner tries to pin a problem on you by saying that you should have "coordinated" it, protest. Demonstrate that you *have* coordinated by taking the designer's (bad) information and distributed it in a timely manner so that everyone had their piece of the problem—properly coordinated. Don't stand for attempts to shift responsibility for a bad or incomplete design to you. Make the owners realize that they are being cheated by the design professional's refusal to accept proper responsibility for the design.

Understand this distinction very clearly. Don't ever take this kind of abuse at any level of project administration—not at **job meetings,** not in **correspondence,** and not at any higher-level contact. Coordination is not the vehicle by which contractors become responsible for design errors. Don't let it become one.

Correspondence

Contents

Related Topics

The KISS Formula

Remember the "KISS" formula. KISS in communications means "Keep it straightforward and simple."

Follow these simple rules to improve all of your correspondence and communications:

Rule 1: Keep It Short—*Always* No More Than One Page

We're not talking about reports, we're talking about letters. There are three good reasons for this requirement:

1. *Attention span.* Remember that you're dealing with business-people and bureaucrats who are probably very busy, may have motivations that you couldn't possibly anticipate, and represent the entire range of personal and professional capacity—from superhuman to plainly incompetent. For these and other reasons, if you approach your letters with the idea that the recipient's attention span lasts no longer than the introductory paragraph, at least you won't be disappointed. Don't beat around the bush—get to the point.

If your introduction is longer than one short sentence, that's the first problem. Nothing more is normally required than a simple reference to the subject, such as:

- Gentlemen: Per your request of 1/12/97 in regards to (subject), our proposal is as follows:

- Mr., Mrs., Ms.: In response to your letter dated 12/16/97, be advised....

If you are attempting to convince, explain, justify, or notify; use conclusions—not lengthy explanations or references. *Never* quote entire paragraphs from a referenced item unless it is absolutely necessary. For example:

Incorrect: "...Article XIII of the General Conditions of the Contract allows the General Contractor 10% overhead and profit on change order work performed by subcontractors. Since this work is totally performed by one subcontractor, the correct application of this item is 10% of $7000 (from line 1) = $700.00."

Correct: "OH&P on work by sub (per General Conditions Article XIII): $700.00."

Incorrect: "Paragraph 2 of your subcontract #7323 dated March 14, 1984, H.V.A.C. Section 15200 paragraph 15201 1.13, and General Conditions of the Contract Article 22 dictate that the mechanical subcontractor must provide all scaffolding, staging, rigging, small tools, and incidental items necessary for a complete installation of all items in this section. We must, therefore, state that you are responsible for providing and removing your own scaffolding for your work."

Correct: "Per General Conditions Art. 22, Sec. 15201 1.13, Subcontract #7323, XYZ Co. is required to provide its own scaffolding."

Unless your supporting references are unclear, and might be subject to more than one **interpretation,** include only that necessary for *conclusions.* Whatever you are referencing to can be looked up and verified by your target. Let him or her do some of the work.

2. *Don't telegraph all your punches.*   If it is a small, simple problem and your final position can be conveniently explained in a single page, then I suppose you may be allowed to embellish a bit. If, however, you are giving someone bad news, or the subject or issue is an uncomfortable one, or you're in the middle of an all-out war, and it's obvious that there's going to be plenty of correspondence or meetings, or even arbitration—don't give your hand away. If it is absolutely necessary, give one (maybe two) short reasons for your position—but only the minimum information. The reason for this is simple: if you conveniently organize and catalog all your aces, it gives your opponent plenty of time to prepare defenses for each issue. If you know there will be subsequent, possibly higher-level meetings, later is better than now. Hold on to your trump cards. This idea does, however, carry a certain risk. Refer to **surprise** for important related discussion.

3. *Don't risk contradicting yourself.*   The idea is simply this: The longer, more elaborate any correspondence, the greater the risk that you may contradict yourself, not only on that particular letter, but elsewhere in the project record. It doesn't take much imagination to see that this whole area of contradictory statements and confusing or unclear positions creates a field day for **attorneys.** Don't let it happen to you.

**Rule 2: Use Simple, Straightforward Language
That Anyone Can Understand**

If you're not a lawyer, don't try to be one. If you, as a lay person, attempt to throw legal jargon without direct advice from your lawyer, you run a serious risk of misapplication. At the very least, you might appear to be trying to be something that you're not. A word that seems straightforward to you may have a page of legal definition and precedence behind it. The incorrect use of such a word not only may change the entire message of a particular letter, but also may go so far as to render the whole thing senseless. Be careful.

If you've got your degree in journalism from Harvard—hold back a bit. Business correspondence can stand small doses of creativity and eloquence, but not much more. Think about not only the person to whom you're targeting your letter, but also his or her staff, any of several levels of subcontractors, the bureaucracy, and anyone else who might provide input for a response.

For example: You send a letter to the Chief of Construction Section, Bureau of Public Works, notifying of a **change order** required by a design error. It is likely that the construction supervisor (jobsite owner agent), the manager at the district level, someone from both the Design Review and Cost Review Sections of Public Works, and of course, the architect will all be involved to define, explain, verify, or defend items in your letter.

Tips for Clear Communications

1. Keep each project separate.

2. Confine the subject to a single issue or *closely* related group of issues.

3. Confine letters to a single page if at all possible. If it's not possible, reconsider and try to make it possible.

4. Avoid redundancy. Do not repeat the project name, letter subject, or contents unnecessarily.

5. Use outline form. Break a series of events or subissues into easily identifiable pieces.

6. Keep each discussion simple and to the point.

7. Use cause-effect style. Set up arguments to arrive at logical conclusions.

8. Stay factual. Leave out rumor. Forget your emotions.

9. Stay cool. Keep the response professional and focused on the proper *result*.

10. Get to the decision maker. Know who is calling the shots, and get your issue to that person's attention.

11. Respect your contract. By your *actions,* let everyone know that you're reading the deal—and you expect them to be doing the same.

12. Guide the decision. Draw conclusions from the facts, and support the idea that your conclusion is the only logical one.

13. Require specific action by a particular date. Have some kind of consequence associated with the failure to meet the date.

CPM/PDM Schedules

Schedule Considerations

Schedules vary greatly in their complexity, level of detail, ability to actually display the plan, documentation capacity, and ability to display cause-effect relationships.

See **scheduling, logic diagrams,** and **bar charts** for important related discussion.

CPM/PDM Description

CPM, or *critical path method,* has become an overused buzzword in the industry. It is usually (but not necessarily) a computer-generated schedule that accommodates each activity's start and completion points, duration, dependency on previous activities, and relationships with succeeding activities. The activity relationships are generally defined into the computer, and the computer is given the job of figuring out the resulting "network"—the location where each activity will actually fall in its complete set of relationships and against the calendar. As the job progresses, information regarding actual start and completion dates, durations, logic corrections, changes, additions, and deletions is added to each activity's information, and an update or "reschedule" is generated by the computer. Displays are either "activity-on-arrow" or "activity-on-node." A time-scaled **logic diagram** is an effective way to display a CPM schedule so that its information is visible and understandable.

PDM, or *precedence diagraming method,* is an "enhanced" version of CPM that adds an attempt to provide probabilities of success to the various baseline and update schedule scenarios. PDM may still be used in other industries such as aerospace and chemistry, but has generally been abandoned in construction because its complexity is wholly unnecessary for our needs—even in the largest of projects. The remainder of this section will focus on CPM only.

Advantages

1. CPM can be carried out to any level of detail. Originally developed as a method to accommodate very large or complex schedules (building a missile system, for example), CPM can handle levels of detail more than adequate for any type of construction project. The schedule size is limited only by computer memory, which is no longer an issue.

2. It can accommodate any number of changes to the program, such as simple corrections to logic, change orders, and delays.

3. It will display all activity relationships that define the original schedule and can change it. The logic of all "before and afters" is left intact.

4. There is great flexibility for adjustment throughout the baseline schedule development.

5. Computer programs can provide many types of reports to managers, which can be tailored to exactly match each manager's needs.

Disadvantages

1. CPM does require a computer, specialized software, and basic computer familiarity. The need for specialized training used to be a significant drawback. These days, however, the software is very straightforward and "friendly." A little initiative and a dose of faith (if you are not familiar with computers) should be all that is really necessary to be trained (or to train yourself) in a reasonably short period of time. This "disadvantage" is becoming less of one each day.

2. By itself, CPM has very poor visibility. Unless combined with a **logic diagram,** or something similar, CPM diagrams themselves display no relationship to **time.** An activity requiring 5 days to complete will take up as much space on the diagram as one requiring 100 days. Even the most accomplished CPM purist therefore cannot get any sense of where the schedule really is by simply viewing it. The information must be studied, clearly understood, and visualized by the reviewer. All analysis is accordingly left to straight consideration of tedious lists of dates. This is by far the most serious disadvantage for any manager or communicator. As the number of activities increases, the total understanding of the project's status—even by the individual who prepared the schedule—plummets dramatically.

3. It must be revised completely—from start to finish in all its detail—each time it is updated. This is not the large task that it initially appears to be, and so this is really a serious disadvantage.

4. Each update generates essentially an entirely new schedule. The set of original activity targets, dates, and milestones can be too easily (if not conceptually) lost after just one or two updates if the manager is not careful to take definite steps to prevent this effect and uses some method to keep attention focused on the original schedule targets.

Conclusion

CPM logic is the basis for all effective scheduling methods. Its earlier forms, used on computer with limited graphics ability, were more prone to the visibility disadvantages listed above. Later forms combined the CPM logic with the improved visibility of **logic diagrams** and even **bar charts.** These combined forms are the most effective management planning and scheduling tools available.

Cut-and-Paste

The Spec Writing Process

Cut-and-paste describes the process by which too many specifications are "written." Whether prepared manually or electronically (using word-processing equipment), most specifications begin with some general standard format, perhaps some existing specification that the design professional used in the past for a similar project, or perhaps a commercially prepared standard general format [such as the one produced by the Construction Specification Institute (CSI)]. In any case, there is a very good chance that your specifications did not at all start out from the ground up with just your project in mind.

Cut-and-paste then begins, and continues until the specifications are "complete." If done manually, the process is literally to cut out those paragraphs and phrases that supposedly do not apply to the current contract, and paste in those additions that (hopefully) will add the new requirements that do apply. If done electronically, the process is still the same although slightly neater and faster. The problems that each technique will breed, however, are identical.

During this time-saving cut-and-paste process, there remains a very high risk that language that does not apply to a particular contract will remain, important inclusions that are necessary for comprehensive treatment will be overlooked, redundancies will be compounded, and multiple treatments will lead to numerous inconsistencies and conflicts in the specification's instructions.

Probability of Error

Two factors that increase the probability that cut-and-paste will directly cause errors in the documents are

1. *Technical specifications may at times be a design professional's secondary priority.* Engineers may have a slightly different perspective than architects, but both are subject to the same outlook: the act of designing is the reason why they became designers in the first place. At least in the beginning, the designer didn't intend also to

become a lawyer. That reality is forced on the designer by the nature of the industry. Throughout the process of design development, the designer is deeply involved in the materials and their configuration. It is only when the design is complete that the technical specifications and the contracts themselves are finally assembled. The contracts and specifications do not seem to have high priority during the design effort, but instead are looked on as an unfortunate, tedious necessity by the design professional. Characterizing work on specifications as a "secondary effort" may be a bit severe, but is probably close to the mark. In any event cut-and-paste is looked on as a fast, inexpensive way to get it over with, even though it is not the most effective method of comprehensive preparation of an important legal document.

2. *The technical specifications and their front-end documents may be assembled at the eleventh hour.* The design process often seems to continue up until the last possible moment. Too often, it is when the deadline of the bid solicitation date looms that serious attention is sharply focused on completing the specification. The specifications then become likely to be "written" during long evening or weekend sessions, and to be fit in between the "real" design work. Junior designers, and even clerks, may be enlisted to prepare certain portions of the documents—even if they are all finally assembled by a "spec writer."

It is difficult enough that the documents you are working with probably originated on someone else's project, and were made to "fit" your job. Add to this the hectic secondary effort described above, and it is easy to see how the probability of errors and confusion can increase exponentially.

Cutting and Patching

Contents	Related Topics
Incidental Work	As-Built Documents
Standard Subcontract Provision	Boilerplate

Incidental Work

Conventionally applied, *cutting and patching* is a requirement of a contract normally included with the idea that the contractor will be responsible for the openings and closings necessary to install the work and to connect to existing and contiguous construction. It is reasonable to assume that such cutting and patching is nonstructural in nature and does not involve handling hazardous materials. If the designer knows that cutting and patching would require invasion and modification of structural elements, that designer has the responsibility to address the structural modification directly as part of the design. While it is true that the designer is not normally responsible for "means and methods" of construction, the design of a structural modification is much too significant to leave outside the scope of the design package.

If there is any doubt as to the application of cutting and patching in your own contracts, take advantage of your opportunity to clarify the contract prior to signing by including a specific provision that, unless specifically indicated otherwise in the contract documents, all cutting and patching in the performance of the work is considered to be nonstructural and nonhazardous and requires no special design or special permits. You might include additional clarification that, if it is determined prior to or during the performance of any cutting and patching that any affected work is in fact structural, hazardous, and/or requires special designs or permits, the owner will be responsible for: (1) the determination of all technical, design, and legal requirements for proceeding with the work; (2) contractor's cost of mobilization, performance, and demobilization for the added work; and (3) all time required for items 1 and 2.

Standard Subcontract Provision

Include in your own subcontracts a standard provision in your **boilerplate** that requires the subcontractor to be responsible for all cutting and patching associated with its work. If you find yourself negotiating a subcontract that does not require cutting and patching, or if you have otherwise determined that the cutting and patching will be provided by other means, your standard language can be negotiated out rather easily. If, on the other hand, your scope review led you to initially believe that no cutting and patching would be required, and you therefore did not include such a provision in your subcontract, subsequently discovering some small amount of cutting and patching would leave you on the hook for the extra cost. If you had a boiler-plate provision in your subcontract, you would be covered for that oversight.

Daily Field Report

Contents	Related Topics
Description	Correspondence
Value	Documentation
Components	Management Reporting Systems
Uses	Notice
"Daily" Means *Daily*	Photographs, Preconstruction, Progress, and Special
A Final Irony	
	Scheduling
	Time and Material (T&M)
	Value of Work—Actual Cost

Description

The *daily field report* is the fundamental document that records on-site progress, together with all conditions that affect the work. It is the focal point of an organization's standard reporting at the source of all causes and effects—the jobsite. Properly designed, the daily field report will catalog not only all the conditions of your own labor, equipment, and materials, but also the complete interaction of all parties to the contract, and of the regular set of all outside influences on your performance.

If actually prepared daily, the daily field report is generally considered to be one of the best of all sources—if not *the* best—available for all job information. This is because it is prepared as the information is being generated, with no appreciable lapse in time. The information is therefore fresh, accurate, and complete. In addition, the information is prepared by individuals with a certain amount of authority and responsibility for the work, people who are familiar with the intricacies of each component of work activity. They have a significant incentive to maintain the accuracy and comprehensiveness of the complete report. They witnessed the work and are qualified to describe all circumstances relating to that project on that day.

Value

If managed correctly, the daily field report will be the most detailed, accurate, and complete record of all jobsite events. It will become the cornerstone of support for every contention because it presents streams of legitimate, verifiable, and believable facts.

Components

Arranged in proper format, and maintained as they should be, the data included on each daily field report should include:

1. Descriptions of each work activity, separated and clarified as to the specific physical locations and extent.
2. Actual labor forces broken down by subcontractor, locations, and major work activities.
3. Equipment on site, and whether the items of equipment are being used that day or are in fact idle.
4. Site administrative staff and facilities.
5. Weather conditions and temperatures at key times of each day.
6. Any **change order** or potential change order work accomplished, with all relevant details.
7. Any work performed under protest, or under any other "cloud" that would require the issue to be revisited.
8. Any **photographs (preconstruction, progress, or special)** taken during the day, along with their subject identification, location, direction, purpose, and photographer.
9. Visitors to the jobsite.
10. **Job Meetings,** discussions, commitments, and conversations.
11. Safety compliances
12. Internal and external communications with respect to **scheduling,** production, productivity, and similar considerations.

Uses

The Daily Field Report is intended to record history, not necessarily to perform any particular ongoing job coordination activity. It is therefore often an easy target from which to steal time when job activities squeeze the time of the jobsite staff. If they are not genuinely accorded the respect they deserve, some employees may get the feeling that the daily field reports are not being used for any real purpose. In such cases, the field report information can become compromised, to the point where it is first unclear, then unusable, then missing altogether. If this happens, you are guaranteed a painful revelation when suddenly you need to fall back on your field reports to verify important pieces of information in order to resolve a major problem, and discover that your field reports are almost useless.

"Daily" Means *Daily*

Because it is impossible to tell in advance which items will become the most important information component, the Daily Field Report must be approached *each day* with the idea that every category must be religiously maintained. It is up to the central office project administration, whatever the particular authority structure is within the organization, to regularly police the reports. You must exercise the *discipline* to verify the completeness and accuracy of your field reports often, to be certain that all information is regularly being properly recorded—each day, on every project.

The idea that the reports are actually completed *daily* cannot be overstressed. If they are allowed to be lumped together for completion even weekly, the accuracy of the information degenerates exponentially. The volume of information similarly is very dramatically reduced.

When on site, senior management should refer to the reports obviously and often, during conversations, issue research, and so on. It is important to let every member of the project team know that the information is depended on, reviewed, and used. Consider some procedure that requires the jobsite staff to fax or mail the day's field report to some central administrative location *each day,* as an additional incentive to complete the reports on time.

A Final Irony

It is true that many sizable projects today are being constructed without such daily reporting efforts, or with field reporting so poor that it borders on being a complete waste of time. If this is going on in any of your projects, understand—particularly in these litigious time—that the lack of some kind of verifiable historic jobsite data can actually be flipped around and used as an example of irresponsible project management. If you do field reports, be sure that they are in fact being used as they are intended. If you do not do field reports, develop a form *now,* and begin using it *today.*

Deadlines

Real and Unreal Deadlines

Human nature being what it is, the deadline for an event is the earliest date by which you can expect it to occur. Deadlines do force action, and it is definitely not an accident that Christmas presents are bought on December 24, income tax returns are filed on April 15, and a 2:00 p.m. bid is delivered at 1:59.

Those are some real deadlines. Examples of some other deadlines that may or may not be real are activity completion dates, purchase order execution dates, payment due dates, and even court dates. Deadlines can pressure us into making a decision, or we can use them to put pressure on others. If we manage to meet the deadline, we can get the emergency over with. If we don't, the consequences are unpredictable.

It's easy to determine the "legitimacy" of a deadline, but the fact is most deadlines are not real. The day and time for a government bid is probably real. We know this because history bears it out. But even April 15 does not have to be real; all that's necessary is to file a form in order to get an extension of the deadline.

If someone tells you, "On Wednesday I'm giving the order to somebody," what that person is probably really saying is, "On Wednesday I'm going to determine what's best for me; and if waiting until Thursday is what's best for me, that is what I'm going to do."

The Power of Deadlines

There is, of course, a risk in not believing a deadline. A report promised on Wednesday doesn't get you fired if delivered on Thursday; but it might. If you are being told that "if you give me the order today, I can guarantee delivery" it might be best to give the order today.

The more you know about the other party's organization, production schedule, inventory picture, money pressures, and professional and personal motivators, the better you will be able to determine if their respective deadlines are real.

An established deadline does focus attention on a tangible date and time. It does compel action. Because, however, we have all been trained that deadlines are in fact not real, people do conduct their operations with the *intent* to make the deadlines established for them, but most don't lose any sleep if the deadline is missed to some reasonable degree.

Give Deadlines More Power

Assuming absolute **integrity** on the part of the parties, subcontractors and suppliers may genuinely believe that they are organizing themselves to achieve the series of deadlines imposed on them—the completion *schedule*—but because of their own problems with the labor force, material deliveries, lack of detail planning, lack of contingency planning, or for any number of reasons, intermediate schedule activity deadlines are missed routinely. Ultimately, it is your own conduct that gives your own deadlines the power that they should have.

Left on their own, subcontractors and suppliers, with their time-squeezed days, will not even consider beginning some activity earlier than it is scheduled. The series of deadlines that you refer to in progress **scheduling** will carry with it a very low probability of achievement unless you intervene.

Arrange your series of deadlines early. Be sure that each activity start is represented at its absolute earliest possible date. Have a mechanism for bringing such activities to the attention of your army of subvendors as early as absolutely possible. Through your conduct, give your own schedule legitimacy. If you tell your vendors "The order is going to be placed on Wednesday," place it on Wednesday. Develop a history of complying with your own deadlines. Look for early opportunities in your own progress schedule to monitor performance, and demand compliance. Communicate to your subcontractors the seriousness with which your entire organization regards the series of deadlines.

On each **change order proposal,** *always* include a proposal acceptance date, beyond which the particular change order is void and the price likely to go up. Do not, however, assume arbitrary dates. Consider them very carefully, and make them real enough to allow you to actually follow through on those imposed deadlines. When the time passes on such a deadline, be sure that you have arranged it in such a way as to allow you to take the action highlighted as the consequence of a delay.

Look for early opportunities to make even deadlines for minor events as real as possible. Do your best to comply with every deadline imposed on you by those parties with whom you are doing business, so that you maintain the upper hand and the right to expect deadline compliance from the owner, design professionals, and subvendors.

Deadlock

Contents

Related Topics

A Powerful Tactic

Deadlock can be a very powerful approach in **negotiation**. There is nothing wrong with deadlock in itself, and there is almost nothing like a deadlock to test the resolve of an opponent. Most people are afraid of a deadlock in negotiation, and whether they realize it or not they do everything they can to avoid it. Accordingly, if you are not apprehensive of the problems that they can create, you might be able to take the upper hand by demonstrating your own firm resolve.

Problems with Deadlock

The truth is, a bad settlement of an issue is easier to explain to your upper management than a deadlock. Because all of us at some time have reached a deadlock in a negotiation, we all know how uncomfortable it is. Having approached a negotiation with the objective of achieving some kind of an agreement, a deadlock leaves us open-ended. If we're not careful, we might begin to lose confidence in our own judgment. We might begin to ask if we could have said or done something differently, if there were other concessions that could have been made, how the deadlock will affect our reputation, and how our own organization will look at the deadlock. We'll wonder whether we should have accepted the last offer.

Problems for Your Opponent

Don't fail to recognize that all the things that are making you so uncomfortable with your impasse are probably having at least the same effect on your opponent and your opponent's organization. Negotiators who do not have the full support of their own management will hesitate to deadlock even if it makes sense for them to do so under the particular set of circumstances. Because it is such a frustrating experience and can leave an organization with some sense of failure, if we are secure in our own team play on our side of the deadlock, we stand a very good chance that the pressure of a deadlock will divide our opponent's organization.

The power of a deadlock lies in our appreciation of how it affects both parties. Although there is no question that a deadlock softens up both organizations to some degree, we need to remain aware of the specifics of the effects on both sides. After some time, both organizations will be willing to reach some amount of compromise, especially if there is a face-saving way out. Refer to **acceptance time** for related discussion.

Breaking a Deadlock

In order to break an impasse that you don't want, consider the following actions:

1. Put some time between you and the resolution, if you can afford to. There is a very good chance that time will make an impasse even more uncomfortable, and force your opponents to look for ways to end it themselves. Look for some small (perhaps intangible) **concession** that you might give as a means to reopen discussion.

2. Change the time shape of uncertainty. Postpone some difficult parts of the agreement for renegotiation at a later time. Change the risk-sharing formula. Look for areas of potential confusion, and offer clarifications.

3. Change the negotiator. Sometimes simply a new face is all the excuse needed by the other party to allow a concession. Change the shape of future satisfaction by offering additional guarantees. Separate the problem into components. Approach each component as an individual problem. Try to solve the pieces, and you might actually wind up with the sum greater than the parts (refer to **detail** for important related discussion.)

Defective Specifications

Defective Specifications

To a layperson, the term *defective specifications* simply refers to a document containing flaws. The practical definition, however, conveys the idea that a defective set of plans and specifications somehow contains requirements that either cannot be achieved or in some manner do not operate to achieve the intended result. The specified components either will not work together properly or, once they are working together, they do not achieve the design intent.

Sources of Defective Specifications

Defective specifications can originate from many sources, and can include specifications that have either incorrect designs ("complete" designs that just don't work) or incomplete designs (designs that might work if some missing items were included in the complete specifications). Defective contract documents are usually a result of some deficiency in attention to the complete design or the design coordination by the design team. In fairness to the design team, its members are often under severe time pressure to produce the complete set of documents for bidding by some aggressive date. This pressure, combined with competitive design budgets, can be the root cause of many defective specifications. Related causes may include such practices in the creation of the specification as **cut-and-paste, strange specifications,** and **old age (specifications).**

The Spearian Doctrine

A significant case related to defective specification was that of the United States versus Spearian, 248 U.S. 132 (1918). There are many books which describe the intricacies and the specifics of the Spearian case, but suffice it to say that Spearian, as decided by the U.S. Supreme Court, is considered one of the most significant cases on the subject of defective specifications.

The essential decision confirmed in Spearian was simply but profoundly that "… the duty to check plans did not impose the *obligation* (on the contract) to pass on the *adequacy* to accomplish the purpose in view." It was accordingly Spearian that provided the idea that the owner furnishes the contractor an *implied warranty of the adequacy of the plans and specifications.* It left the contractor responsible to construct that which is clearly indicated, but relieved the contractor of the responsibility for its performance with respect to the design's intentions.

This is a landmark case with which every contractor should be intimately familiar.

Delay

Definition

In the calculation of the net effect of a delay on the project end date, the subject of *concurrent delays* must also be considered. Concurrent delays are those in which two or more delays are caused simultaneously by both the owner and the contractor. To the extent that both delays clearly overlap, the mutual responsibility for the delays is recognized. Accordingly, the law provides that neither party will be charged for that portion of the delay.

As you can imagine, it all comes down to **documentation,** the project record, the history of communication, and your ability to convincingly display all related facts in a cause-effect analysis.

In general, the concept of *delay* most often implicitly refers to delay in completion of the project beyond the original specified contract completion date. This is a net effect on the project end date, and it is not necessarily equal to the actual total delay to an intermediate activity or series of activities.

If an activity is on a project's *critical path,* a delay to that activity by definition would equate to an equal delay to the project end date. If, however, a delay is affecting an intermediate activity that is not on the critical path, the delay might be said to also absorb at least a certain amount of available *float* on that path.

For this section, it is important only to note that there is a distinction to be made between an activity delay and project completion delay.

Compensation Categories

All delays are very costly to every party to a contract, as well as to any party connected with the contract (refer to **change order components** and **consequential costs** for important related discussion). Depending on the facts of the situation, the particular circumstances, and the actual contract provisions, a delay may be *compensable* or *noncompensable.* All this means is that when you've managed to provide complete and adequate justification that a delay to the project is in fact not the responsibility of the contractor, the contract itself either will allow you to be paid for the delay or may simply wind up granting you nothing but an "extension of **time.**"

Noncompensable Delay

Noncompensable—or excusable—delays are considered to be the fault of neither party to the contract. In such situations, the owner must grant an extension of time, but the contractor is not entitled to any reimbursement for its cost associated with the delay. It is significant, however, in that once having granted a time extension, the owner may not assess **liquidated damages** or actual damages, may not default the contractor, and may not demand that the contractor adhere to the original schedule of completion by **acceleration.**

Noncompensable delays are usually defined by the contract. In many instances, the term is nearly interchangeable with *excusable delay,* because, if a contractor is looking to be "excused" for a problem to the project, implicit in that request is the idea that the core of the issue is neither the fault of the contractor nor of any party to the contract.

This category of delay is usually of the **force majeure** variety, including "acts of God," and other things such as fires, floods, strikes, national emergencies, inclement weather (under certain circumstances), or other "causes beyond the contractor's control."

Note, however, that other "causes" of noncompensable delays may be defined in the contract, but might actually be of the compensable variety, given the particular facts of a situation and your ability to document and display the cause-effect. Examples in this category include such "noncompensable delays" specified in the contract as "any act or neglect by the owner or architect, or by any separate contractor employed by the owner, or by changes ordered in the work, or by delay authorized by the architect, or by any cause by which the architect shall decide to justify the delay."

Delays in these types of categories that are defined in your contract to be "noncompensable" might not actually be.

Compensable Delay

A compensable delay is one that is caused by some performance or performance failure on the part of the owner or design professionals, or by other causes within the control of the owner.

The law clearly recognizes that one party to a contract may not do anything (either directly or through negligence) to prevent the other party to the contract from fulfilling its obligations.

Examples of owner-caused delay include:

- Failure to approve shop drawings within a reasonable period of time
- Failure to coordinate a project when prime or separate contracts are awarded
- Delays caused by defective design
- Directed suspensions in the work, or portions thereof
- Failure by the owner's design professionals to perform their duties in a timely fashion (submittal approval, requisition review, inspections, etc.)
- Any other delay caused by the owner or its representatives

Concurrent Delay

Multiple and continuing delays to the project can quickly add up to a complicated, cryptic, and confusing scenario in which it is impossible to sort out the individual effects on the project. The ability to boil it all down to a clear demonstration of either linear—or concurrent—delays, and the relative amounts of each, is simply and directly related to the amount of attention given to (1) the development of an adequate baseline construction schedule and (2) the incorporation of all changes and delay effects of the project into the schedule on a continuous basis.

Refer to **three schedules: as-planned, as-built, and adjusted** for important related discussion.

Records Used to Determine Delay

The best project **documentation** that can be used to determine delay is that which is contemporaneous: generated and distributed as the respective events are occurring. Such documentation routinely helps you comply with **notice** requirements of a contract, and is a more genuine and legitimate support for any factual representation.

The types of records that you might consider to prepare contemporaneously as the project progresses, or that you may need to secure after the fact, or prepare as an analysis, might include the following:

1. The as-planned schedule
2. All progress schedule updates, with any transmittals noting distribution and any significant remarks
3. A cash-flow projection, based on the relation of the approved **schedule of values** to the baseline as-built schedule

4. Each periodic application for payment

5. An S-curve analysis; which displays the anticipated cash flow against the actual cash flow

6. All **change order** documentation; including proposals, negotiation notes, and final change orders

7. All **RFIs (requests for information)** and related documents

8. **Meeting minutes**

9. Special meeting minutes

10. **Daily field report**

11. Shop drawing logs, with supporting shop drawing transmittals

12. **Correspondence**

13. **Contract documents**

Assembling all these records does not guarantee success in the delay analysis or delay claim, but will certainly put you in the best possible position to succeed.

Delay Damage Categories

The items that follow are categories that should be considered when assessing costs resulting from a job delay. The list is a general overview, and should be used only as a guide for you, your attorney, and possibly your claims consultant to use as a starting point from which to develop the detail of your ultimate presentation:

1. Increased labor cost

   ▪ Increased hourly wages and benefits
   ▪ Increased number of hours due to out-of-sequence of work, acceleration, disruption

2. Increased material costs

   ▪ Absolute value of price increases
   ▪ Increased shipping and handling
   ▪ Storage and rehandling

3. Increased equipment costs

   ▪ Increased rates for equipment and operators
   ▪ Increased hours due to out-of-sequence work, acceleration, and disruption
   ▪ Idle equipment costs
   ▪ Demobilization and remobilization costs

4. Increased direct (jobsite) overhead cost

    - Increased supervision cost at the site
    - Field offices and field facilities
    - Temporary field utilities: power, heat, light, etc.
    - Extended bond and insurance coverage
    - Miscellaneous costs associated with continued on-site presence: cleanup and maintenance, erosion control, temporary protections, etc.

5. Increased home office overhead

    - Allocated **home office overhead** costs
    - Home office administrative overhead costs

6. Opportunity costs associated with reduced capacity; lost profits

7. Reduced bonding capacity; lost profits on work which otherwise might have been obtained and performed, but for loss in bonding capacity, as that capacity is tied up in the delayed project

8. Cost of capital

    - Carrying costs for retainages and other payments that would otherwise be due but are now late because of the project delay
    - Loss of use of money

9. Attorney's fees and expenses related to pursuing damage recovery

10. Punitive damages

Delegation

Contents

Related Topics

Delegate Importance

Plenty of managers give delegation lip service, but few actually delegate authority in important matters. They delegate details and dog work, but decisions are kept closely held. One who practices real **leadership,** however, participates in details and dog work and is in the best position to recognize where the work can be done without, or how it can be done faster or better. The real leader delegates as many important matters and decisions as possible, because that fosters a climate in which subordinates can grow both personally and professionally.

Accountability and Authority

If a task can successfully be delegated to a subordinate, that success is usually rooted in the idea that it is the subordinate who is closer to the point of use. The subordinate will be more personally and immediately affected by good or bad performance, and if given the tools and expectation, the subordinate can see more clearly why it is in his or her best interest to rise to the occasion and complete the task thoroughly and on time.

The great stifler of delegation is that *accountability* is often delegated, while the *authority* to make related decisions is not. The subordinates are thrown into the situation—to the wolves—with one or both arms tied behind their backs. Their performance with respect to a situation is left closely tied to decisions, input, or some other connection which must still flow down from the top. When the ultimate resolution is adversely affected by some lack of performance on the part of the superior, somehow these poor subordinates are still held accountable—responsible—to an unfair degree by those same superiors who have failed to hold up their end of the plank. As unreasonable as this example may seem, it is precisely this situation that is occurring minute by minute in every construction company. It is precisely this situation which regularly and routinely undermines everyone's effort to delegate.

Accordingly, if you have made the decision to delegate an item of work or important decision, simultaneously make the corresponding decision regarding the specific limits of authority that you will actually invest in your subordinates. Discuss those authority limits explicitly with the subordinates, be clear in your expectations, and determine the explicit criteria by which the subordinates' performance will be judged. In this way, the subordinates know where they stand and can assess whether they have enough tools, information, and resources available for the task. Because the performance criteria are specific and measurable, the subordinates can understand and be responsible for decisions made. This is effective delegation.

Department Delegation

Consider two executives as an example. The first executive operates in a fairly traditional manner within the legal department. He reads some contracts very carefully, and makes detailed notes. He returns other contracts with a question, implying that he has read the contract carefully, but has not really done so. In other cases, it appears that he simply signs contracts, not necessarily having read them thoroughly. There is generally a feeling throughout the department that the executive reviews all the documents anyway, and so the documents stack up on the executive's desk directly from the department's own **boilerplate** machinery, with little to no review, preparation, or thought given to those documents by the executive's subordinates.

The second executive notifies his general counsel that he does not want to read any legal documents covering specific transactions previously approved. He clearly instructs counsel that if he is to execute a contract, then he expects the document to be initialed by the legal counsel for the legal aspects. In addition, the executive has the Estimating Department head or other appropriate person review and initial the contract for scope of work and other operating considerations. The executive makes it clear to both of those individuals that if it is sent to the executive with those two sets of initials, the executive will sign it without reading those criteria.

In this way, the second executive places the accountability where it belongs while keeping the company better protected by having those close to the particular aspects personally review those aspects. It minimizes oversight, reduces internal memos, and results in a cohesive, thoroughly managed work product. Everyone participates, understands each role in the total transaction, and is appropriately made responsible for that portion of the total outcome.

Delegate the Whole Job

In some companies, delegation can work this way: The superior starts the job, hands it to the subordinate for the difficult or boring part, takes it back when it's completed, and modestly takes the credit.

A leader's delegation, however, should look for the chance to give a subordinate an opportunity for doing an entire job, and for receiving the credit if it works. If done this way, a bored or frustrated subordinate can come alive when given an entire project, and that individual's abilities can take a surprising leap. Such an approach can begin to transform a moderate or mundane individual, first into one with a pulse, and then possibly into a real performer.

Look for the opportunities to make assignments that give your people character. Give your subordinates complete and important assignments. Ask them to report back to you in ways that focus on the need to respect the organizational reporting system, rather than on ways that imply that you are chasing them around making sure that they're "doing their work." Generate a dialog with subordinates with respect to the assignment as if you are equals. If you occasionally offer your assistance with tasks related to the details of the assignment, you might be surprised at how often subordinates will refuse to share the dog work with you to demonstrate their ability to pull it all together.

Deliberate Errors

Contents

The Problem

Low Risk

Be on the Lookout

Related Topics

Contract versus Contact

Geotechnical Information

Integrity

Liars

Power of the Standard Form

Spying

The Problem

This section is not intended to suggest that anyone should intentionally introduce errors into pricing, negotiation, or any other business dealings. It is intended only to suggest the possibility that people with whom you do business at any level may, at any time, be considering this unethical idea.

For those without any moral scruples, deliberate errors can serve a significant purpose: they misdirect and deceive. People

- Add wrong

- Multiply wrong

- Leave out words

- Misplace decimal points and commas

- Make incorrect statements

- Change clauses after agreements have been made

- Add or delete language in bodies of documents

A very subtle word change can alter the context of entire meanings.

Low Risk

From the error maker's point of view, the potential risk associated with the introduction of such errors is very low. If the error is discovered immediately (or early), there is really nothing to lose; "anyone can make a mistake." A simple indication of **surprise,** combined with a little look of "confusion," can leave the person who discovered the "error" quite unsure (or unsuspecting) of the real situation.

If a person discovers such an error much later, someone in the organization must then have the courage to reveal it to upper levels of management and explain why the error was not discovered in the first place. From the error maker's point of view, the odds become

very high that the later the error is discovered, the greater the probability that those who finally discovered it won't do anything about it.

And so from the error maker's perspective, the potential for any kind
of a direct penalty is extremely low, whereas the potential rewards may
be extremely high.

Be on the Lookout

Be on the lookout for such errors. Force yourself to check the arithmetic, read the fine print, compare final drafts against the original
drafts word for word, and confirm every understanding. If you do discover an error and determine it to be deliberate, get angry. Consider
carefully everyone to whom you should direct your protest, and then
follow through immediately. Never assume that everything is right.
Be skeptical. Check.

Design-Build

Contract Relationships

In the design-build project delivery method, the owner contracts singularly with a design-build firm. This type of firm can generally offer both in-house design capability and in-house construction capability. It can be a design office that affiliates itself with a construction company, or a construction company that affiliates itself with a design firm. Whatever the details, the owner sees only the design-build firm contractually. There is no distinction made as in **general contracting** with separate contracts between the owner and construction force and the owner and the design force. The subcontract relationships to the construction side of the design-build firm are identical to those of the general contractor.

Communications

Communication between the construction and the design entities can be transparent to the owner. Communication between the design-build firm and the owner is likely to be confined closely along the lines that would be expected in the relationship between a design firm and the owner; that is, the owner's input is of course involved during the design development process, selection of alternative pricing, and final authorization to proceed with any changes. As far as a subvendor is concerned, communication should be a one-stop process. Instead of providing submittals, for example, to the general contractor, who must then provide them to the design professionals for their reaction, the subvendor provides its submittals to the design-build firm, which will very likely have the design component review the submittals immediately. Such a process makes the review efficient and quick.

Advantages and Disadvantages

The principle advantage to the owner with this arrangement is simplicity of composition. Only one contract entity need be dealt with, and responsibility for all performance is as clearly pinpointed as possible—directly and to a single company. In this way, the owner relieves itself to a large degree of the kinds of contests that are common in the traditional **general contracting** arrangement. This method of project delivery is therefore attractive to an owner because of its apparent speed and its single-point accountability.

A serious disadvantage from the owner's point of view is that there is no sensible watchdog mechanism that confirms the proper performance in all the details of the design-build company. Whereas a separate, independent design firm would perform submittal review, inspection, payment application approval, and other important functions on behalf of the owner, a design-build firm has many opportunities for abuse, if appropriate safeguards are not built into the owner–design-build agreement. Inspection of the work, evaluation of changes, and so on can be a complicated, ineffective operation if the owner does not have complete confidence in the **integrity** of the design-build firm.

These notable disadvantages, and the apparent disadvantages of the traditional general contractor arrangement have led many owners to consider the various forms of construction management, specifically **construction management with a guaranteed maximum price (GMP)** and **agent construction management (ACM).**

Design Duplications

Related Topics

As Indicated

Boilerplate

Cut-and-Paste

Defective Specifications

"Equals" and "Substitutions"

"Fat" Specifications

Interpretation—Right to Choose

Old Age (Specifications)

Strange Specifications

Issue

Design duplications can appear anywhere in the contract documents: the plans, specifications, general conditions, or referenced standards. They can manifest themselves in several ways:

1. Specifications for the same or similar items in two different specification sections

2. Specifications for different items intended for the same function included in two different specifications

3. Descriptions of different items intended for the same function included in the same specification

When a duplication is identified, the owner and design professionals invariably take the position that the work is absolutely included in the contract. After all, it's specified "twice." If it's substantial, expect a request for a credit proposal.

Specified Twice, or Not at All

Just because an item may actually be specified twice, do not assume that it has actually been provided as any portion of the contract. If, for example, you have bought two separate items per plans and specifications, and there is justifiable reason in each specification for that party to consider that the item is provided in the other specification, there may be justifiable reason why *neither* party included the work item. In such a case, the net result would be that there was either a clear or a sublet which ultimately caused the item to not be specified at all. Refer to **coordination** for important related discussion.

Response Guidelines

These effects are subtle but real. Understand them completely before you give in too quickly. Follow the recommendations below in order to help you confirm the case and proceed accordingly.

1. Determine all details of the apparent duplication. Determine whether each description is complete, and, if so, whether it is consistent with the other. Determine whether the descriptions are in different specification sections (with different subcontractors involved), whether they are included in the same specification (both under the responsibility of the same subcontractor), or whether the duplication offers different treatments, supposedly to accommodate the same function.

2. Of the different items and/or methods apparently called for, is one version more sensible or preferred? If so, determine how you would like the situation to be handled. Which situation would, as a practical matter, work best within the job quality and schedule constraints?

3. Review all contracts, plans, and specifications. Determine if any or all contracts are of an **adhesion contract** nature. Identify **ambiguities.** Determine if the affected subcontracts are "per plans and specs" or if the scopes of work are segmented.

4. Determine if "rules of precedence" or "correlation of contract documents" is clearly provided in the specification to help you point to the rules that should be used in the ultimate **interpretation,** or if you need to rely on applicable contract law.

5. Analyze the duplication as objectively as possible. List for yourself all the reasons why each subcontractor should or should not have carried the work in its bids. Determine if each of the potentially affected subcontractors has been aware of the work, but reasonably construed it to be accommodated by another trade. Determine if each duplication is clear in itself, or if its use is strained or otherwise incomplete.

6. Find out if anyone contacted the owner prior to bid with a request for clarification regarding the item. If anyone claims this condition, determine whether there is any **documentation** to support the contention.

7. Determine your preferred solution. Does the solution involve a commitment of your own money, time, and effort, or does it strictly involve subtrades? Confirm the dollar estimates for each solution to the problem. Consider the timing of each solution with respect to the effect on the construction schedule. Evaluate the potential of the affected subcontractors to accept the extra work without a significant battle. Consider if any solution makes more sense than others, given design, cost, schedule, and quality considerations.

8. Determine if any grounds exist to convince the owner and/or design professionals that the duplication was reasonably not included in your general bid and that the price increase you're proposing is therefore appropriate.

9. If you find your position weak, or your ability to convince the owner lacking, do not make the final decision yourself. Refer to **conduit theory** for important related discussion. Submit a request to the owner or design professional as your contract requires for interpretation and direction. Require the owner or design professionals to give you the complete basis of the determination and the name of the responsible party, specification section, and other appropriate contract reference.

10. If your review of the situation reveals a strong position that could be handily substantiated, back up your contentions with specific contract references. Be sure to include the technical plan and specification descriptions that support your position, references to the conflicting details, the contract provisions that dictate the manner in which ambiguities are to be resolved, and your summary conclusion logically deciding the issue. Follow up with a change order proposal, including the time required for acceptance before project impact occurs.

Detail

Simplicity versus Complexity

Throughout our industry, there appears to be a resistance to providing detail. People who price changes or other project components most commonly pursue, at least initially, some avenue that will allow them to present their pricing in as few lump sum components as possible. The lump-sum values are always larger than the approver would otherwise wish them to be and offer little or no indication as to how they were obtained.

The next obvious step on the part of such a would-be approver is to simply ask for more detail. That detail is accordingly given over the phone, on the back of an envelope, or in a more formal correspondence, but in the final analysis *is* given to some degree—just late, and possibly fragmented. The degree of resistance in providing an adequate amount of detail seems to be inversely related to the probability that those lump sum values will be approved in their first submitted amounts.

The irony in pursuing the lump sum option to avoid pricing detail is that, in most cases, the detail will ultimately become a requirement. Accordingly, the failure to initially provide detail serves only to delay ultimate approval, and may give your approver the initial impression that you are trying to hide something.

Detail = Approvability

There seems to be a direct correlation between the complexity of pricing substantiation and the likelihood of securing price approval at maximum levels and an inverse correlation between the volume of detail with supporting backup and the likelihood that all the supporting detail will actually be reviewed and checked.

Over and over, it seems that, as long as the cost component summary is clear, the fatter and more complex the backup and the more minute the level of detail included in each calculation (along with references to other appropriate sources, etc.), the more likely it is that the data will be assumed to be correct. Even if an item does not initially lend itself to any precise calculation, it will probably be to your advantage for you to display the manner in which you did arrive at the particular price.

Large Number of Small Items

Almost without exception, it will be easier to secure approval for a large number of small items than for a small number of large ones. Psychology aside, it has been proven in the final test over and over again. Realize right at the beginning that no one but you can visualize the complicated sequence of events in the complete detail, with all its interferences and contingencies, in the way that *you* can visualize them. The challenge in ultimately securing approval for a price, however, is that it is exactly this visualization that you must achieve in the mind of the approver in order to force a complete understanding of the reasons behind your pricing. It is only at that point that your approver will be able to sign off with the feeling that your price really is fair and reasonable. It is up to you to get others to appreciate your point of view. You've got to destroy their possibly oversimplified preconceptions and educate them to your way of thinking. The concept of **equitable adjustment** is closely related to these ideas.

If you think through all of the individual sequences involved in the achievement of an otherwise lump sum activity, and list them in complete detail, you may surprise yourself with the actual amount of effort that goes into achieving a particular item. Think through and include all the classic time-killers that are often overlooked in such considerations. For example, before you will be able to get into an area to remove and replace a window, do you have to notify the room occupant to leave and wait for it to happen? Do you then need to move the furniture out of your way and remove the window treatments? Does it all need to be replaced when you are finished? Will you have to vacuum the rug? Do you need to hand-carry the old window down two flights of stairs to a dumpster behind the building?

After itemizing every conceivable subactivity, consider each activity individually. Think about the actual logistics of the day, including coffee breaks, safety meetings, and all the other things that steal time. Price each individual component reasonably, but separately. If you pursue this type of exercise consistently, you *will* arrive at a price which is higher than the simple lump sum that you would have arrived at without such detailed consideration. Although the total itself might be larger than anyone is expecting to see, your subsequent **negotiation** can be directed to the item's individual components. A simple consideration of whether or not the particular subactivity is actually required, along with a very obvious review of your reasonable subprice component, will go a long way to securing approval of the individual item. The smaller unit numbers may be easier for your approver to accept, and if you do need to negotiate them, you might be able to modify one without necessarily affecting the others. Refer to **concessions** for related discussion.

Dispute Clause

Description

The dispute clause is the contract mechanism that provides a specific procedure for resolution of serious differences. It recognizes that construction disputes are of a unique breed and can occur in various degrees of seriousness. Properly designed, it should consider not only issues that are clearly in the dispute category, but also those provisions of changes that have not been resolved in accordance with the **change clause.** In this situation, it can apply to either the entire change or simply those components of the change which did not wind up in final agreement.

The dispute clause may actually be combined with the change clause in a particular agreement, or it may be separated for clarity.

Composition Possibilities

A good dispute clause should not only provide basic procedure, but should also allow the complete determination of outcomes that would apply in the various situations within the realm of possibility. If you're drafting your own dispute clause, consider the issues that follow. If you're considering a dispute clause that is provided to you as part of an agreement, the way that it addresses, or fails to address, the issues below may give you an indication of the care that has gone into the preparation of your agreement.

1. *Describe the basic resolution procedure.* **Arbitration** might be provided as an option, or mediation, or other procedure that might ultimately conclude with litigation if agreement is not reached along the way.

2. *Include complete and comprehensive procedure for the dispute resolution mechanism.* If arbitration is provided, for example, be sure to spell out the conditions of arbitration, and the rules of engagement. If a recognized arbitration body is mentioned, reference to the published rules of that arbitration body may be sufficient. If not, great care must be taken to provide for such a procedure in the

clause. Methods for resolving things such as arbitrator selection, venue, and discovery should be specifically considered.

3. *Is the dispute mechanism (other than litigation) "binding"?* If that is the intention, there should be language confirming that any award resulting from such specified procedure shall be final, and the judgment may be entered in accordance with applicable law in any court of competent jurisdiction.

4. *Is the dispute mechanism intended by the party to be the resolution mechanism?* Has it been precisely so defined, or is it vague enough to allow creative attorneys to circumvent the true intent? Is there any language, for example, specifically clarifying that the dispute resolution mechanism is a condition precedent to any legal action?

5. *What happens to the project during a dispute?* Is it clear that the contractor (or subcontractor) has the right to stop work pending resolution of dispute? Or is it clear that the contractor (or subcontractor) must continue the work that is the subject of the dispute?

6. *Is there a "good faith" requirement for submitted disputes?* Is some kind of personal certification required on the part of a company officer to affirm that the claim is made in good faith, and the supporting data are accurate and complete?

7. *Are bond claim procedures affected?* Can a bond claim be made simultaneously while a dispute is pursued in accordance with the contract provisions, or is it very clear the dispute resolution procedure must be run out in its entirety before a bond claim may be pursued?

8. *Are housekeeping issues properly addressed?* Is venue, disposition of legal fees, appeal proceedings (if allowed), conflict-of-interest, consolidation, and every other significant issue specifically addressed, or are they left to become the stuff that legal fees are made of?

Dispute Resolution

Intent of the Parties

The dispute resolution mechanism in a contract often appears to be clear but unfortunately, in practical terms, can be more often very far from the case. If the contract is silent with respect to any specific dispute resolution procedure, litigation of the dispute is an implicit option, although **arbitration** or **mediation** can be an option if the parties subsequently agree to it. Other contracts provide an explicit procedure for arbitration, mediation, or some combination, providing only that the award rendered in such an arbitration is enforceable by any court of competent jurisdiction. Whatever the detail, the result is an explicit written intention of the parties that a particular dispute will be resolved by a certain procedure. In other words, if we have included an agreement to arbitrate, we intend to arbitrate. As simple as it sounds, this basic principle is being perverted daily as attorneys continue to posture and concoct scenarios that are outside the explicit dispute-resolving intention of the agreement.

The "Real" Procedure

For example, if an agreement provides for arbitration as the mechanism to resolve all disputes, and the contractor has provided a 100 percent payment performance bond as security for such performance, and the subcontractor agrees to this condition, is it fair or equitable for a subcontractor to place a lien on the property before even the beginning of the dispute resolution procedure described in the contract? Similarly, is it fair to pursue a claim on the bond, simultaneously with or before proceeding with the prescribed resolution procedure, without first confirming the legitimacy of the subcontractor's position through the clearly described due process?

Despite all our efforts to clarify the intention of the parties with respect to dispute resolution, day after day we continue to allow attorneys on both sides to pervert and distort the true intention of the parties.

One Solution

If your contract or subcontract provides for **arbitration** or some alternative form of dispute resolution, and that is the true intent of the parties, it is unfortunately necessary to clarify how that true intent will be applied. (Refer to **agreements versus understandings** for important related discussion.) In order to achieve this, you might improve your subcontracts, for example, to include provisions that address the following:

- The prescribed dispute resolution mechanism (arbitration for example) is the *exclusive* remedy, which must be pursued *as a condition precedent* to any legal action *whatsoever.*

- If you have provided the owner with a payment performance bond, clarify that your own subcontract bond claims may be pursued only under the conditions that: (1) you have received payment from the owner on behalf of work performed by the subcontractor—assuming that is a requirement of the subcontract (refer to **pay-when-paid**); (2) the subcontractor has in fact fully complied with all its responsibilities with respect to its subcontract (refer to **schedule of values**); (3) the dispute resolution pursuant to the contract (arbitration for example) has in fact been conducted; (4) an award pursuant to that dispute resolution mechanism has been granted in favor of the subcontractor; and (5) you have not complied with the requirements of such award.

- If the subcontractor pursues any legal action, or submits claims on the contractor's bonds before first allowing for the process described above, the subcontractor's account will be adjusted by a credit change order to offset the amounts owed to you to cover your costs and expenses associated with your administrative, personnel time, legal fees, and other costs expended in responding to such inappropriate actions on behalf of the subcontractor.

Clarify your agreement with a clear understanding. Follow up with a clear, step-by-step resolution mechanism that will keep your remedy reasonable, and without subject to further interpretation. Keep your chosen dispute resolution mechanism intact, and ensure that it operates in the manner intended.

Documentation

Get It In Writing

It's been said that it's more important to be documented than to be right. Every attorney will tell you that every case is determined not on the "facts," but on the *documented* facts.

Even with absolute **integrity** on the parts of both parties to a construction agreement, misunderstandings, misinterpretations, misapplication, and just plain miscommunication are compounded over the duration of a project simply by the sheer number of transactions. Even with the best of memories, and the most honest intent, only the most significant and clear issues have any chance at all of being remembered the way they exactly happened. Beyond that, there is virtually no chance at all that the date and time of the occurrence would be remembered. I'll leave it to you to determine the relative possibility of determining and demonstrating—and quantifying—the resulting cause-effect on the project date and your cost of completion.

If it's part of your job—and part of the company responsibility—it is now a major part of *your* responsibility to write it down, and get it distributed.

No Excuse

In contemporary contracting, there is virtually no excuse for any level of inadequacy in your project documentation. There are so many vehicles available to us—**scheduling,** schedule revisions, **meeting minutes, RFIs (requests for information), photographs, videos, change orders,** memos, faxes, e-mail, **daily field reports,** production reports, inspection reports, and on, and on, and on—that each minute of every day allows us to conveniently incorporate the facts of the situation on a relevant document, and to get that information contemporaneously incorporated into the formal project record.

Attend that job meeting and get your remarks in the meeting minutes. Fill out the daily field report with the remarks made to you in an on-site conversation—and distribute a copy of that field report to that party. Include the reasons for each schedule interference on your schedule revision updates—and distribute those schedule updates with those incriminating notes to all project participants. Get it all down, and get it distributed.

Think on the Fax

Approach your project with the idea that the only reason that you are having "conversations" at all is so that you can begin your fax with "Confirming our conversation of ...." Refer to **notice** for important related discussion. Get intimately familiar with your company's fax-transmittal form and the **RFI** form. Train yourself to ask every question by writing directly on one of these two forms. Get in the habit of faxing those questions to the individual who is responsible for responding to you.

Cross-Correlation

Develop your own methods to tie your documentation together in an interrelated network. If your construction scheduling update method allows you to provide remarks on the status of the activity performances, include in those remarks references to **job meetings,** letters and memos, **RFIs, change orders,** and other components of the project documentation that would provide the detail to support your summary remarks.

Follow the same procedure with the other components of project documentation. Start each item in the job meeting minutes, for example, with your RFI designation number. The effort you put into the cost-correlation of your documentation will pay off huge dividends in every single instance where you need to research any issue. You will be guided immediately and directly by the progressive series of detail that can support any justification of your analysis.

Be Responsible

Look for opportunities to assume the official responsibility for project documentation efforts. If, for example, there is any option to you, volunteer—yes *volunteer*—to provide the job **meeting minutes.** Control of the job meeting minutes is control over the most important and respected portions of the entire job record.

Look for other ways to transform your own ongoing documentation records into "official" status. Consider, for example, offering as a "convenience" distribution of your own **daily field report.** A simple gesture, this procedure can result in a quantum leap in the legitimacy of your daily information both in terms of factual content and **notice.**

If some other party (the owner representative, design professional, etc.) is otherwise responsible for some "official" project documentation—such as the job meeting minutes—don't relax. You must exercise the discipline to keep your notes, almost with the anticipation that the distributed official documentation will regularly be overly aggressive, guilty of significant omission, and even misrepresentative. You must force yourself and your people to regularly maintain complete and accurate notes that you will use to immediately check the accuracy of all distributed "official" information.

Be sure that in the next job meeting you force the inclusion of information that had been conveniently omitted from the meeting minutes. Don't be shy about clarifying a statement in the minutes so that it more accurately reflects the conversation as it *really* happened. If such abuses continue, react accordingly. Don't be afraid to highlight your concern about the legitimacy of the information as it's being presented, and demand that the information be presented completely and correctly.

Be sure that you and your company are completely and accurately documented, and you will have taken a giant leap toward raising your own professional level of responsibility.

Duty to Inquire

Clarifying Ambiguities

A contractor will not be permitted to recover additional costs resulting from complying with an owner's interpretation of the contract if the contractor knew—or should have known—of an ambiguity or a design defect before executing the contract, and failed to bring it to the owner's attention at that time. The rules and circumstances regarding **ambiguities** and **interpretation** are closely related and are very relevant to this topic.

Reasonable Interpretation

The laws that apply in determining the reasonableness of a contractor's interpretation of certain contract provisions and indications depend on the factual circumstances of the case. In common law, a court deciding an issue with respect to ambiguous contract language might attempt to determine the most reasonable interpretation, and then apply that interpretation to the issue. In making such a determination, the court might rely on the rules regarding ambiguities and interpretation. Even under these circumstances, however, there does remain the risk that the court might agree with the owner's interpretation if it is *more* reasonable than the contractor's. Under federal government contracting principles, however, the contractor's interpretation is likely to be followed if it is a reasonable interpretation—and not necessarily the *most* reasonable interpretation available. In such a situation, it might be recognized that it is in fact possible for more than one reasonable interpretation to be available; in such cases the law provides that the contractor should have the right to rely on its own reasonable interpretation.

Duty to Inquire

If a contractor's interpretation of a situation is in fact reasonable, the contractor is under no obligation to further research the documents to determine if any other "reasonable" interpretation is available. If the owner subsequently forces its own interpretation on a contractor, the contractor should be able to recover the additional costs associated with the performance of that interpretation—*unless the contractor knew or should have known of the ambiguity or defect in the* **contract documents**. In such a case, the contractor has an obligation to bring the ambiguity or defect to the attention of the owner in order to secure clarification or direction before submitting its price to perform the contract.

Another situation that imposes an obligation to inquire on a contractor is when there is no "reasonable" interpretation available. If a construction detail, for example, omits important components, or a section of the work cannot be tied into some other portion of the contract, and there is no information available in the contract documents that would allow a contractor to interpret or interpolate, the contractor has a duty to inquire—to at least ask the owner how it intends to complete the detail. It is important to know, however, that the duty to inquire in these cases is more closely related to situations regarding **patent errors** (obvious defects). The contractor should not be held responsible to inquire regarding circumstances that are the result of either **latent defects** or lack of adequate **coordination** in the design itself.

That a bidder fails to recognize a discrepancy in the contract documents does not mean that a successful bidder *should not* have recognized such a discrepancy. If the discrepancy would have been discovered by a competent contractor performing a reasonable review of the documents—very close to the definition of discovering a patent error—the contractor would probably not be relieved of its duty to inquire about it in the contract documents.

Economic Loss Rule

Definition

The economic loss rule provides that when a party suffers an economic loss (as opposed to personal injury or property damage) in a commercial transaction, that party can seek recovery only against the other party to the contract. Accordingly, strict application of this rule in a typical construction situation requires that the general contractor has no cause for action against the project design professionals for extra cost caused by defective plans, improper inspection, or other acts of negligence. In the same manner, a subcontractor is limited to an action against the general contractor, even if the subcontractor's claim is based on actions or inactions of the owner or design professional.

Exceptions

Exceptions to the principle are most commonly based on the theory of negligence. They might apply in cases of defective documents or some level of negligent supervision. Such theories are based on the argument that a design professional has a duty to protect those construction parties who foreseeably could be harmed by the design professional's negligent performance (contractor, subcontractor, suppliers). It is recognized that a duty of care arises. It is beginning to be more consistently recognized that the design professionals are thrown together with the construction force in a very intimate relationship in a way that—even though no contract exists between them—makes it impossible for the construction force to perform in the face of improper conduct on the part of the design professionals.

Conflicting Principles

Taking the approach that a design professional has a legal duty to protect parties who *foreseeably could be affected by negligence* clearly expands the duties established by conventional contractual relationships. For this reason, conflicting legal principles can be involved when a court is asked to apply or disallow the economic loss rule.

Further considerations include the idea that the design professionals and the construction force are thrown together in such a relationship that emphasizes the mutual duty of care. A design professional approves show drawings, inspects the work, certifies payment applications, and performs numerous other duties such that it is impossible for the contractor to perform to any acceptable degree without significant care and consideration on the part of the design professional.

From that point, the conflicting principles are much more than theoretical. It is not uncommon, for example, for a subcontractor to be faced with an insolvent owner, questionable lien rights or bond rights, and a claim. Unless the court of jurisdiction recognizes some kind of negligence theory against the design professional, the subcontractor and contractor simply find themselves without any remedy. The recognition of this all-too-common but severe inequity seems to be finally turning heads of the courts to look for ways to restore equity in the reality of the relationships.

Practical Reality

Although these developments may seem encouraging, it is definitely appropriate to proceed in this area with extreme caution. Applications vary widely, and the confirmable facts of the particular case bear very heavily on the ultimate outcome.

As more situations evolve where a design professional exercises substantial amounts of control over the contractor, giving orders about the project and providing procedures on how to correct deficiencies caused by **defective specifications,** more courts are beginning to recognize causes for action against the design professional. They recognize that even though no privity of contract exists between the parties, the direct control exerted by the design professional over the contractor during the construction process can be determined to be sufficient to create a legal duty not to act negligently.

This encouraging news must, however, be tempered with the reality that the fact that a design professional has prepared defective plans and specifications is *not* likely to create any legal duty as described. Apparently, it is the ongoing *actions and activities* of the design professional throughout the construction process that weighs most heavily on the final determination.

Enumeration of Contract Documents

Document Enumeration

It has been customary in construction contracts to include some provision that enumerates the contract documents, specifically listing each document and its corresponding date within the agreement. The plans and specifications, addenda, proposal forms, price schedules, general conditions, supplementary conditions, special conditions, insurance forms, bond forms, and so on are all listed in complete detail.

To Enumerate

If you are the contractor in an owner-contractor relationship, or a subcontractor in a contractor-subcontractor relationship, specifically enumerating your contract or subcontract documents should be gospel. Your agreement thereby will clearly represent the specific understanding—the basis of your bid. In other words, if it isn't listed, you haven't priced it. In addition, by indicating the specifics in such detail, you will have taken all the steps you can in ensuring that the responsibility for the correlation of documents, coordination of all those documents which comprise your own bid package, and identification of omissions in preparation of the bid package will remain with the other party to the contract.

Not to Enumerate

If you are the owner in an owner-contractor relationship, or perhaps more important, the contractor in a contractor-subcontractor relationship, don't necessarily jump to provide such a clear enumeration of the documents. If your agreement provides language that requires that the other party perform not only the specific work described but any additional work within that general description necessary to "create a fully functional and complete project," or some similar catchall language, your effort to enumerate the specific documents described may run the risk of unnecessarily limiting this objective. You may unknowingly narrow the specific definition of the subcontractor's assignment and thereby clearly relieve that subcontractor of its responsibility for determining its requirement for a "fully functional and complete project."

Look for ways to describe your scope of work that do not bear any risk of limiting the description. If you must enumerate the documents because a clear, general description of the scope of work is not possible without doing so, then go ahead. Take one last look, however, to see if you really can proceed without enumerating the documents.

"Equals" and "Substitutions"

Common Misapplication

In practice, the ideas of "equals" and "substitutions" are often misapplied not just by owners and design professionals, but by contractors as well. Much too often, both equals and substitutions are automatically dumped into the *substitution* category. At this point, it might appear to be nothing more than semantics, but the difference in treatment might mean the difference between having an available product correctly approved for use, or having it rejected or allowed only after some reimbursement.

Contract Clarifications

Many contractor-owner agreements in the public sector (federal, most states, some municipal) and only the most complete private agreements may provide specific definitions of what products may be considered "equal" and what will be considered as a "substitution." If such specific definitions are not available directly in your contract, you may need to rely on the Uniform Commercial Code, perhaps in combination if the issue as defined by **trade practice.**

In any of these cases, the operative definitions (at least in principle) should be as follows:

Equal: The recognized equivalent in substance, form, and function, considering quality, workmanship, economy of operation, durability, and suitability for the purpose intended, and not constituting a change in the work.

Substitution: A replacement for the specified material, device, or equipment which is sufficiently different in substance and function to be considered a change in the work.

Examples of *equals* might include

- A specified concrete surface hardener has a mix design of 50 percent metal filings and 50 percent portland cement. The "equal" product has a mix design of 50 percent metal filings, and 50 percent portland cement.

- The specified 2- × 6-in, 16-gauge structural steel stud is manufactured by ABC Corp., and the equal product is a 2- × 6-in, 16-gauge structural steel stud manufactured by XYZ Corp.

Examples of *substitutions* might be

- The specified concrete surface hardener has a mix design of 50 percent metal filings and 50 percent portland cement, whereas the substitution has 40 percent metal filings and 60 percent portland cement.

- A 2- × 6-in, 16-gauge structural steel stud manufactured by ABC Corp. is specified; the substitution is a 2- × 6-in Douglas fir wood stud.

Different Contract Requirements

The decision that has to be made is a very important one, because your contract will go on to treat the two cases very differently. Equals may be clearly allowed. In government contracts, equals must be allowed in order to comply with the legal requirement that the specification not be a **proprietary specification.** In such cases, the contractor should have the right to submit equals for approval during the normal course of the submittal-approval process. But there's more; because the equal is recognized to be an equivalent, the item is not considered to be a *change* in the contract. Accordingly, any owner request (or demand) for a credit **change order** should not enter the picture.

In the case of a substitution, however, the documents may indeed require very special treatment. The **contract documents** may, for example, require that substitutions be substituted within a certain number of days after contract award or after the bid, or even with the bid. In addition, because substitutions are considered to be a change in the work, prepare yourself for **negotiation,** if you are the one proposing the substitution for your own benefit. Even if you find yourself proposing a substitution because of a job reality or out of job necessity—for reasons not your own doing—you might still find yourself needing to explain why this is the case, and why you accordingly require additional compensation by having been forced to make such a change. Refer to **implied warranty** for related discussion.

Two Perspectives

Your particular contract will be a barometer with respect to your right to submit equals or substitutions for approval.

If you are a general contractor making a submittal on your own behalf to the owner, know what your specific rights are according to your contract, and comply with any prescribed procedure as closely to the letter of the procedure as you can. Understand how any distinctions between equals and substitutions are treated, and be prepared to have to clearly explain it all over again—even to those who drafted your contract. Know in advance what your action is supposed to be, take it early, be definitive, and be firm in your position.

If, on the other hand, you are a general contractor who is being asked by your subcontractor to push through a substitution, be careful. If there is no legitimate reason for a substitution based on some project reality, understand that on balance, the only thing a general contractor stands to "gain" by pursuing substitutions on behalf of its subvendors is a delay in the project resulting from delay in approval of the substitution, and possibly an assumption of an increased amount of liability associated with both the design and the construction of the substituted item.

Accordingly, if there is an economic or some other benefit to the general contractor, so be it; proceed accordingly. If, however, the substitution attempt is really nothing more than the subvendor's effort to achieve a higher profit margin through the use of a cheaper product, proceed with extreme caution.

Application of Equals

A true equal should be subject to a very straightforward submittal and approval process. Before proceeding with your submittal, however, consider these ideas:

1. Know the specific language in your contract with respect to equals and substitutions. If there is a procedure prescribed, follow as closely to the letter as possible.

2. If you are working on a public contract, your right to submit equals is fairly clear. There are, however, specific instances where a public owner has a right to specify a proprietary product. In such cases, an equal will not be allowed. Understand the concept of **proprietary specifications,** and understand what your rights are with respect to this particular specification section.

3. Be prepared to have your submission treated as a substitution, with the result that the first reaction by the designer might be a rejection on some inappropriate grounds, or an immediate request for

a credit change order. Look for ways to head off this time-wasting posturing by anticipating the situation, and preparing a complete equal submission that will guide the design professional to the proper determination.

Application of Substitutions

If you are considering submitting a substitution for approval, consider it carefully, and proceed with process.

1. Take a second look. Is the item in fact a substitution? Is it really a *change in the work?* Is there a way to redefine the substitution as an equal? If so, the probability of approval can take a quantum leap.

2. Consider the project design for reasons why the substitution is legitimate. See if you can justify the substitution as one required by some difficulty in the **contract documents** rather than one *you* want to make. Perhaps:

- The material described in the specification is no longer available.

- It can be reasonably demonstrated that the material described in the specifications is inadequate, inappropriate, or will not otherwise serve its intended purpose.

- Late material deliveries or other problems related to the specified material or equipment or its supplier will cause unacceptable erection/installation schedules, or will otherwise affect continuous construction (refer to **implied warranty** for related discussion).

3. After you've confirmed how you intend to proceed with the substitution/submittal, comply explicitly with any and all stated submission requirements for substitutions. Consider the specified procedure for the time of submission, the correct number of copies, the form and content of all submittals, and any requirements for comparative information to be simultaneously submitted that will allow comparison with the specified item.

Equitable Adjustment

To Make "Whole"

"Equitable adjustment" is a concept that a contractor be made "whole" in the event of a change condition that affects the work. The contractor should be left in a condition that it otherwise would be in had the change not occurred.

Contract changes do much more than alter the scope of work. They disrupt orderly sequences, interfere with planned activities, void prior coordinations, change schedule logic, and change methods for work not otherwise directly addressed by a change. They can cause a contractor to remain mobilized on the site longer than originally anticipated, and can contribute to disproportionate administrative costs resulting from backtracking and rework. In theory, the contractor is entitled to recover these and any other direct and indirect costs that occur as a result of the mere existence of the change.

Concept

When considering any change or claim situation, step back for a moment and consider the complete condition. Become aware of all those things that you now find yourself doing that are strictly a result of the change only. The fact, for example, that you now have to drive to the site to review a specific condition is an activity that you otherwise would not have had to involve yourself with had the change not existed. The fact that your retainage on the entire contract balance is going to be delayed for an additional month because of the change is not a condition that you otherwise would have to bear.

Catalog all of those things that you otherwise would not have had to deal with, had the change not been in existence, and you may find yourself with a negotiation **agenda** that at the very least can give significant ammunition to negotiate your best outcome. In a claim situation, it may provide you with a very legitimate itemization that will maximize your entitlement. Refer to **concessions** for related discussion.

Exculpatory Clauses

To Shift Risk

Exculpatory Clauses are those specifically designed to "Exculpate" a party. They are designed to shift the risk of an issue from one party—typically the owner—to another—typically the contractor.

Although unpleasant, some categories of risk dealt with by these types of clauses can at least be apparent to contractors. An example (discussed further later) can be a clear disclaimer of subsurface conditions. It will only be clear, however, if the writer of the provision at least had the decency to be up front about the intention to provide for such a shift in the project risk. On the other hand, many other categories, however, can be more of a challenge to detect. They can either appear to be benign, or have the power to hypnotize by their legalistic, "industry-standard" appearance. These types of contract provisions are correspondingly too often given cursory review by contractors during their bidding or contract review/execution processes. They can, however, ultimately be the most expensive clauses in an agreement for a contractor who has not clearly understood the complete condition.

The Most Dangerous Clauses

Exculpatory Clauses are a category of contract provision that can be innocuous in appearance, but actually create the greatest risk to a contractor or subcontractor. Certainly, contract agreements have become increasingly sophisticated and complex. Contemporary contracts contain language that has been strained through layers of legalese, and has become quite creative in the ways that the language has departed from the conventional mainstream industry treatment of various issues. Even the mainstream has taken on a new set of teeth in recent years.

This is not a surprise, and it may not even be offensive in one sense of fairness. Clauses that go on to elaborately describe some new fantastic condition in elaborate detail at least have a way of making their presence known for those who are taking a responsible approach to reading their contracts before signing them. At that point of realization, you will have at least been given the opportunity to understand the new condition, to find out about the meanings and ramifications of such a provision, and then make your own risk analysis and determination of your willingness to positively assume that new level of risk. And so Exulpatory Clauses are dangerous enough in their new levels of risk that they add to a contract, but the danger does not end there.

Even more importantly than the idea that the new clauses may not have been any part of your understanding at the time of your bid is the fact that the most dangerous type of these new clauses are those that are present "by default." These are the clauses that by the *omission* of language, or by a subtle change in wording dramatically alter the risk of the relationship. These are the clauses that you don't see.

As an example, consider a **"no damage for delay"** clause. This is a provision that describes a situation where, if the contractor is delayed on a project for any reason that is not the fault of the contractor, the contractor will be entitled to an extension of **time** (so that it would not be charged damages for the delay) but specifically goes on to provide that the contractor shall not be entitled to any amount of *compensation* for the added time. When these types of clauses first appeared, they were clear in their intent, often requiring from a paragraph to a page of language describing the condition in clear detail. Even though some might consider such a condition to be inequitable, at least it was explained in clear language and presented to a contractor under a spotlight. Today, however, the same legal effect is more likely to be accomplished with a simple statement that the contractor shall be entitled to an extension of time "... as its exclusive remedy." By simply adding the word "exclusive" or "sole" to the phrase, it *limits* a contractor's right of recovery *dramatically*. If you knew enough to strike the single offending word from the phrase *before* you signed the contract, you will get your extension of time *and* preserve your right to recover the added expenses associated with it.

It's this sneaky approach to these risk-shifters that push their risk to whole new levels.

Although a contract may be riddled with numerous individual paragraphs, phrases, and individual words throughout the document that create exculpatory relationships, they all boil down to a few major categories. Once the principle and intent of the categories are understood, recognizing their various incarnations in the language can be a straightforward process. Their application is summarized here.

No damages for delay or acceleration

This condition was summarized in the example above. There are typically extreme costs to a contractor associated with delay. Such clauses may go on to specifically delineate those categories of delay that will be noncompensable, or may be broad conditions applying to all categories of delay. Refer to **"No Damages for Delay"** for important related discussion.

Disclaimer of subsurface or other concealed conditions

These provisions are attempts by an owner to place the risk of unforeseen physical conditions on the contractor. In a conventionally worded "differing site conditions" clause which has historically been provided in many industry-standard and government contracts, the risk of these unforeseen conditions is left with the owner. If such a clause has been eliminated from your contract, or the contractor has failed to include a simple replacement either directly in the contract agreement or as a condition of its proposal, the risk may indeed be shifted to the contractor. This is precisely the kind of risk that can create a $300,000 problem on a $200,000 contract. Refer to **Subsurface Site Conditions** and **Unforeseen Conditions** for important related discussion.

Disclaimer of Documents

This category is a contemporary version of exculpatory language that is strange, inequitable, and underhanded. Simply put, it is a phrase or paragraph that plainly states that some document—often geotechnical information, for example—that is part of the *bid* documents will *not* be considered to be part of the *contract* documents. It may go on to state that such information has been provided for "informational purposes only," "is not to be relied upon by the contractor," and "will not be the basis of any claim ...."

Indemnification

Most contractors will not have difficulty with the historical industry-standard approach of requiring a contractor to indemnify the owner against damages arising out of the contractor's operations—including the operations of those under the control of the contractor (the subcontractors). This is fair, reasonable, and logical.

The new breed of indemnification, however, now goes on to specifically require the contractor to indemnify the owner against damage to the owner caused by actions, omissions, and negligence *of the owner and its design professionals*. I can't believe that there is a person on the planet that really believes that this is *fair*, but there are sure to be a number of them—judges, arbitrators, contract review boards—who will take the position that fair or not, it is a written provision that was agreed to by the parties. Refer to **Indemnification Clauses** for important related discussion.

Notice

I've included "notice" in the exculpatory category because of the "ambush" characteristic that notice provisions can impart to an agreement. The Agreement portion of a contract (refer to **Contract Documents**) may contain a notice provision or two—both the time required for notice for certain conditions, and how notice can be served. It may contain many more than a few. The general conditions and even portions of any technical specification may also contain numerous additional notice requirements. They're everywhere. Sometimes they are in conflict with each other, but many times they are sinisterly synergistic—complementing each other in a way that creates different, complicated, and confusing applications for different situations. The worst types are those that seem to give direction in one place, but are changed in another for a specific condition. In such cases, an unwitting contractor will be left with the feeling of compliance having found the first one, only to later find out the hard way that a claim is lost on a strained technicality after applying the second one.

Triers-of-fact love technicalities. Such technicalities allow a correct legal decision, [the appearance of] a "professional" approach, [the appearance of] a cause-effect, logical development to a determination, and therefore the *appearance* of fairness. Technical notice provisions are very dangerous if they are not implemented properly. Don't get caught by them.

Enforceability

Many categories of exculpatory clauses are indeed clearly enforceable. The "no-damages" and "notice" variety most often fall into this category. A contractor might in some other situations take some consolation in the questionable enforceability of other types of provisions—but this situation is changing for the worse every day.

When first introduced, for example, a written disclaimer of documents did indeed appear to the world to be as underhanded, unreasonable, and devious as it is. Courts had actually reasoned that the information was obviously included in the bid documents for a purpose, which could only be that they were to be used in the preparation of the bid. Add to that the idea that (in the case of geotechnical information, for example) recognition that the owner is the only one in the position to take soil borings and perform other relevant studies while all bidding contractors are not, and reason determined that it was patently unreasonable to then hold the contractor responsible for errors and omission in the owner's documents.

But today, this is changing. A contractor cannot rely at all on any possible or probable lack of enforceability based on any measure of "reasonableness." Today, the attitude is more likely to be "you read it, you signed it, you agreed to it, you own it."

There are still some varieties, for a while at least, that may still preserve their "unenforceability" through their patent unreasonableness. An indemnity of a party against its own negligence still seems to fall into this category. So far, even the legal system seems to still consider this blindside to be unreasonable, and ridiculously unfair. But don't count on it.

Power to Negotiate

Now the good news. Fortunately for contractors, there remains significant power to negotiate these terms *when they are discovered*—at least in nongovernment contracts. The power to negotiate these terms to bring them into some semblance of fairness lies in their intrinsic unreasonableness.

Consider the indemnity situation described above. It is genuinely so unreasonable to require a party to indemnify the other against himself that when the issue is brought to that party's attention there is virtually no good explanation as to why the requirement is fair and reasonable. In such a situation, the party will move off the requirement. If not, you will have been given a very clear indication of who you are about to (try to) do business with.

The actual degree of unreasonableness translates directly to your ability to negotiate a better provision. But before you can even do that, you have to know what they are, be able to recognize them, and find them in all their incarnations and variations throughout each component of the entire agreement.

Expediting Material Deliveries

Related Topics

Backcharges

Concessions

Documentation

Hostage Taking

Joint Checks

Liars

Pay-When-Paid

Surprise

The Expediting Mindset

Not any of us with any production responsibility should have a problem with the idea that we should approach each project with the attitude that it is *always* necessary to expedite *everything*. Too many areas of our business seem to be founded on the squeaky-wheel concept. If *your* wheels aren't squeaking, you can be sure that your subcontractors and suppliers will be responding to all the other wheels that are squeaking. There seems to be no correlation of the size or level of "sophistication" of the subvendor and any tendency of that subvendor to provide lip service instead of delivery service. Just because a subvendor is larger than you are, for example, there is no reason to relax at all.

Organize yourself and your company to approach each relationship with a subvendor so that you exert effort every step of the way to improve the odds of exceptional material deliveries. This attitude must be applied not just to purchase orders (those cases where materials are being delivered strictly on your own behalf), but to your subcontracts as well (those cases where the respective material deliveries are not really your "responsibility" because they have to be delivered to a subcontractor to enhance *its* total performance). If you and your project staff are complacent and comfortable in the belief that just because the material delivery is under the "control" of your subcontractor and it shouldn't be much of a problem, you're setting yourself up to become very frustrated.

Instead, approach each supply contract and subcontract with the clear idea that it is up to *you* to verify all information for *yourself* from the best sources available. It is up to *you* to eliminate as many middleman interruptions in the information chain as possible. From there, organize your activities to be that squeaky wheel, to show your subvendors just how seriously you're taking these requirements.

Communicate the degree of detail to which your entire organization is tracking the performance, and of the level of tenacity with which you will ensure that *your* project will be serviced to the level of the written commitment in the subvendor agreement.

Expediting Action Lists

Certain specific activities have proved to be very useful in helping a project staff expedite material deliveries both from supply vendors and through subcontractors. They can be applied to various situations in order to help avoid delivery problems in the first place, or to bring problem deliveries closer to the original schedule.

The items that follow are not intended to be implemented in any particular order, but are a catalog of separate suggestions that might serve as a menu from which to select actions that are appropriate to a particular situation:

1. *Identify the true source.*   Begin in your own subcontract form, by including a clear requirement that the subvendor provide you with a certified list of all subsubvendors for the project. Require a clear disclosure of all actual sources of materials, equipment, and components.

2. *Get a list of all material suppliers.*   If you are not provided with the subcontract execution, send a form or a letter to each subvendor immediately on the execution of the subvendor agreement requesting the list of all subsubvendors. Note the subcontract requirement, and that your subcontract stipulates that the delivery of such a list is an express condition of the first payment to the subvendor.

3. *Establish contact with the direct source of material delivery as early as possible. Identify the key individuals in each supply organization.*   Contact them early to verify that all information given to them by the subcontractor regarding scope of work, specification requirements, and material deliveries is accurate and complete. Try to develop these relationships as early as possible.

- If a subsubvendor wants to be sure of prompt payment, it usually realizes that it is in its best interest to communicate with you to the extent appropriate for this particular contract. Call attention to the fact (if appropriate) that you are the one with the payment bond, and that you are the one that will be processing payments and has the power to determine a joint-payment structure.

- Once such direct communication is established, the first result should be that the reliability of your delivery information will improve dramatically. You will also be able to use this direct information as a gauge to allow you to determine the reliability of the delivery information that you have been getting from your first-tier subcontractor. When significant discrepancies become apparent, you might want to turn your attention to information that the subcontractor has been giving you with respect to other provisions of its subcontract.

4. *Confirm the relationship of the subsubvendor with your first-tier subvendor.* You may, for example, discover that there really is no "relationship" to speak of. It might turn out that the subsubvendor is really very happy talking with you, because its concerns for payment were at least equal to your concerns for delivery. Just like you, it may be very happy to be talking with the "source."

5. *Determine the specific payment terms between your first-tier subvendor and the subsubvendor.* Similarly, you will probably discover that the payment terms between your first-tier subvendor and your subsubvendor may be dramatically different from those between you and your first-tier subvendor. For example, you may have a **pay-when-paid** provision between you and your subvendor, whereas your subvendor is likely to have a 30-day or other finite time limit for payment between that subvendor and its subsubsupplier. Although technically not your problem, the fact remains that there is a certain probability that your subvendor will be obliged to pay its supplier well before you are responsible to pay your subvendor. This situation is perhaps the beginning of the most common delivery problems to general contractors. (Refer to **hostage taking** for important related discussion.) If you know of such a situation involving a major supply item, and turn the other way in the naive belief that it just isn't your problem, you're setting yourself up for it to become your problem at some point. Instead, use your new relationship with that subsubvendor to discuss the situation openly and look for a way to ease the subvendor's concerns over the almost inevitable delay in payment because of the gap in the payment terms. Taking the "high road" approach directly with the subsubvendor will not work every time, but you just might be surprised how many times the subsubvendor will respond very positively to your early open discussion of the issue. One **concession** (that really isn't one) may be to use that discussion as an opportunity to offer the subsubvendor a **joint check,** or copayment agreement, specifically sent to that subsubvendor, allowing a **pay-when-paid** relationship with the first-tier subvendor. Such an offer may provide the subsubvendor enough peace of mind to get your materials delivered to your jobsite unaffected by a payment issue.

6. *Consider the fabrication location.* When you're told "The parts are on the shop floor," consider responding "That's fantastic, I'll be

there this afternoon—you can show them to me." Your response will either immediately confirm that the information is real, or that you have been given a "check-is-in-the-mail" answer all along. And if the latter turns out to be the case, from that point forward that particular vendor ought to be very careful with the information given to you. You might at least elevate the information out of the "what you want to hear" category and into the "realistic" category.

7. *Visit the fabrication location.* Even if you've managed to confirm that all the information given to you is absolutely real, the simple act of just visiting a remote location to see your materials communicates a genuine concern for the efforts of the hard work on the part of that subsubvendor to get you your parts and materials on time. Many times, the situation may need nothing more than this simple act of appreciation to give that subvendor's production operation the added incentive that keeps *your* material moving forward through the shop. Without any doubt, the mere act of a shop visit has consistently been *the* most powerful and successful tool of all expediting efforts.

8. *Relate material deliveries to project payment cycles.* Point out that if the item is delivered by the end of the month (or by the end of whatever your pay period is), it will go on that pay period's pay application to the owner. In other words, if the item comes in 1 day later, everyone is going to have to wait an additional 30 days (or whatever) to even submit the invoice.

9. *Determine whether the shipment to your site is done directly or by common carrier.* Many shipments are either waiting for a full truckload, or will be consolidated by common carrier. It is often reasonable to consider the up-charge to get your materials on their own direct truck.

10. *Consider accelerated payments.* If, for example, the supplier is on a 30-day or even a pay-when-paid payment term, consider offering a COD or other advanced form of payment. Don't necessarily give it away, however. Even though it might speed up delivery, it would also be justification for a further price discount, as well.

11. *Consider advising the subsubvendor that you are thinking about changing the item.* If the delay is the fault of the subsubvendor, consider doing what you can to develop the idea that it might lose the order altogether. Do this with extreme caution, however. Make it believable and be sure that you are *actually ready to do it,* or you might find yourself in a deeper hole if the vendor subsequently drops *you.* Throughout all these efforts, those changes that become necessary as a result of your first-tier subvendor's failure will be chargeable to that subvendor if you design your subvendor agreements properly and your **documentation** is properly maintained. Refer to **backcharges** for important related discussion.

Experts

Use

Pitting "your word against mine" and other situations that rely heavily on the experience or credibility of any participant too often result in a **deadlock** that needs to be jarred loose. In such cases, experts can be brought in to add authority and guidance.

Experts have been defined in many ways. There is a justifiable healthy criticism that expertise should not be taken at face value. Many "experts" are really not all that they may appear to be. Some experts are real, scientific, and secure in their knowledge, while other "experts" are unsupported, fearful of contradiction, or just plain phony.

Individuals who are thought to be authorities in their fields usually exert greater influence than those who are not so recognized. People tend to be intimidated by experts who are also opponents. When a recognized authority speaks, others of less acknowledged stature may be reluctant to challenge the expert's statements and assertions.

The Credibility Ladder

Those experts with the most credibility are people who have done original and controlled experiments. Below that are those who have accomplished some independent analyses. Those who categorize and redefine information and spend their time with semantics are next.

Beyond absolute knowledge, the credibility of an expert is influenced by the expert's age, appearance, and a manner that is or is not threatening to others. Experts who express themselves with confidence, organization, clarity, and directness exert greater influence.

The effectiveness of an expert may also be influenced by the level of academic degrees, number of publications, and level of national recognition. The higher any of these categories, the easier it is for that expert to sell a viewpoint.

Even the manner in which an expert is introduced into a situation may be significant to a negotiation outcome. Those experts who are introduced in a positive, credential-enhancing manner exert greater influence than individuals with equal qualifications who have not been so emphasized.

Types

Experts come in almost any field imaginable. Law, claims analysis, accounting, project management, **scheduling,** estimating, design, engineering, **delay** analysis, soils, and every conceivable technical matter will have its own contingent of experts ready to address your problem. With a little effort, you will be able to find a recognized expert in almost any field.

Best Use

The less technically oriented an expert's field, the greater the possibility of your dissatisfaction with the eventual work product. The reason for this is simple: the further that you are away from a specific technical assignment, the more subjective, judgmental, and broad your actual—or implied—assignment to the expert might become (refer to **agreements versus understandings** for related discussion). The need for a technical soils analysis, for example, is fairly straightforward. A technical analysis by a qualified consultant is needed to serve a very specific, well-defined purpose. The assignment is clear, the results are measurable, and the authority is supported by the credibility of the individual, probably through a recognized degree or certification credentials.

On the other extreme, consider a legal issue. Although many lawyers are notorious for not being the best businesspeople, and will be vocal in telling you that they are giving you legal advice, not "business" advice, somehow you may still find yourself getting business advice anyway, in legal advice's clothing.

As a further example, if you ask your lawyer (the legal expert) for a broad work product, such as a contract, you may find the response falls in a range of acceptability. If, however, you asked the same attorney to give you an opinion as to the legality of the manner of expression of a particular clause in your subcontract—a clearly defined, narrow, and specific assignment—the probability of your satisfaction with the response goes up exponentially.

And so the best use of any expert will be that for which you will be able to narrow the description of that expert's assignment as much as possible. Focus the assignment to the completion of a specific task, along with a particular expected outcome, and the probability of your being satisfied with the final work product of that expert will be high.

Defense

If you find yourself facing an expert, don't get rattled. There is no need to overreact. Resist all feelings of intimidation whatsoever. Acknowledge that all experts have their limits, and that there are probably specific responses that will work in your favor. In dealing with an expert, consider the following:

1. Don't confuse apparent qualifications, wealth, or recognition with true expertise.

2. Do not assume that the individual's expertise is actually appropriate to the particular situation. An expert in one area is not likely to be equally expert in other areas. Expertise is not transferable. It's been said that experts and consultants are coming to know more and more about less and less until they will eventually reach a point where they will know virtually everything about nothing. Maybe this is an extreme viewpoint, but maybe not.

3. Explore the subject. While some experts know more and more about less and less until they know virtually everything about nothing, other experts know less and less about more and more until they know virtually nothing about everything. Explore the subject to determine the specific areas of the individual's expertise, and look for ways to move your negotiations to the fringes or outside those limits. Look for ways to introduce areas that are clearly—and to the acknowledgment of the expert—outside the limits of the individual's expertise.

4. Be skeptical. Look for ways to introduce questions or otherwise get responses from the expert that will test his or her expertise. Get responses to questions to which you know the answers, in order to gauge the accuracy—and actual competence—of the expert. Keep a catalog of incorrect responses that you might later use to chip away at the credibility of that expert's remarks.

5. Approach the same issue from different directions. Don't be afraid to ask the same question five times in five different ways. Keep looking at issues from different angles, and probe for the answers that you're trying to get. Experts don't always have common sense. Many experts enjoy their expertise, and might be made to ramble on with very little urging. If the expert is inclined to talk, encourage as much dialog as possible. If you are successful, look for confusion, contradictions, or other questionable remarks.

6. When all else fails, consider one of your most expensive alternatives; get an expert of your own. It's been said, "For every expert, there is an equal and opposite expert." Don't try to be "equal"; try to get yourself a better one.

"Fat" Specifications

Contents	Related Topics
Development	Ambiguities
The Good News	Boilerplate
Response Guidelines	Contract Documents
	Cut-and-Paste
	Defective Specifications
	Design Duplications
	Interpretation—Right to Choose
	Old Age (Specifications)
	Strange Specifications

Development

"Fat" specifications develop over a period of time at a design professional's office. Each year, more projects are completed, more battles are won and lost, more arbitrations and litigations occur, more change orders are given up and more disputes are resolved for better or for worse. Each subsequent specification attempts to gain from the experience by adding more **boilerplate,** rhymes, reason, guesses, **interpretation,** diversions, and directives. With each disclaimer, qualification, and quasi-legal reference, the pile grows.

For a contractor confronting such a specification, it's easy to overact to initial appearances. The specification, with all its elaborations, may make no effort to hide the fact that it's an attempt to dramatically alter the risk-sharing formula. It can seem so ridiculously stacked in the owner's and/or design professional's favor that it may be very difficult to see how any person of sound mind would ever sign such a document.

The Good News

There may be, however, a significant difficulty for the owner and design professional with a fat specification. All the extra baggage accumulated in a piecemeal fashion over an extended time may not have been coordinated properly or completely with existing documents, or with each successive layer of nonsense. Each extra creative clause has most likely been added *as* each individual piece has been drummed up. Coordination of the new language with existing language may be less than adequate, resulting in numerous conflicting treatments of the same or similar situations. A different kind of problem can compound the difficulties for owners and design professionals, because the new language may be placed out of design context. A newly determined treatment of an issue may be based on an intention that may be different from the original intention of those who have prepared the document in the first place.

The ultimate result can be a complicated, cryptic, and confusing collection of contract clauses that will be riddled with overstatements, understatements, contradictions, ambiguities, impossibilities, unreasonableness, and in some cases just plain ridiculousness. The ultimate accomplishment of such an effort might ironically be an increased probability of numerous errors leading to changes and claims.

Response Guidelines

It is generally easy to spot a fat specification, particularly on a smaller project. A quick review of the documents reveal:

1. A "front end" of the **contract documents** (general conditions, special conditions, etc.) that's fatter than the actual technical specifications themselves.

2. Extensive duplication, restatement, and redundancy in the general provisions.

3. Descriptions and instructions that are much longer, labored, and more complicated than necessary. When, for example, a sentence would sufficiently describe a responsibility, a paragraph is used instead. Efforts of a design professional taking a "lawyerly" approach toward document design are obvious.

4. The presence of many clauses describing requirements that are not normally encountered in specifications for the type of project being considered.

Don't be intimidated by an overly ambitious-looking specification. Be cautious, but be prepared. The excess language is frequently nothing more than an indicator that the design professional and the owner do not really know what they're doing, and of their attitude toward their dealings with the contractor. It is therefore much more a clue as to *whom* you're doing business with than of a firm treatment of a contract document.

Do make the effort to become intimately familiar with every nut and bolt of the specification content. Because of the dramatically increased probability of a document error, develop the ability to quickly spot the duplications, ambiguities, and contradictions for what they are. Learn where such problems are encountered in the documents, keep them organized, and deal with them directly and decisively.

Force Majeure

Unforseeable Delay

Force Majeure defines a category of delays that are not forseeable by either party to the contract. Typically, the category is thought of strictly as "acts of God" (the literal interpretation of the phrase), including such things as weather and natural catastrophe. The category can, however, also be expanded to include other genuinely unforeseeable conditions or effects on projects, such as strikes or a national emergency.

Applicability

The key to an issue's applicability does not simply lie in the existence of a certain type of condition. It lies in the fact (or lack of the fact) that the condition was not known to either party—and that neither party *should have known*, or have been aware of, the condition.

"Rain" and "snow" do not by themselves constitute unforeseeable conditions. If, for example, the contract contemplated performing concrete foundation work in January in the northeastern part of the United States, it is probably reasonable to expect that the contractor should anticipate having to deal with at least a characteristic amount of snow and freezing ground condition during the concrete placement. Similarly, if deep earthwork is bid to be performed in the summer in Florida, it is probably reasonable to expect the contractor to anticipate a certain amount of characteristically wet conditions. In each of these cases, the principle of Force Majeure will probably apply if the subject conditions are fairly common because at least one party, the contractor in these examples, should have "foreseen" these conditions. Even in the case of a strike, if a key union agreement expires during the critical production cycle—structural steel, for example—it might be argued that the contractor should have been aware of the condition and incorporated the anticipated strike into its bid.

And so Force Majeure is not necessarily so clear after all. For it to apply, it must be demonstrated that the specific condition was not—and should not have been— known to either party. In the above examples, Force Majeure might apply if the snowfall or rainfall was four (or some other significant factor) times the average (expected) amount, or if the strike was at a fabricator's plant in a third-tier supplier in a remote part of the country, of which the contractor could not be reasonably expected to be aware.

Excusable, Not Compensable

A genuine Force Majeure item is by definition the fault of neither party to a contract. Accordingly:

- The delay or other effects on a project are not caused by either party, so neither party should be held responsible. The effect is therefore "excusable." The contract time should be extended for the duration of the delay for the contractor, and the owner should not be held responsible.

- Any damage suffered by one or both parties because of the event was also, by definition, not caused by the other party. For this reason, the damaged party is not entitled to compensation for the problem from the other party.

Contractual Entitlement

To obtain an extension of contract time or other similar remedy for a Force Majeure or other type of excusable delay, there should be a clause in the agreement portion of the contract or in the general conditions which affirmatively permits an extension of time for such excusable delays. In the absence of such a contract provision, the common law rule that usually applies is that if a contractor executes an obligation containing a time-is-of-the-essence provision, the contractor will be held responsible to perform that obligation on time unless such is rendered impossible by an act of God, the law, or the other contracting party.

If there is a specific provision for either Force Majeure or for the more general category of "excusable delays" in a contract, it is necessary to proceed with extreme caution. The language (and even the basic intent of the law) may have actually been modified in an unusual and expected—but fully enforceable—way that might leave an unwary contractor with the wrong kind of surprise. Refer to **Exculpatory Clauses** for important related discussion.

General Contracting

Contents

Contract Relationships

Communications

Advantages and Disadvantages

Related Topics

Agent Construction Management (ACM)

Construction Management with Guaranteed Maximum Price (GMP)

Contract versus Contact

Design-Build

Economic Loss Rule

Implied Warranty

Contract Relationships

General contracting is the traditional method of project delivery. In its form, the owner contracts directly (and individually) with the general contractor, and simultaneously contracts separately and individually with the architect (or engineer).

The general contractor is typically responsible to provide all labor, materials, equipment, supervision, and incidentals necessary to complete the entire scope of work as defined in the **contract documents** to meet all quality requirements, and to do all this within the time frames specified. The architect (or engineer) generally produces the contract documents, which include the plans, specifications, general and other conditions, other appropriate documents, and even the agreement itself between the owner and the contractor. Upon the production of the contract documents, the design professional most commonly provides construction services on behalf of the owner as well. These services typically include reviewing shop drawings, reviewing and approving the contractor's payment applications, inspecting the work, and interpreting the documents.

The owner may retain the architect or the design professional during the construction phase, may retain the design professional in a supplementary or some kind of support capacity, or may choose not to retain the design professional at all during the construction phase, opting instead to provide the construction phase services by itself, to the degree it deems necessary. In any case, the design professional's services—as far as the contractor is concerned—are really part of the owner's responsibility anyway. Contractually, the general contractor sees only the owner in terms of rights and responsibilities. Refer to **implied warranty** for important related discussion.

The general contractor enters into individual agreements with its subvendors, the army of subcontractors and suppliers that will make up the construction force. Many contemporary construction contracts require that the general contractor perform a minimum of 20 percent of the value of the total contract with its own forces, in an attempt to assure the owner of some significant amount of "equity" directly in the project on the part of the contractor.

Even though there may be dozens of separate vendors involved with a project through the general contractor, the owner looks only to the general contractor for satisfaction of total performance. Accordingly, the general contractor's dealings with its subvendors should in theory be transparent to the owner. The subcontractors and suppliers in turn look directly to the general contractor for satisfaction of performance; even if any difficulties in that relationship arise directly from the use of the contract documents that were prepared by or for the owner. Refer to **economic loss rule** for important related discussion.

Communications

Communications between the owner, contractor, and design professionals necessarily overlap to a great extent. Specific contracts may vary in this regard, but generally speaking, most owners and design professionals prefer that communication to the owner from the general contractor go through the design professional. Similarly, communication between the subvendor force and the design professionals should be maintained through the general contractor.

Although these relationships are usually based upon the noble motivations of effective **coordination** of the information, the general contractor is still wise to be very careful. If all communications are specifically maintained to the owner through the design professional, and the design professional "interprets the documents," the general contractor should confirm the formal limits of authority bestowed on the design professional by way of the general contractor/owner agreement. If there is any doubt, the general contractor will be within its right to insist on important determinations to come from the owner, if that's what the contract says.

Advantages and Disadvantages

Since general contracting is the traditional arrangement, most industry participants are familiar with the relationships and understand many of the difficulties associated with it. An owner's concern, for example, will be the reliability of the general contractor in forwarding appropriate payments to its subvendors, and thereby not only keeping the construction force happy and working, but also keeping the property title free from liens and encumbrances. General contracts have developed in many creative ways in attempts to provide the owner with these protections. The basic general contract holds the general contractor completely responsible for its subvendors. Contemporary construction contracts, however, tend to go into much detail in an effort to provide greater "control" on behalf of the owner. Because of the new relationships they create between the design professionals and the construction force, such construction agreements have removed large amounts of control of the general contractor over its own construction force. As a result, serious problems can develop because owners insist on the responsibility of the general contractor for the performance of its subs, while general contractors protest that the construction agreement has removed their ability to control their subs; the responsibilities for lack of performance are thereby at least shared by the owner.

Because of the inherent difficulties with general contracting, various other project delivery methods have been getting increasing amounts of attention. Examples of the major forms of competing methods include **design-build, agent construction management (ACM),** and **construction management with a guaranteed maximum price (GMP).** Refer to those sections for important related discussion.

Gentlemen's Agreement

Dangerous Deals

Gentlemen's agreements—sometimes referred to as *handshake deals,* have a well-deserved reputation for failure. Gentlemen's agreements between two individuals with the best of intentions break down for a number of important reasons, such as:

1. They have not been forced through any discipline that will require consideration of all the bases and resolution of every potentially important subissue. Between "friends," it is at least uncomfortable to discuss and negotiate certain contract mechanisms that would apply to a default of the other party. Because such things are not discussed, there are no clear understandings of each component of the agreement. The huge gray area left in a gentlemen's agreement will guarantee that any problems that do arise will become much larger than they otherwise might have been.

2. The two "friends" with the best of intentions have two different viewpoints about the particular deal to begin with. The words *reasonable time* may mean 5 days to one person and 1 month to the other. *Adequate crew size* may mean two individuals for 4 hours a day to one person, and 10 workers at 6 days a week to the other. And so without committing a deal to writing, we will begin the deal with two distinct "understandings" (or "misunderstandings") about each component of our new deal.

3. The people who make the gentlemen's agreement are not the individuals who must make the deal work. The contractor's superintendent, project manager, subcontractor's foreman, owner's representatives, design professionals, and project engineer must implement and manage the particular deal, and the mix is impossible. In such a case, if the deal is not clear and explicit, somewhere between two and six additional judgments are applied to the meaning of a *good job.*

As an example, let's say your good friend, the framing contractor, agrees at the bargaining table to install temporary wood stairs in your building in order to help construction along if for some reason the permanent steel stairs coming from another supplier are late. If you do not write that specifically into your deal, the only guarantee you will have is that at the time you are asking him to begin construction of the wood stairs your "friend" and his foreman will recall the discussion, but will also recall that "It was never resolved" (or that "We agreed otherwise").

Different "Gentlemen"

Gentlemen's agreements are very dangerous. Even if the party with whom you have made the agreement has absolute integrity, and you have even managed to get clear and distinct understandings on both sides as to the components of the deal, a good possibility still exists that your friend may, at some point, be removed from the scene of the deal before the deal has a chance to be consummated or concluded. The clerk of the works, for example, may be changed by the owner, a general contractor may change the superintendent, and so on. People get shifted to other areas of the organization, they get promoted, they get fired, they might not completely understand the agreement, or they just plain go back on the deal.

To whatever extent practical and/or necessary, get your deal documented—even if it is nothing more than a note in the job meeting minutes. Get *your* deal in *writing*.

Refer to **agreements versus understandings** for important related discussion.

Geotechnical Information

Description

Geotechnical information is most often provided by an owner as part of a set of bid documents. It is a result of some amount of subsurface investigation performed physically at the site to determine to some reasonable degree the composition of materials that can be expected during the excavation and other preparations for the building structure. This subsurface information is generally gathered by making a series of soil borings. In this procedure, representative locations are selected (presumably by an engineer) and test cylinders are drilled to varying depths below the surface. When the cylinders are extracted, the composition of the earth is determined with precision. It is important to note, however, that "precision" applies to the specific location of the bore at the time of year that the bore was taken.

Whatever geotechnical information is provided by the owner as part of the bid documents, bidders typically rely on it in determining their bids. Not just obvious things, such as the presence of rock, but data about the composition of soils and the water table provides a bidder with significant information for determination of certain necessary construction procedures, such as the need for haul roads and for dewatering in excavation.

Locations

Whatever conclusions are drawn from the information as it is provided, it is wise to be aware of the boring *locations* relative to the actual construction.

If, for example, the geotechnical information is given around the site perimeter, a bidder would have no choice but to extrapolate that information throughout the interior of the site. If conditions subsequently are encountered that differ materially from that which can be inferred directly from one boring location through the site to the other, the facts would probably serve as a basis to substantiate compensation for a **change order.**

If the bore locations are grouped in an area, or provided for areas outside the building's footprint, or conspicuously absent in other areas of the building footprint, proceed with caution. There may be legitimate reasons for the apparently odd condition (for example, the building location might have been shifted after the original borings were completed, and no supplemental borings were provided). There may, however, be other reasons for the strange and/or missing information. Unfortunately, the prudent bidder is forced to also consider the possibility of either intentional or inadvertent omission of information from the bid set that is in fact available to the owner. Refer to **deliberate errors, patent errors, latent defects,** and **knowledge** for related discussion.

Time of Year

Be critical of water table information given. If the boring was done in late August in the northeastern United States, you might be surprised when you dig something deep in the spring. Whatever the reason, the effects can be severe, and justification for extra costs may be predicated on the lack or inaccuracy of information originally provided.

Disclaimers of Subsurface Information

These days, more and more owners include provisions in their contracts that expressly require that the contractor assume the risk of unforeseen physical conditions. For example, there may be a statement in the bid documents or in the contract itself that the contractor, by submitting a bid on the project, represents that he has undertaken a complete site inspection. The statement might further explain that, by virtue of this inspection, the contractor assumes the risk of conditions that would be readily observable or discoverable through such a complete inspection.

The second type of creative clause being introduced in contemporary contracts is a statement in the conditions that the contract documents actually *exclude* from them any information provided by the owner regarding subsurface conditions. Such clauses go on to state that any geotechnical or subsurface information is provided for "informational purposes only," or some other ridiculous remark. They further go on to state that, accordingly, the contractor is *not to rely on this information in the preparation of its bid.* The owner would argue that sheer technical information should not be considered as a representation of the actual geotechnical conditions on the site, and that such data should not be considered to be part of the contract documentation.

Yet another type of disclaimer is a statement in either the conditions of the contract or the contract itself that the contractor shall not rely on any subsurface information provided by the owner in the preparation of the contractor's bid.

These disclaimers of subsurface information and **unforeseen conditions** are examples of **exculpatory clauses.** Refer to those sections for important related discussion. They are blatant attempts by the owner to shift all risk of subsurface conditions directly to the contractor. They may be unfair, but they must be dealt with.

Enforcement of Disclaimer Provisions

Fortunately, most courts to this point have been reluctant to construe these disclaimer clauses strictly against the contractor, especially when the contract also contains a changed or differing site conditions clause which specifically allows contractor recovery based on conditions that are materially different from those represented or reasonably anticipated. These courts have reasoned that the owner obviously provided the geotechnical information to the contractor for a purpose, the most obvious purpose being to provide a mechanism for a contractor to formulate an accurate bid without extreme contingencies. Beyond this basic logic, some courts have gone on to confirm yet more of the obvious: that the owner is in a far better position to conduct a thorough geotechnical investigation than any of the various bidders can conduct on their own. Related to this is the idea that it is not at all reasonable to expect any bidder to invest the time and the money in performing such complete investigations if it has no assurances—or even a probability—of being awarded the contract. Even though these clauses have had a history of unenforceability, it would be prudent to take no comfort in this fact. These types of clauses have been given so much attention, that new, creative input by **attorneys** may introduce language that will force reconsideration by these same courts. If you're not careful, you might find yourself on the edge of or part of a test case that will be a rude awakening for our industry.

More important, if you observe this type of clause in your contract, a red flag should go up. Even if you are comfortable with the idea that the clause itself is not enforceable, don't stop there; go back through the entire contract and look for other **exculpatory clauses.** The one you just found is a pretty clear indication of the manner in which your new contracting partner intends to do business. Read your writing on the wall.

Guarantees and Warranties

Distinct Terms

The words *guarantee* and *warranty* should not be construed as interchangeable, as many of us in our industries tend to do. They have different and distinct meanings, and should be treated accordingly.

A *guarantee* is a promise that does not impose any primary liability on the guarantor, but binds the guarantor to be answerable to the default of another.

A *warranty* has been defined as an absolute liability on the part of the warrantor, and the contract is void and listed as strictly and literally performed.

A guarantee:

1. Binds a third party to the terms of another's contract (for example, a performance bond)

2. Implies present or past liabilities

3. Usually has a stated time limit

4. Applies to indebtedness or performance of one's duties

A warranty:

1. Binds a party to the terms of its contract

2. Implies present or future liabilities

3. Has no time limitation on the liability if it is unrestricted, but can have a time limit if it is a restricted warranty

4. Applies usually to products and their qualities

Dates of Beginning Coverage

Contracts differ not only in the guarantee and warranty periods specified, but in the manner that they treat the date of beginning coverage. Some contracts are clear and specify either substantial completion or full completion as a start of coverage, but some careless contracts manage to remain silent on the issue.

If your contract is silent with respect to the date of beginning coverage—implying only a completion date—you might be in your rights to rely on the idea of **trade practice** in order to support your contention that the substantial completion date should be the effective date of beginning coverage.

Express Warranties

Many products carry a standard written "express" warranty:

- It is enforced for some prescribed period of time (most often 1 year, sometimes 2, but occasionally 5 years or more) from the date of *shipment.*
- It does not cover damages in shipment or abuse by other trades before acceptance.

It can be difficult to get a product manufacturer to provide for all the specific components of a required warranty after the order has been placed. Even if the subtrade responsible will positively make up the difference in such warranties, these supplements may not be accepted by the owner, and your payment may be withheld as a result.

Be sure that the complete product warranty provisions are a part of every purchase agreement that you have in effect in the first place, either directly to that vendor, or passed through the subcontractor. Refer to **pass-through clause** for important related discussion.

If reliance on your pass-through clause is your situation, don't rest in the belief that your subcontractor takes this issue as seriously as you do. Insist at the onset that your subcontractor provide you with written substantiation that the respective product vendors will provide all guarantees and warranties as specifically required.

Implied Warranties

There is often an implied warranty in a transaction or a contract, unless the documents clearly state otherwise, that requires the products or goods to be reasonably fit and sufficient for the purpose for which they are to be used. There is an *implied warranty* that each product will perform as required for a purpose that its manufacturer had represented and the product was designed for.

The same situation applies to the **implied warranty** on the part of the owner to the contractor that the plans and specifications will be sufficient to achieve the desired results, that the project *can* be built as designed, and that all specified materials *can* be ordered and delivered within the time frame necessary. Accordingly, if you cannot get your specified materials in time because they were not available through no fault of yours, the owner (through its designer) will have violated the designer's implied warranty of availability of such products within the time required to complete the contract.

Health

Contents

Related Topics

Good Health

You can't do good if you don't feel good.

Good health is the single greatest gift given to you at birth. Its value is never appreciated by many people until they have it no longer, like those people who need to be imprisoned to understand the value and meaning of freedom.

Is your body a high-performance machine that you tune up for the LeMans or the Grand Prix, or is it a clunker, parked by the curb to get you from birth to death any old way? Are your brain and liver pickled in alcohol? Are you fat and sluggish? Do you puff going up a flight of stairs? Are you gaunt and nervous? Do you fuel your body up with high-test meats or with low-octane burgers, fries, and hit-and-run junk food? It's been said by many people about the body that if you abuse it, you won't get to use it for very long.

Schedule an Exam

Schedule an appointment now for an annual physical and then keep it. Be sure it's complete—not just a reflex-urine test, thank you, exam—but the works: x-rays, EKG, blood test, and so on. Get a prevention check before the engine knock or dead battery. If you have any reason to think your health might be less than excellent, schedule yourself every 2 or 3 years at a major medical or health clinic for an even more thorough examination.

Home Office Overhead

Cost Recovery

Home office overhead is one of the most significant of all contractor costs relating to delayed **time** of completion, and yet the most intangible and difficult to support. *Overhead* means different things to different people. Light, heat, and other "fixed costs"—the "soft costs"— are most commonly thought of as overhead; but beyond those obvious categories, the issue can become blurred. Is a office-bound project engineer overhead? Are long-distance phone calls made specifically on behalf of an individual project overhead?

Direct Cost Isolation

The first step in beginning to get a handle on effectively dealing with this cloudy cost category is to look for ways to isolate those cost issues which might otherwise be defined on a project-specific basis. Is there a way, for example, for a project engineer to report his or her salary time on a project-by-project basis? Is there a way to catalog long-distance calls and other overhead-appearing items in ways that can assign them to the job as direct expense? To the extent that this can be achieved, those otherwise soft costs can be elevated out of that category and properly placed into the much more specific direct-job-cost category.

As the organization's ability to perform these cost assignments improves, the relative value of overhead which must be left to be allocated among the jobs by some prorating accounting function is reduced.

Home Office Overhead Calculation

Perhaps the most well-known of all home office overhead calculations is the Eichleay formula. "Eichleay" has been accepted in many legal venues, but in its strict application has not been accepted in others. Even where it is not accepted, however, similar formulas are relied on. Whether strictly accepted or not, it does apply an important principle.

Eichleay and similar formulas are relatively straightforward accounting conventions that provide for the total home office overhead of an organization to be prorated among the organization's projects over each project's time period, while considering each project's size relative to the company's total output.

In one case, the United States Court of Appeals through a Federal Circuit Court ruled that the Eichleay formula is the only method recognized for the computation of unabsorbed home office overhead on federal construction projects. It reasoned: "Because it is impossible to determine the amount of unabsorbed overhead caused by the delay of any particular contract, and because the Eichleay formula provides an equitable method of compensating a contractor for unabsorbed overhead without costing taxpayers more than they should pay, we hold that the Eichleay formula is the exclusive means for compensating a contractor for unabsorbed overhead."

The Eichleay formula proceeds in three steps, and is stated as follows:

$$1. \quad \frac{\text{Contract billings}}{\text{Total billings for contract period}} \times \frac{\text{total overhead}}{\text{for the contract period}}$$

$$= \frac{\text{overhead allocatable}}{\text{to the contract}}$$

$$2. \quad \frac{\text{Allocatable overhead}}{\text{Days of performance}} = \text{daily contract overhead}$$

3. Daily contract overhead $\times$ days of recognized delay = amount recoverable

Presentation Problem

Even though Eichleay and similar types of calculations arrive at values that should be accurate in a given circumstance, one difficulty with such formulas is that, although recognized to be equitable, they arrive at numbers that can be very large relative to the original claim. While it is true that the sheer size of the home office overhead burden should underscore the dramatic damage actually being felt by the contractor, the resulting calculation is so large that often it appears to be unbelievable. A jury or an arbitration panel can quickly get the feeling that slick accounting is inflating numbers to an unreasonable degree.

Presentation Solution

In order to shore up an otherwise accurate home office overhead calculation, and increase the probability that the value will be seen as reasonable, it is important to create an impression of the project as it actually impacted the construction company's office on a very practical—and damaging—level.

Simply put, Eichleay and similar accounting formulas neatly prorate overhead values strictly based on the value of the job. In reality, however, a delayed job drains increasingly disproportionate resources from the entire contracting organization. When a job is sick, many levels of management, up to and including the senior levels, are routinely—sometimes *exclusively*—involved on the problem job. While Eichleay gives a neat prorating value, the truth is that disproportionate amounts of time, energy, and effort from the entire organization are regularly diverted away from the company while it attends to the problems of the delayed project.

Considering this real-world scenario, the argument becomes one that characterizes Eichleay as *not* being equitable to the contractor, and that it actually *understates* the true cost to the organization. The even-handed accounting distribution does not consider the resource-draining effects of the problem job on the contractor's entire organization. The contention is therefore that the Eichleay and similar formulas do not do the contractor equitable justice in their oversimplified distribution of overhead. Paint *this* picture, and the Eichleay values for the delayed project may begin to look more reasonable to the trier of fact.

Hostage Taking

Contents

Industrial Kidnapping
Risks to the Kidnapper
Resolving a Standoff

Related Topics

Arbitration
Breach of Contract
Claims Awareness
Deadlines
Deadlock
Documentation
Expediting Material Deliveries
Integrity
Liars
Spying
Surprise

Industrial Kidnapping

In construction, kidnapping—the taking of hostages—can be almost a daily occurrence. Although never a person, "hostages" typically include money, materials, labor to install work, and even completion schedules. They can include paperwork, property, or a good person's reputation.

Hostage taking can take obvious and subtle forms. One obvious example involves material suppliers. Every material supplier knows the particular materials that will become critical to the progress of the work at some point. Through your regular communication, the supplier is well aware of the pressure on your own organization for the delivery. And then it happens, almost magically. Two days before your long-anticipated critical delivery, your supplier advises you that a higher payment for the materials is now required, because of some circumstance that is not entirely clear to you at the moment. The supplier is well aware that you have run out of time; you have no time or other opportunity to renegotiate a deal with another supplier. The supplier has pretty much got you exactly where it wants you.

A variation on the above example: Two days before your anticipated critical delivery, the supplier contacts you advising you that it now needs a resolution of a problem on *another project* (and another time) the supplier's way—now—or the supplier will be "forced" to cancel the current order.

Another common example: A subcontractor has failed to perform to the standard of all the requirements in the subcontract agreement. In such a case, the subcontractor may have submitted an invoice which is either directly inflated, and/or is not justified because of that subcontractor's failure to comply with specific provisions of the agreement that are beyond the simple installation of work, such as delivery of certified payroll reports, production of **as-built documents,** delivery of safety **meeting minutes,** or delivery of operating and maintenance manuals. The situation might even be worse because of the subcontractor's substandard installation, or you may have other problems—the owner is withholding a payment to you, you need to correct defective work, and so on.

And then you get the famous statement: "Give me a check, and I'll show up," to which you respond: "Show up, and I might arrange for a check." And so the standoff is solidified with the subcontractor's completion of work being held hostage.

Risks to the Kidnapper

If you are thinking of becoming the kidnapper—the hostage taker—understand the extreme risks you are putting yourself at, in both the short and long term. These risks not only relate to a permanently damaged reputation or relationship with the kidnap victim, but also may leave you in a significant and intense legal situation.

It is interesting to note that a common characteristic of the hostage situation is that the kidnapper is usually not justified in its extreme, unethical, and **surprise** tactics with respect to the rights and responsibilities between the kidnapper and the victim.

In the subcontractor standoff above, it is very likely that the subcontractor is experiencing its payment issues because it has genuinely not lived up to its end of the bargain. That sub goes on to fail to recognize the ripple effect of the series of problems that its noncompliance has created first for the general contractor, and then for the owner by late completion, substandard work, etc.

And so the kidnapper—or would-be kidnapper—would be wise to reconsider the requirements of its agreement, or become aware that it may be doing nothing more than creating a substantial breach of its agreement that is clearly tied to the project's critical path. The kidnapper thereby nails itself down as the specific reason for the entire project's late completion. To the extent that this effect can be demonstrated by the general contractor, the ultimate exposure to the kidnapper can be hugely disproportionate in relation to the importance of the original hostage.

To compound this idea dramatically, the other risk to the kidnapper is that it is guaranteed to stir anger and then determination in the victim's entire organization. Even if there is some way that the hostage situation might even be justified in principle, the problems that it generates for the victim's organization are intense, immediate, and dramatic. The line being walked by the kidnapper is a very narrow one indeed. Pushed a shade one way or the other, the victim's organization can flip in a moment from quick acquiescence to the demands of the kidnapper in order to preserve the project to an energetic, determined focus on overcoming the problem caused by the hostage taking while not giving in to the kidnapper's demand.

If this second occurrence should happen, the kidnapper is suddenly jolted into a very bad position. Not only will it be stuck with the subject of the kidnap, which has now become worthless or at least of marginal value, but it can now brace itself for everything that the victim's organization is about to throw because of the extreme damages caused. These situations have a way of very quickly escalating out of the business decision arena, where a strict cost of doing business is the primary consideration, to a matter of principle, and someone is about to be taught a lesson almost without regard to the costs involved in such a lesson. In a hostage situation gone wrong, the would-be kidnapper should buckle up for a very rough ride.

Resolving a Standoff

Business kidnapping is not as difficult to deal with as a human kidnapping because life is not at stake. In resolving a hostage situation, a few ideas that can help include:

1. Anticipate a hostage situation in the development of your own standard agreements (refer to the **power of the standard form** for important related discussion). Put very clear, but very severe, penalties in your standard agreements for these unethical, **surprise** situations.

2. Stay calm and cool. Do your best to keep your emotions out of the picture. Reread your agreement with the kidnapper. Take a moment to fully understand all the professional and personal motivations of the action.

3. Do your best to anticipate the possibility of a hostage scenario. Don't wait until the last minute to confirm material deliveries. Break up your material deliveries into sequences to test your relationship with your supplier. Keep your eye carefully fixed on that last delivery, and plan it well enough in advance of your actual need specifically so that you are not up against the wall, being forced to make a quick decision because of an immediate deadline. Refer to **expediting material deliveries** for important related discussion.

4. Get your own hostage. If a subcontractor is withholding work, the reason for the kidnapping is its ransom—the current check that it is looking to receive. I assure you, that payment is significant to that subcontractor's life at the moment. Don't underestimate the true value of that payment. Understand the real effect on the subcontractor's organization of your continued withholding of the payment; it may be

much larger than the absolute value of the payment itself. Do some research, and try to establish the reality of this particular situation. Breaking the hostage crisis may be nothing more than calling the kidnapper's bluff. Refer to **spying** for important related discussion.

5. Protest to a higher level (or to some other level). If your current problem is with the credit manager of a supplier organization, consider calling the vice president of sales. The credit manager is only concerned with payment; and not necessarily concerned with the supplier's continued relationship with your organization. That is not how the performance of the credit manager is evaluated. The sales manager, however, would be *very* concerned with the continued relationship with your organization. That *is* how the sales manager's performance is measured. Bringing the credit manager's unethical approach to the sales manager's attention may be all that is necessary to soften the standoff. Refer to **deadlock** for important related discussion.

6. Have someone high in your organization resolve the issue with someone high in the kidnapper's organization. Even if the entire kidnapper's organization is corrupt, people at the top understand the value of not *appearing* to be corrupt. Their egos might be attached to the issue at some upper level; probe for that level. Have the president of your organization contact the president of the kidnapper's organization. Be sure, of course, that your president has some real facts at hand. There is some chance that the president of the kidnapper's organization can be made to appear "petty," and may even acquiesce to an equitable resolution if only to avoid damage to his or her ego.

7. If you must pay the ransom, be very clear in your **documentation.** Prepare a clear communication to the kidnapper that includes an itemized list of the reasons why the kidnapping is wholly unsupported by your agreement, a specific description of the damage to the project and your company that is a direct result of the hostage situation, and even a request that the kidnapper provide its written substantiation as to why it believes its action is justified. If the kidnapper actually provides you with a written response, there's a very good chance that it might be *the* written documentation that will clearly nail your situation down in your eventual litigation or **arbitration.** There is a very good chance, however, that your written request for a written response will actually go unresponded to or will be inadequately responded to. This might be okay, too. No answer might be a very clear answer.

Unfortunately, the payment of a ransom encourages kidnapping. Unscrupulous businesspeople who try it and succeed develop the idea that it is a regular approach to business and look for other victims. Take such situations seriously, and do your best to resolve them equitably and on principle.

Implied Warranty

Constructibility

If a contract specifies a product and requires a contractor to use that product, the contractor has the right to rely on the owner's *implied warranty* that the intended, or "satisfactory," performance will result. Accordingly, the contractor who is so directed to use a specific product or a particular brand which cannot or will not perform as specified, or as intended, should not be held liable for the resulting failure, defect, or other unsatisfactory result.

Such an owner's implied warranty of constructibility may apply only to **proprietary specifications** and may not extend to performance specifications (see **"performance" and "procedure" specifications**).

The specification provision, for example, that requires the **quality** of a product to be the equivalent of a specific brand name product or "equal" product is a performance specification. In such a case, there may be no implied warranty of constructibility on the part of the owner.

Product Application

As an example of the owner's implied warranty of constructibility with respect to the physical performance of a product, consider a contract in which the owner specifies a particular architectural light fixture and names that product by manufacturer and model number. If it subsequently turns out that the light fixture cannot fit in the ceiling space after the contractor has exercised proper **coordination** of the components of the total construction, the owner will bear the responsibility for the failure of the specified product to "perform as intended."

Time Consideration

The owner's implied warranty of constructibility with respect to the time of performance of a contract is divided into two basic aspects: a straight time consideration, and a schedule sequence consideration.

With regard to straight time, if a contract requires total performance within a prescribed period of time, the owner implicitly warrants that the project can in fact be constructed within that stated time. As an example, consider a contract which requires completed performance within 100 calendar days. If the owner had specified a boiler that cannot be delivered before 120 days, the owner can be said to have breached the warranty of constructibility by directly creating the situation that will prevent the specified contractual result.

With regard to schedule sequence, the owner's specified product should not interfere with the contractor's reasonably (and competently) planned construction sequence, which is logically necessary to perform the requirements of the contract. Consider the construction of a fire protection pump house that has the same 100 calendar day requirement of the first example. In this case, the boiler is available within 100 days. In addition, two large foam storage tanks need to be installed for the fire suppression system. Consider further that the remaining 20 days is apparently sufficient to complete all boiler mechanical and electrical connections and all storage tank connections to the fire pumps. The problem in this example is one of logical construction sequence. The storage tanks are too large to fit through the designed overhead door, so the only logical construction sequence requires that the tanks be placed in the structure before the roof joists are installed. In such a case, either the tanks need to be delivered to the site much earlier than a normal construction sequence would have required, or sufficient time must be available after the actual tank delivery date to complete the basic building structure. Either way, the specified performance with respect to the contract **time** has again been interfered with, and the owner's implied warranty of constructibility has been breached. Delivering the tanks to the site within the 100 days that (to the owner) initially seemed to be sufficient won't allow performance within the original contract time.

Refer to **time** and **force majeure** for important related discussion.

Impossibility and Impracticability

Excuse or Abuse?

It's been said (some courts have held) that there is no excuse for non-performance due to "misfortune, accident, or misadventure." Having said that much, however, the courts do realize that in many instances this blanket approach can leave a contractor with a result that is far too harsh. Exceptions to the rule have accordingly been explained in terms of **constructive changes** or "implied" conditions.

Evolution of the Concept

The doctrine of impossibility of performance is still evolving. One modern application has been determined as follows:

> A thing is impossible in legal contemplation when it is not practicable; and a thing is impracticable when it can only be done at an excessive and unreasonable cost.

The doctrine attempts to deal with the gray area left by the court by giving latitude to consider specific circumstances whereby the sensibleness of having the contract language strictly enforced is weighed against the commercial sensibleness (or senselessness) of requiring the particular performance.

Practical Application

If the concepts of impossibility or impracticability are considered in order to try to resolve an issue, it may prove to be effective to incorporate the concepts with the idea of demonstrating that the performance being demanded is required (actually or constructively) by some change in circumstances in a process that may involve the following steps:

1. A "contingency"—something unexpected—has occurred or might have occurred.

2. The risk of the unexpected occurrence must not have been allocated to either party, either by agreement, or by "custom." (Refer to **trade practice** for related discussion.)

3. The occurrence of the contingency must render the performance being demanded commercially impractical.

Note that although extreme impracticability (financial hardship) is the essential basis for the argument, the existence of mere "unanticipated difficulty or expense" not amounting to impracticability is not at all within the scope of this application.

The greatest hurdle in a practical application of these ideas toward problem resolution is the ability of the parties to agree on items 2 and 3 above.

Example

As an example, consider a situation where a concrete slab is placed that varies approximately $\frac{1}{2}$ in in a 10-ft dimension. Is it "reasonable" for the design professional or owner to insist that the slab be removed and replaced because the specification stated that all concrete slabs *shall* "be level within $\frac{1}{4}$ in in 10 ft in any direction"?

Even though the cost of removal and replacement is very high, it might actually be reasonable if the contract contemplated subsequent installation of scientific equipment or the installation of some following construction that required those tolerances. It may not, however, be so reasonable if it is a shop floor that is only going to get beaten by tow motors and heavy equipment.

Inadequate Design Detail

Contents

Shifting Design Responsibility
Forms of Missing Information
Problems with Missing Details
Corrective Action

Related Topics

Ambiguities
As Indicated
Coordination
Cut-and-Paste
Defective Specifications
Duty to Inquire
"Equals" and "Substitutions"
"Intent" versus "Indication"
Interpretation—Right to Choose
Patent Errors
RFI (Request for Information)

Shifting Design Responsibility

There are basic reasons why any particular design may contain insufficient detail for proper coordination and construction. The designer may not have spent enough time to complete the design and coordinate it with all other design interfaces. Or the omission of detail in the design may actually be intentional; it might be an attempt to shift the burden of the remaining design onto the contractor or construction force under the guise of **coordination.**

Forms of Missing Information

Missing or inadequate design information can take many forms, from obvious omissions to more subtle approaches. For example,

- Insufficient dimensions are provided, so that even an elaborate calculation cannot locate portions of the work correctly.

- Descriptions are incomplete, introducing questions or subjectivity into the scope of work. (Is the blocking "continuous," "16 in on center," or "as needed"?)

- Mounting details are not considered. (Do you want stainless steel brackets or rubber bands holding up the limestone?)

These kinds of problems at worst cause the contractor to assume a certain amount of responsibility for design, and at best just add time (and a little confusion) to the construction process.

Problems with Missing Details

The problems generated for a contractor and the construction force by missing design information and inadequate levels of design detail are too often disproportionately larger than the problems that the designer would have had in completing the detail. Such problems include the time required to resolve questions, redundant efforts expended by the contractor to secure and coordinate new information, and the risk taken by the construction force of assuming a responsibility for a portion of the design which should not be theirs. Shop drawings are returned with "by GC" or "GC coordinate" notes on them instead of the dimensions and details that should come only from the designer. Field time is wasted each time a situation involving inadequate design information is encountered. Work stops and answers are needed immediately.

Corrective Action

Remember that the word **coordination** means arranging in order; it does *not* mean *inventing* information—that's design

Be intolerant of missing information. Always get the missing design information from those who are responsible to provide it. Even when the answer may be obvious, establish a correct and complete design with the designer; but be sure that the final direction is coming from the designer—not from you. Refer to **RFI (request for information)** for important related discussion.

Scrutinize the "clarification," or whatever the design professional chooses to call the missing design information after you finally receive it. Compare it to your original **interpretation** of the detail at the time of bid. Determine if the completion of the detail is what could have been reasonably inferred with the original set of design documents. Is the detail subject to more than one interpretation? If so, you may not have to accept a "clarification" that is really an embellishment of the contract. Refer to **interpretation—right to choose** and **ambiguities** for important related discussion.

Indemnification Clauses

Description

An indemnification provision in a contract is a type of **exculpatory clause** that requires the contractor to compensate the owner for any damages whatsoever that arise for the performance of the work by the contractor, or for other reasons that are within the control of the contractor. It can be all-encompassing.

Similarly, an indemnity provision in a subcontract protects the general contractor from damages of every type which arise from the performance of the work by the subcontractor, or from any conditions that are otherwise within the control of that subcontractor. (Refer to **pass-through clause** for important related discussion.) The pass-through provision in the subcontract will provide a contractor indemnity if the owner-contractor agreement provides for a contractor-owner indemnity. Even so, do not leave these important issues to the pass-through clause. Simply be sure that your own subcontract incorporates an adequate indemnity provision.

Example Clause

Indemnity provisions come in various sizes and shapes, but contain similar operative language. The basic indemnity provision will include language to the effect that:

> The contractor shall indemnify, hold harmless, and defend the owner, design professionals, their representatives, servants, agents, and employees, from and against any and all claims, suits, demands, actions, cost, and damages of every kind whatsoever including injury or death arising from or resulting from the performance of the work of this agreement.

The provision may go on to provide that the indemnification obligations are not affected in any way by any limitation on the amount of damages, compensation, or benefits payable by or for the contractor or for any subcontractor under worker's compensation, disability benefits, or employee benefits.

It might also go on to provide the specifics of any number of other situations, given the disposition of the particular attorney who drafted the clause.

An Unfair Twist

The example language described above can be considered "fair," and is almost sure to be enforceable by the courts. Indeed, the compensation does seem equitable, and there is enough history and precedent to protect the owner from liability on claims caused by acts of the contractor, subcontractors, and employees.

We do, however, begin to walk on the edge of fairness when the clause goes on to provide that the contractor also indemnify the owner for claims caused by the actions of third parties *not under the control of the contractor or its subcontractors.* Not only does this not seem fair, but is on the edge of enforceability, as well.

Clauses which have clearly stepped over the fairness line now appear much more commonly in construction contracts. They are buried in legalese and are tagged onto the ends of otherwise innocuous-looking sentences.

These are the clauses which require that the contractor indemnify the owner from claims and damages which are caused by actions, omissions, and blatant negligence by *the owner,* its employees, and/or the design professionals. In other words, you would be forcing me to protect you from yourself. Refer to **"conspicuous" contracts** for important related discussion.

To this point, courts have been generally reluctant to permit a party to indemnify itself against claims caused by its own negligence, and accordingly have not permitted these types of unfair, aggressive clauses to be enforceable. **Attorneys,** however, are getting better every day at drafting new and improved language that is specifically designed to circumvent the specific reasons given in judicial opinions for such lack of enforceability. In other words, some day soon it shouldn't be a surprise to see a poor contractor finally being held responsible for some owner holding a gun to its own head.

Don't be the test case. Force yourself to read every indemnification provision provided in your contracts, and strike out what is usually little more than a single sentence—that line which goes on to require that the contractor protect the owner from its own negligence. Strike it out, and insist that it is a deal breaker. Because of the blatant unreasonableness of the language, "negotiating" the issue is often not much more than simply telling the contract drafter that the provision is not acceptable. By a simple stroke of the pen, you will have protected yourself and your company from an incredibly outlandish amount of additional liability that should not be yours at all.

Integrity

Contents

Related Topics

The Old Days

When two construction people get together in conversation—particularly when the subject of negotiating a contract or subcontract comes up—one or both will probably lament "the old days" when only a "handshake" was necessary to close the deal.

Such remarks are a slur to the integrity of the individuals in our business; they imply that the reason why handshake deals no longer work is simply that no one can trust anyone else. We stare at the 21-page agreement in print too small to read, and wish we went to law school when we had the chance.

Meeting of the Minds

Assume for a moment that there is absolute integrity on the parts of both parties to a pending agreement. Assume further that each party actually intends to live up to its side of the bargain to the fullest extent that it possibly can, that it intends to pursue this relationship with energy to genuinely satisfy the other party. The problem then is not really one of integrity at all, but one of a true meeting of the minds.

Compounding Differences

The problem begins with the simple idea that my idea of a "good job" is not exactly what your idea of a "good job" is. We both intend to do a "good job," but we are already beginning the relationship on two separate pages.

The problem is further compounded with the ideas that we are both going to exercise **delegation** by assigning the performance of our handshake deal to two other individuals. Those two individuals also intend to pursue the agreement with absolute integrity, to the complete satisfaction of the other party. Those two new individuals, however, have still two additional ideas as to what "good" performance is.

So, we begin the handshake deal with four well-meaning individuals, energetically pursuing *four distinctly different performances,* all with the very *best of intentions.* Given this scenario, it should be easy to see that the odds of any party being happy with the results have plummeted dramatically. It has absolutely nothing to do with the integrity of the parties, or with the lack of any party's intention to live up to its end of the bargain. It is only the result of a well-intended but very simple and complete misunderstanding.

Details Solve Differences

The straightforward way to avoid this type of ironically bad situation, to keep friends friends, to encourage satisfactory performance, and to raise the odds of mutual agreement is to clearly define each component of the relationship in writing, with a corresponding precise expectation of performance. To the extent that you can clearly define each component, you will successively remove the possibility of misunderstanding related to an "impression" of performance. Details solve differences. Remove the subjectivity from the relationship, *clearly define the mutual expectations,* and your friendship stands at least some chance.

"Intent" versus "Indication"

Intent or Indication?

In a scope-of-work dispute, the "intent" of the contract is very likely to be raised at an early point of discussion. Design professionals might attempt to divert attention to what they *meant* to say if they can't find anything in their **contract documents** to indicate precisely what they wanted their specifications to say. In contemporary contracting, nearly every specification written—whether provided by some standard authority (such as the American Institute of Architects) or fully written from the ground up—contains numerous examples of language that attempt to cover the contract gaps and thereby induce the contractor to perform work that the designer "meant" to include. Refer to **cut-and-paste** and **boilerplate** for related discussion.

Response

Whether design intent can be used as a means to fill gaps left in a contract specification description boils down to the words *reasonably inferable*. If the missing work can be reasonably inferred to be necessary to complete the detail, and the gap is so obvious that a professional contractor would not normally overlook it, then the designer may actually be able to use the design intent to require the contractor to perform the work in question. Refer to **patent errors** and **duty to inquire** for related discussion.

Defense

In order to test the applicability of design intent as a legitimate inducement to the contractor to perform work not specifically indicated, consider the following tests:

1. Can the remaining work be completed without the extra work in question?

2. Is there more than one way to complete the extra work in question?

3. Is the extra work not usually encountered by the trade now being considered to construct it?

If you can answer "yes" to any of these questions, it will throw into serious question the applicability of intent as a work requirement that the contractor should be responsible for. For intent to apply, it would need to satisfy the same test as that for **trade practice.** That is, the missing intended work must actually be necessary with *absolute regularity* and *consistency.* It can be considered to be reasonably inferable; it *must* apply in the specific case considered, *can* or *might* apply is not enough.

Example

If, for example, a concrete slab is placed and varies approximately 1 in within 10 ft, is it reasonable for the architect to insist the slab be removed and replaced because the specification required very clearly that the concrete slab shall be level within $\frac{1}{4}$ in in any direction?

The cost of such replacement is very high. It may actually be reasonable if the slab is intended for installation of scientific equipment that requires very close tolerances. It may, however, not be at all reasonable, if the application is a shop floor that is going to be beaten by tow motors, or be subject to other work not requiring close tolerances.

Accordingly, the success of this application might be related to the context of the work, not just the literal specification language.

Interpretation—Right to Choose

Contents

Principle

Example

"Reasonable" Interpretation

Responsibility to Investigate

Related Topics

Adhesion Contracts

Ambiguities

Coordination

Duty to Inquire

Exculpatory Clauses

Trade Practice

Principle

In its simplest form, the general rule is that if **adhesion contracts** (take-it-or-leave-it deals) contain any provision that may be subject to more than one clear, *reasonable* interpretation, the contractor has the right to choose the reasonable interpretation that will be applied in the specific circumstance.

In a manner similar to that for the principle of **ambiguities**, the law assumes that those who are responsible for drafting construction contracts not only provide for their own interests but have had every opportunity to be sure that the contract documents are clear and complete. If through all that effort they have not been able to produce a set of documents that are clear in their instruction, it is not reasonable to hold a contractor to any higher standard that would essentially require the contractor to correct for the design's mistakes or confusions.

Example

Consider a design detail that provides a statement that the contractor should provide "Blocking as Required." The intent of the designer might have been for the contractor to provide "continuous" blocking. The contractor, however, may have had experience (possibly even with the same client, as can be the case in government contracts) that the condition only required blocking in the specific areas of each fastener for the item to be supported. Moreover, the contractor may have (at least in his or her experience) actually installed the work according to *its* interpretation, and have had the work inspected and paid for.

Under these circumstances, the contractor's interpretation should probably be considered reasonable *enough*; and barring any other clarifying language in the contract, the contractor will be entitled to rely on that reasonable interpretation.

"Reasonable" Interpretation

It is important to understand that this principle applies as long as the contractor's interpretation is in fact a *reasonable* one. It does not, however, have to be the "most" reasonable interpretation, or even "more reasonable" than any competing interpretation. It only needs to be "reasonable" in its own right.

Responsibility to Investigate

Once a reasonable interpretation of an issue has been discovered by or otherwise been made available to the contractor, the contractor is under no obligation to continue to search the documents in an attempt to try to discover if any other reasonable interpretations might exist. If a contractor has been able to positively determine the complete instruction required to complete a design detail, it has satisfied its requirements to coordinate its construction and secure adequate direction before proceeding. A contractor is required to coordinate its *work*—the contractor is not required to coordinate the *design*.

Refer to **Ambiguities, Coordination,** and **"Intent" versus "Indication"** for important related discussion.

Job Descriptions

Freedom within Limits

It has been said that in order to develop children with healthy attitudes and positive self-esteem, it is necessary to give them "freedom within limits." Contrary to many beliefs, children do not want—and do not need—absolute freedom. By giving children a clear indication of reasonable limits, you give them a better understanding of their roles in your family, a sense of what is and is not expected of them, and even an indication of how they are being measured in your eyes. With all this comes an increasing sense of security because you have reduced a significant amount of confusion in their own lives.

And so it is with your employees. If your method of job assignments boils down to handing someone a title—"project manager," "project engineer," or "superintendent"—with little more than implicit assumptions about the meaning of those titles, then it will also be wise to prepare yourself for the inevitable confusions and conflicts that will arise from the difference in perspective between you and your employees. Refer to **agreements versus understandings** for important related discussion.

What is more, consistently in the construction industry, **authority** is rarely given to the same limits as *implied* responsibility. In other words, in the overwhelming majority of cases, employees in the construction industry feel that, even though they do not have the authority to determine certain actions, when something goes wrong, it is still their fault.

Assuming an adequate level of competence on the part of an employee, these confusions and inconsistencies regularly breed feelings of self-doubt, insecurity, dissatisfaction, and inadequate performance. The worst irony of all this is that these employees generally are doing their best, with very high levels of **integrity,** to serve their company—as they are trying to figure out how their company would like to be served.

Performance Effectiveness

Well beyond the idea that you simply "owe it" to your employees to provide clear direction, probably you will dramatically increase the effectiveness of every employee by giving a clear description of responsibilities. Define the limits and clarify the "freedoms." Catalog each responsibility with a corresponding level of **authority.** Describe how each function correlates with and fits into your organizational system, and how each job relates to the others within that job's sphere of influence. Describe, for example, how the project engineer's activities relate to those of the site superintendent, and how the activities of each will coordinate under the control of the project manager.

Use organization charts with lines and boxes that clearly describe the reporting chain. Have a list that clarifies document-signing authorities, communication responsibilities, and **documentation** requirements.

Review the job descriptions, along with the specific responsibilities and limits of authority, with your employees. Look for those aspects that make the employee feel more comfortable, and try to identify those that make the employee more uncomfortable. Look for any possible confusions or dilemmas that might be caused by discrepancies between a written description and a practical operating reality in the field. Encourage open dialog. Use the process to further refine the collection of job descriptions for a period of operation within your organization.

Work to define the specific responsibilities and the particular freedoms along with their appropriate limits, and you just might find yourself with employees who have clear ideas about how to handle daily operating situations, who can move methodically through the workday, and who can resolve outstanding issues instead of procrastinating them into growing in-baskets.

Job Meetings

Contents

Meeting Purpose

Day and Time

Location

Participants

Action Rules

Related Topics

Agenda

Change Order Files

Conduit Theory

Documentation

Letter Wars

Meeting Minutes

Notice

Meeting Purpose

Job meetings are held to *solve problems*—not just to massage the same items that you discussed last week. They are critically important to the quick and complete resolution of every item affecting the project—if they are *managed,* and not avoided. They are not there simply to record history, but to force action, pinpoint accountability, and support your actions.

Day and Time

Mondays and Fridays will be sparsely attended. Even if you manage to ensure participation, attention spans will be divided, and you might have some difficulty maintaining any consistency from meeting to meeting without constant bird-dogging of all required participants.

Tuesdays or Thursdays are best. Whenever the rest of the world schedules anything, it is almost certain to be on a Wednesday, creating the inevitable conflict. Wednesdays do, however, remain much better than Mondays or Fridays.

Insist on morning meetings starting between 10:00 and 11:30 a.m. This will:

- Allow a few precious minutes for last minute preparations.

- Give people a chance to get to the meeting without having to fight morning or noon-hour traffic.

- Catch attendees before the rest of the day is allowed to interfere with their schedules, thereby promoting consistent attendance.

- Leave the rest of the day to act on critical issues before they're allowed to cool.

- Improve your chances of catching people "in," if you need to phone or visit them today to resolve something.

- Leave time to force others to change their plans for the rest of the day in order to resolve current problems now.

- Keep everyone working toward getting through the agenda and finishing the meeting. The closer you get to lunch, the quicker things seem to get resolved. In marked contrast, meetings held after lunch are conducted in slow motion; they're sure to be partially attended, move at half-speed, and close with most of the original **agenda** still intact. You can't have a full head and full stomach at the same time—one of them has to be empty.

Location

Always meet at the site. Don't waste time arguing over who's project it is, or get caught in the one-upmanship game of showing authority by contesting the meeting location. Heads of bureaucratic government or quasi-government agencies, for example, have a habit of trying to arrange meetings at their own offices, or at some other locations convenient for them.

The jobsite is where the issues live. Get out of the field office, walk to the problem, point at it. Misunderstandings that everyone had will be cleared up in seconds, and you'll move closer to resolution.

Participants

The absolute minimum should be the owner's representatives, design professionals, construction field personnel (superintendent, project manager), and construction administration (project manager, project engineer). Unfortunately, it is getting more common on small and midsized projects for the mechanical, electrical, and structural engineers not to attend—usually because the owner–design professional agreements pay these consultants on an hourly arrangement during the project's construction phase. But that's *their* problem, not yours.

It may work in the unlikely event that you have no engineering problems. If you do, however, their lack of attendance is your guarantee that a minimum of a week will be added to any related design resolution. If your agenda has design-related problems, insist on these individuals' attendance. If they then do not attend, you will have every right to call foul, and highlight the potential schedule impact resulting from the extra delay in resolution.

Action Rules

1. *Schedule meetings as frequently as* you *need them to be.*   During the job start-up, shop drawings are flying, construction and bid pack-

age coordination efforts are being compressed into small time frames, and resulting questions are multiplying. Insist on weekly meetings. Too often, those responsible for acting on a job meeting item will not look at the item until the day before (or the morning of) the next job meeting. **Deadlines** seem to be the earliest that you can hope for any action. Get these deadlines (the next meetings) as close together as possible. As the project settles into a pace, it's up to you if you think it will be all right to relax into biweekly meetings. If, however, you get any hint that there is too much time between issue and resolution, immediately get back to the weekly schedule.

2. *Always start on time.*   Regardless of who's late, and regardless of how many times that person has been late, start the meeting at the scheduled time. Having to sneak into an ongoing meeting one or two times will usually cure a tardy attendee of the problem. If it doesn't, chronic offenders should be confronted at the meeting. Let those who do get there on time know that you appreciate their efforts.

If for some reason you can't start (the owner's rep is driving in from another city and the design professionals refuse to start), consider stating at the actual start of the meeting that you now need an adjustment in the **agenda** to hit the important topics because you must leave on time. Get and keep control. Let everyone know that your time is valuable, and they need to learn to respect that. You've managed to keep your commitments; you have a right to expect others to do the same.

3. *Enforce mandatory attendance.*   Do not tolerate absence or neglect. When an expected attendee is missing, it disrupts the agenda and loses time. When the agenda item comes up, call the person right in the middle of the meeting. If a speakerphone is available, call him or her on it. Preface your conversation with "We expected you here, but since you're not we've got you on the speaker, so ..." and move right into the issue. A mild reprimand for the person's lack of consideration (a strong one for repeated offenders) is definitely appropriate. Be matter-of-fact and businesslike. The person will be caught at least a bit off guard and embarrassed enough to be sure not to go through it again.

4. *End each item with a* resolution.   If the issue itself is not finalized, end with a determination of a specific action to be made by a particular individual (by name) by a certain date. Nail it down.

5. *Keep ongoing, complete records.*   Use methods that keep:

- The project record clear
- Everything on the front burner
- Everyone accountable for his or her actions (and inactions)

Refer to **meeting minutes** for additional related discussion and action rules.

Joint Checks

Issue

The practice of writing joint checks has become common throughout the construction industry. It is usually seen as a reasonable method to ensure proper payment through multiple contract tiers, thereby minimizing lien and payment bond claims. Conflicts arise, however, because of different approaches taken by courts as to the effect of an endorsement of a joint check by a subcontractor or supplier.

The joint check arrangement usually arises when the ability (or intention) to pay a party in the payment chain is questionable. A general contractor, for example, may elect to issue checks payable to a subcontractor and one of its suppliers, specifically in order to minimize the risk of that supplier filing a lien against the property or pursuing a claim against the general contractor's payment bond. Similarly, the supplier may request a joint check arrangement when that supplier has concerns regarding the financial condition of the subcontractor to whom it is supplying material.

The Problem

Contractors who issue joint checks usually do so with the idea that they are eliminating their liability for the amounts of the joint checks to either—or both—of the parties to whom the joint checks are issued. Unfortunately, however, the subcontractor's or supplier's handling of a joint check can vary, depending on the law applicable to the specific situation.

Typically, when a general contractor issues a joint check it intends that the subcontractor endorse the check and turn it over completely to the supplier. Problems immediately result when the subcontractor does not follow that procedure. For example:

- The subcontractor endorses the check and turns it over to the supplier, but instructs the supplier to apply the payment to accounts other than those intended by the general contractor.

- The subcontractor endorses the check and manages to deposit the check without the coendorsement.

These types of problems dilute or dissolve the protections originally sought by the party issuing the checks.

The Solution

Never prepare a joint check and deliver it to the first payee with the expectation that the payment will simply be endorsed and turned over to that party's supplier and the entire payment amount will be properly applied to the correct account. Instead, require that the first party endorse the check, but retain the check in your possession. Retain control over the particular payment, and arrange for the delivery to the second party yourself, along with an exchange of appropriate waivers and releases.

When the intent of a joint check is to pay *both* payees to the full amount of the check, obtain a written acknowledgment *from each of the joint payees* that their endorsement of the check constitutes a waiver for the full amount of the check of both payees' rights against the payment bond if any, or their right to file a lien.

Taking positive custody of the check and carefully directing it to its intended recipients, along with clear account application, finalized with appropriate waivers and releases, will leave you with the best chance of preserving your initial intent intact.

Deliver a statement with the check (along with an appropriate note on the face of the check) clarifying the specific accounts that the payment is to be applied to. Go one step further and secure a written confirmation *from both payees* that the payment is being applied to those accounts.

Knowledge

Contents

Obligation to Disclose

Superior Knowledge

Related Topics

Deliberate Errors

Duty to Inquire

Exculpatory Clauses

Geotechnical Information

Implied Warranty

Liars

Patent Errors

Surprise

Unforeseen Conditions

Obligation to Disclose

The party preparing a construction agreement (the owner) has an absolute duty to disclose to the bidder superior knowledge of the item that may either directly or indirectly relate to the work, where that knowledge is either unknown, or is otherwise unavailable, to the contractor.

Consider a contract that provides boring data or other subsurface **geotechnical information** as part of the bid documents. Assume that the boring locations are shown in one area of the site, but the building footprint has been shifted during the design development process, leaving a significant amount of the building footprint over an area not represented by the boring data. Assume further that subsequent to the bid, but prior to contract award, additional borings in the other area had been taken, and the owner is now aware that the conditions of the soils below the surface are materially different than those that can be inferred from the boring data given in the original portion of the site. A "nothing-to-lose" attitude that the contractor might somehow absorb the cost of working through the undisclosed condition may leave such an owner bordering on fraud.

Whether the situation is the result of an inadvertent omission, or the result of a bet that the owner will either definitely pay you now or maybe pay you later, the contractor is entitled to compensation for the changed condition. In the latter case, the approach is definitely abusive. Refer to **exculpatory clauses** and **unforeseen conditions** for related discussion.

Superior Knowledge

If the owner's superior knowledge of a factor, such as the unavailability or inadequacy of a specified material, would lead to a reduced cost or improved efficiency, it must not withhold that information from the contractor. In a sense, this obligation to disclose superior knowledge is related to and is the mirrored opposite of the contractor's obligation to disclose **patent errors** and its **duty to inquire.**

Latent Defects

Related Topics

Description

A *latent defect* (or latent **ambiguity**) is one which could not have been readily detected by a competent contractor by reasonable means. There are conditions that, at the time of bid, are unknown at least to the contractor, and may not be known by anyone. (Refer to **knowledge** and **patent errors** for important related discussion.) A latent defect is to be distinguished very clearly from a patent error, which is an obvious or glaring deficiency that should have been detected by the contractor prior to bid.

In the condition of a latent defect, proper information relevant to the condition is probably not obtainable by a contractor through any reasonable means. The information might have been obtainable by the owner if it had chosen to expend the time and money necessary to investigate the matter, but the fact remains that the information is simply unavailable to anyone. In such a case, the presence of a latent defect may actually be nobody's "fault."

An example of this type of condition might be the requirement of a contractor to incorporate in its bid all conditions for those effects that are indicated in the **contract documents,** or that might be "readily apparent" on a reasonable site investigation. The contractor would be responsible for rock, even if it is not disclosed in any boring or other geotechnical information, if visual site investigation reveals obvious rock outcroppings. The same contractor under the same set of bid circumstances would not be responsible for the rock if there is no such physical indication, and if any **geotechnical information** provided by the owner as part of the bid documents did not disclose such rock. In the case where the rock is known to no one, the condition is considered a latent defect.

For these reasons, the legal rules support the idea that the contractor will be entitled to recover extra costs resulting from latent defects.

Common Categories

The two most common categories of latent defects are

1. *Subsurface site condition.*   These are conditions that may be undetected by testing or research, or that lurk beneath the site unknown to anyone because of the lack of any testing or research. Examples include:

   - Soil composition
   - Water table or springs
   - Rock
   - Previous disposal area
   - Organic or other "unsuitable" materials
   - Utility, sanitary, storm, or telephone line locations different from those on record
   - Previous structures that have long since been abandoned

   Refer to **unforeseen conditions** for related discussion.

2. *Hidden conditions in an existing facility.*   In an alteration project, or perhaps where a new project ties into an existing facility, certain conditions may exist that could only have been disclosed by prior demolition. **As-built documents** previously prepared for the area may be corrupt, incomplete, or nonexistent. Examples of such conditions include:

   - Discovery of structurally unsound materials
   - Malfunctions of existing equipment
   - Building configurations that are different from those shown on the existing plan or on as-built drawings

Leadership

Contents

Lead or Follow

Most people in large companies today are administered, not led. Somehow, they are now a "human resource" or "personnel." I'm not any longer sure that they are people. True leadership must be for the benefit of those led, not for the benefit of the leaders. In combat situations, officers eat last.

It often seems that the larger the company, the greater the probability that leadership within that organization is described by the position, rather than the actual attribute. Lawrence Peter and Raymond Hull summed it up in their book *The Peter Principle* (Morrow, NY, 1971; reprinted 1993, Buccaneer Books, Cutchogue, NY) with the remark that "Most hierarchies are these days so encumbered with rules and traditions, and so bound by public laws, that even high level employees do not have to lead anyone anywhere, in the sense of pointing out a direction and setting the pace. They simply follow precedence, obey regulations, and move to the head of the crowd. Such employees lead only in the sense that the carved wooden figure-head leads the ship."

Leadership Styles

In general, there are three styles of leadership:

1. *Autocratic.* This is a dictator's style in which the subordinate has little or no input with regard to the work to be performed. The accomplishment of specific work assignments within confirmed time frames is the management system. Performance is arithmetical. The items of work are either accomplished in the required time frames or not.

2. *Head coach.* This style is most closely associated with sports. The supervisor provides direction, expertise, vision, and a series of goals. The subordinate has input as to how and when work is to be accomplished, and shares in the respective successes and failures.

3. *Autocratic–head coach combination.*   In this style, the subordinates work as the *team.* Many areas of decision making, however, are specifically reserved for the supervisor alone. It is this mix which, in my opinion, is appropriately applied to the typical construction organization. The production authority defines the goals, objectives, methods and procedures—the tools—for each project manager, project engineer, and site superintendent to use while carrying out the various components of each job. Cooperation and teamwork are absolutely essential in order to keep energy focused toward project objectives, and not internal company politics. Final decisions—perhaps based upon a dollar-limit schedule—are specifically reserved for correspondingly increasing levels of **authority.**

Spotting a Leader

Leaders come in all sizes, shapes, ages, and environments. Some may not appear to be overly intelligent, some may actually be very poor administrators, and others may apparently be susceptible to any number of human weaknesses. The true leader can be recognized because somehow or other, his or her people consistently turn in superior performances. Those same people noticeably direct their energy to the outside issues of managing the specific problems or issues, rather than internal issues of authority, politics, and employee relationships.

> As for the best leaders, people do not notice their existence. The next best, people honor and praise. The next, people fear, and the next, the people hate .... When the best leader's work is done, the people say "we did it ourselves." (*From Lao Tzu.*)

Letter Wars

Avoid Abstractions

The more office-bound you are, the more you avoid direct personal contact with those with whom you do business. The more inclined you are to talk about an issue rather than *resolve* the issue, the more inclined you might actually be to escalate a problem into a *letter war.* It's like driving a car. The minute you get behind the wheel, you become a different person. If you know you don't have to look the other person in the eye, it's easy to cut him or her off at the intersection, or not allow the other driver into traffic. Being rude is easy, because it's not really a person that you are dealing with; it's just a car. Similarly, if you are on the receiving end of such a transaction, you will find that if you can manage direct eye contact with your offending competition, the abstraction dissolves, and suddenly you're dealing with another person. Immediately, the situation is transformed, and you are allowed to change lanes.

The same process occurs when writing a letter. Too often, it is too easy to make abrupt statements and determine absolute position if you don't have to look that person in the eye. Related to this is the idea that if you speak when you're angry, you'll make the best speech you'll ever regret.

Solve the Problem

Before you send out your next letter cataloging what you would *like* to say, if only for the personal satisfaction it might give you for the immediate moment, stop. Think for just a moment, and write down everything that you originally intended. At the very least, the process will allow you to get the issue off your chest without unnecessarily forcing your foot into your mouth. Even if you don't send your initial letter, you can file it to record important research that you might have conducted on the subject in order to prepare your missive. The critical idea at this stage, however, is under *no* circumstances send it out.

When the letter is done, put it down and let it cool. Don't even leave it on top of your desk, in case some well-meaning subordinate would mail it for you. Put it in your drawer. If you can afford the time, wait until the following day. After you have had a chance to regain some perspective, reconsider your entire letter. Picture yourself in front of the individual and a group of independent people reading your letter in front of you. How comfortable are you with the information? If your letter is truly a rational response to the situation, it will be equally rational in the morning. If through that reevaluation process a letter stands the light of day, then by all means let it go. On the other hand, a clear head may let you see your initial reaction as more emotional than rational. At a minimum, you might have saved yourself and your company an embarrassment. Beyond that, you might have saved yourself an increased amount of time, energy, and effort to undo at least a portion of the new battle that you might be escalating.

Get things back into perspective, and focus on *resolving the problem,* and not escalating the conflict.

Liars

Contents

Related Topics

Real Lies

I'm not saying that these men are liars; it's just that they have such respect for the truth that they use it very sparingly. (*Watergate Prosecutor.*)

Lies come in all shapes and sizes. Some are outright untruths, with which we usually associate the term, but many lies come in numerous forms of "creative" representations and misrepresentations of information.

Is an exaggerated **time and material** ticket a lie? Is a change proposal that includes cost items that are not likely to be incurred a lie? Is the intentional withholding of information that would more completely describe the true nature of an issue a lie?

Because the gray area surrounding the term is so broad, the sheer momentum of an issue can divert your attention away from the true nature of an interaction. That nature might plainly be that the person with whom you are dealing is simply less than forthcoming, and is not giving you complete or accurate information. In the worst case, of course, the individual may be flatly and totally misrepresenting the information.

Confirming the Lie

One reliable, field-tested method to confirm whether an individual is actually guilty of "massaging" information—or just plain lying—is admittedly abrupt, but effective. It works both in cases where you do have proof and in cases where you have no proof. It is particularly valuable in the latter instance.

The method is this: If you suspect that an individual is "misusing" information, simply *accuse* him or her of doing so. Whether or not you actually do know and can support your position, approach the situation with that attitude. Yes, you do risk insulting the individual. Think about your own reaction to such treatment if someone approached you in this manner. If you were innocent, you would hit the roof. You would be angry, insulted, and determined that you would not accept such unjustifiable, unfair treatment. You would (should) go off like a rocket, demanding a retraction of the statement, or some other appropriate restitution.

If on the other hand you were genuinely guilty, you would more likely react in a weak, sheepish manner. You would, instead of taking the Roman candle approach, ask something like "Who told you that story," or "Why do you feel that way," or something equally lame.

And so if you are the one being lied to (and not the liar), understand these effects. If, after confronting an individual with a situation, you find yourself listening to those golden words "Who told you that story," you should know much more clearly who—and what—you are dealing with.

Lien Rights

The Lien Process

A mechanic's lien is a statutory security device through which unpaid laborers, contractors, subcontractors, and material suppliers who have improved real property may enforce payment for services and materials provided. By creating a lien, these entities can force a judicial sale of the property that is the subject of the lien, if they are not paid as they are entitled to be. To avoid the result, the owner will either pay the lien, compel the contractor (if the lien is filed through a subvendor) to pay or otherwise discharge the lien, or proceed through the judicial process to demonstrate why the claimant is not otherwise entitled to the payment sought.

Lien laws have been widely criticized. They are seen as complex; as creating rights that are unnecessarily redundant where, for example, there are payment bonds on a project; and as oversimplified in their approach. They may compel owners and contractors to pay for goods and services twice, while the real culprits are allowed to sneak from the scene.

Right to Assert a Mechanic's Lien

Although state statutes vary, a lien claimant must generally satisfy these tests:

1. It must be shown that the real property has been improved.

2. The claimant must have supplied materials and/or labor.

3. The materials and/or labor must have been supplied for one or more purposes specified in the controlling statute.

Notice and Filing Requirements

Every state and the District of Columbia have some form of lien statutes. These statutes give unpaid contractors, subcontractors, and suppliers a claim against the property that they have provided good services for. Many of these individuals and companies, however, can easily lose their lien rights because of their failure to comply with statutory notice or filing requirements.

Every state's lien statute includes some notice and filing requirements that are considerably shorter than the statue of limitations for breach of contract. Strict compliance with these notice and filing requirements is necessary to protect the lien. It is because of this that it is critical for contractors, subcontractors, and suppliers to be aware of the statutory requirements in each state where they perform work or provide materials, and it is similarly important to be aware of how the courts of each state interpret their particular statutes.

The majority of the states measure the time for notice and filing from the last day that work was performed or materials were supplied. Some states further qualify this by providing for the last day that "significant" or "substantial" work was performed. This consideration is the basis for the "screen door" principle, named for the situation where the contractor returns to the site to "adjust the screen door" to establish a later date from which the notice and filing date will begin.

Duration and Extent of a Lien

Most lien laws require that the lien claimant enforce the lien by initiating a foreclosure action within a specified time after one of a certain number of events has taken place. These events typically occur on

1. The date when the underlying debt accrued
2. The date when the last item of work was performed (sometimes the last *substantial* item)
3. The date when the lien was filed

Applicable time frames and triggering events vary from state to state. These time frames must be complied with strictly and to the letter, or the claimant will be left without a valid lien.

Even if properly effected, a lien is usually limited as to the enforceable amount. For a contractor in privity of contract with the owner, the enforceable amount is generally limited by the contract price. For a subcontractor or supplier not in such privity, the enforceable amount is generally limited by the reasonable value of the labor and materials provided.

Governing laws may also impose additional limitations by requiring that the sum of all liens may not exceed the contract price less payments made by the owner to the contractor prior to receiving pre-lien notice. The effect of this additional limitation can be significant;

it can work to the effect that, if the owner pays a contractor all or most of the contract price before the subcontractor or supplier gives the required pre-lien notice, the owner may be liable to the claimant only for the difference, if any, between the contract price and the amount paid to the contractor. Although protecting the owner from double payments, such a provision would leave nothing for the claimant if it is a subvendor.

Enforcement

A lien claim is enforced through foreclosure on the property that was improved. The purpose of the foreclosure action is to compel the sale of the property in order to provide the funds to compensate the claimants.

Enforcement of a lien may pit the claimant against other competing parties with interest in the property. Although mechanic's liens can be superior to other liens and encumbrances placed on the property after the filing of the mechanic's lien—or possibly after the commencement of labor or the actual delivery of materials—complex questions of priority may still rise, especially when the total amount of all liens and claims exceeds the value of the property.

Life Saving—The Four Steps to Project Recovery

Save a Life or Save a Dying Project

The American Red Cross summarized its *Four Life Saving Steps* as a quick reference to draw your attention to the immediate needs of the victim, in prioritized sequence of procedure.

For a troubled project—or a troubled company—the principles should speak for themselves:

1. Stop the bleeding.

   - Locate the wound, and use any and all means to stop the bleeding, e.g., pressure or even a tourniquet.

2. Start the breathing.

   - Revive the victim's breathing.
   - Restore pulse.

3. Protect the wound.

   - Prevent infection.
   - Promote healing.

4. Treat for shock.

   - Keep victim warm, comfortable, and reassured.
   - Sometimes the shock of an incident can cause more harm than the wounds.

Does any of this have relevance to any of *your* projects? Good luck.

Liquidated Damages

The Big Misunderstanding

The concept of liquidated damages is one of the most used yet most misunderstood in both its practical and legal applications. To many people, a liquidated damages provision calls attention to a hard number that often appears to be a penalty for failing to achieve the impossible. Individuals on both sides of the contract implicitly consider it to be almost an automatic charge against the contractor's account for each day that the contractor misses the originally scheduled substantial completion date. The reality, however, is that it is very often nowhere near as severe, and on a particular project it may actually be closer to a comfortable limitation on a contractor's ultimate liability.

Definition

The idea of liquidation damages developed because it is recognized that if the owner is delayed in its ability to occupy the project and use it for its intended purpose, it will suffer damage. It is also recognized that it is extremely difficult, time-consuming, and expensive to identify and quantify the actual extent of damages. Accordingly, the liquidated damages provision is intended to do nothing more than provide a stipulation as to the value of those damages if they should occur, thereby eliminating the need to determine an actual calculation at a later date.

Having a liquidated damages provision *in no way assigns responsibility for the damages.* That is up to the due process of the **dispute resolution** mechanism provided elsewhere in the contract. Liquidated damages come into play only after responsibility for the delay and its net extent have been *proved* to be that of the contractor.

Contractor's Liability: Increased or Decreased?

If the delay turns out to be genuinely the fault of the contractor (or the contractor is unable to prove otherwise), liquidated damages may be a curse, but it might also turn out to be a blessing. If a contract, for example, is subject to $500 per day liquidated damages, and the job is delayed for 30 days *clearly* by the fault of the contractor, the maximum damages that can be charged against the contractor would total $15,000. If instead the contract was silent with respect to damage calculation and did not include a liquidated damages provision, it is likely that the contractor would be exposed to a calculation that would include the *actual* damages of the owner. In many such cases, it does not take an incredibly creative attorney to total up both clear and complex cost items and lump them into the "actual damages" category. In such cases, the contractor might find itself exposed to claims which include damages relating to lost rent, abandoned leases, lost profits due to sales not complete, and other such "actual damages" that would dwarf the $15,000 liquidated damages.

For this reason, many contractors look for, and even insist on, reasonable liquidated damages to be provided in their contracts. If this approach appears unusual or even a little suspect, remember that it's only intended to avoid a misunderstanding like that described above.

Not a Penalty

Liquidated damages are not a penalty. The term *liquidated damages* is used specifically to avoid the use of the word *penalty*. It has, for example, long since been interpreted by most courts that if a contractor is working under the threat of a penalty for failing to complete a project by a certain date, then the contractor should correspondingly be entitled to a reward (bonus) to the same extent if the contract is completed prior to that date. What's good for the goose is good for the gander. The use of the word *penalty* is therefore avoided by those who draft contracts in order to preclude the contractor's ability to collect any such reward.

Defenses and Reactions

If *both* the contractor and the owner have contributed to the cause of the total delay, the contract may provide that the responsibility be "apportioned" between the contractor and the owner. Liquidated damages will in this way be assessed against the contractor for its portion of the delay, and the contractor would be entitled to prove its damages for the owner's portion of the delay.

If the contract does not provide for such apportionment, some courts have held that by contributing to the delay, the owner totally waives any claim to liquidated damages. Other courts, however, have held that the contractor is entitled only to a "credit" for that part of the delay caused by the owner—another way of saying "apportionment."

If a contractor breaches a contract by totally abandoning performance, some courts have determined that the liquidated damages provision may not apply. These courts distinguish between a breach by delay and a breach by abandonment, finding that the parties intended to apply the liquidated damages only to the delays when a contractor completes the work. This has not at all been a consistent application. Check with your own attorney if your curiosity requires.

Courts have generally refused to allow liquidated damages if the contractor's performance under the contract has been *substantially* completed by the date specified in the contract and only incidental or detail work remains. Substantial completion has generally been defined and interpreted in a way consistent with that used with the American Institute of Architects as:

> ... the date certified by the architect when construction is sufficiently complete in accordance with contract documents, so the owner can occupy or utilize the work or designated portion thereof for the use for which it is intended.

It is therefore generally recognized that, when the owner has possession or use of the property, an assessment of liquidated damages for trivial details in the work would amount to a penalty.

If a contractor has built or renovated a project and a percent of the facility has been accepted and occupied by the dates stipulated in the contract, it has been successfully argued that the owner is not justified in assessing 100 percent of the value of the original liquidated damages. In such cases, the concept of liquidated damages can apply only when the entire project is delayed. In the case of partial occupancy, therefore, it may not be appropriate to assign even a portion of the liquidated damages.

Be careful in dealing with changes to the original liquidated damages provision in the event of a contractor-caused delay. Left intact, liquidated damages will most likely provide the topside number for your ultimate liability for delay. Playing with the enforceability of application or the straightforward application of the provision might backfire, suddenly exposing the contractor to actual and some "creative" damages. Know what the likely result will be if you are considering arguing the applicability of liquidated damages.

Logic Diagrams

Schedule Considerations

Schedule types vary greatly in their complexity, levels of detail, ability to actually display the plan, visibility, **documentation** facility, and ability to display cause-effect. Refer to sections on **scheduling, bar charts,** and **CPM/PDM schedules** for important related discussion.

Logic Diagram Description

The logic diagram became a natural extension of CPM (critical path method) scheduling as computer graphics became easier and more economical; logic diagrams provide the *visibility* that was badly lacking with CPM.

A logic diagram simply takes the schematic, unscaled activity "nodes" of a CPM schedule, scales them with respect to **time,** and places them in their proper places under a calendar. The result appears visually to be a time-scaled bar chart with dependencies simply drawn in. The bars themselves are often "optimized" in their display—to fit on the paper wherever there is space available. The result is that the activity placement on the display is by schedule logic (as opposed to specification section, as is common on the bar chart).

The logic diagram itself is therefore only a drafting convention. The schedule remains a true CPM schedule.

Advantages

1. All of the advantages of CPM apply. Refer to that section for the complete list.

2. There is greatly improved visibility and *understandability* of all schedule information; much better than even those of the bar chart.

Disadvantages

The problems listed for CPM under the following items remain. Refer to that section for additional related discussion.

1. The computer requirement

2. The need for complete update

3. The potential practical loss of previous information on and attention to prior milestones

Conclusion

Logic diagrams are so significant in their contribution to the development, implementation, and management of CPM schedules, and their software is so available, that no CPM schedule should ever be used without them. The CPM/logic diagram combination is one of the most effective management methods available and must be seriously considered. Its selection, as opposed to the use of **bar charts,** will be determined by the manager's preference, needs, and abilities. Because, however, of the logic diagram's unique ability to make a clear representation of the schedule work, a manager should not overlook this important tool.

Loyalty

The Free Agent Executive

Every manager at some point has uttered words to the effect that "The fundamental problem is keeping good people once you find them." Focus is then directed to all sorts of compensation, with the idea that the way to create loyalty among the lieutenants is to provide the right package of financial incentives, perhaps related to productivity.

With the loss of security in the workplace brought on by business realities of the 1980s and the 1990s, hired team members need to feel some level of consideration beyond perhaps what has been offered in the recent past. This is not at all to say that money is not a (*the?*) primary motivator, but only to acknowledge that the time, energy, and stress associated with the perceived lack of security steal increasing amounts of energy and squander time that should be more devoted to productive tasks.

And so the "free agent" executive is born—a capable individual who sees that contemporary business demands quick reaction in guerrilla warfare, that the corporation needs to make such immediate personnel changes as senior management deems necessary for cost, marketing, and profitability reasons. That very strong, probably justifiable perception, breeds the same feeling that quick reaction and changes are needed in the free agent executive.

Simply stated, the free agent feels that, since the axe can fall at a moment's notice, he or she must be ready to pick up the pieces as quickly as possible in stride. The eyes are always watching for clues from the corporation, feelers are out for alternative job opportunities, and the entire concept of loyalty becomes a fond memory.

The Loyalty Demand

A major problem with this whole question of loyalty is that liabilities lie in virtually every area of operation. Every strategy, goal, policy, procedure, form, form letter, telephone conversation, meeting, and offhand remark is subject to improper treatment at many levels. Dollar volumes are so large that a small percentage swing in a single line item of an account can immediately translate into thousands—or tens of thousands—of dollars for better or worse. Because the liabilities can quickly become so huge, incentives for unscrupulous operators to attempt to influence your own people can multiply exponentially. Refer to **spying** for important related discussion.

Loyalty among the managers and executives within a construction operation, then, is not just a cliché that we can be satisfied to simply lament over. Loyalty must become a fundamental criterion of the relationship among all project team members and a measure by which the performance of each employee will be judged as to value within the organization.

Deal decisively with loyalty. Be clear among your managers and executives that you expect nothing less than absolute loyalty. When hard examples of loyalty failures are exposed, deal with each incident quickly, firmly, and with a punishment that fits the crime. Consider making an example in some way to the remainder of your project teams, in order to reinforce the message to the group of the organization's profound need for loyalty.

Developing Loyalty

Of course people work for money, but different people can be motivated by different things, particularly over an extended period of time. With realistic exceptions, people do not usually change jobs just for money. The real difference between a $5000 or $10,000 salary increase being offered by a competitor is almost insignificant, particularly in the short run. By the time the move is accomplished, the regrouping is done, and the orientation procedure gone through, the increase is all but gone. Even if more money is involved, some lifestyle change is likely to suck the financial gain up relatively quickly. Stock plans are set up for retirement, leaving a subliminal feeling that it really may not ever happen for the individual. We are all really more concerned with the present than we may realize (or admit).

Although it sounds trite, the truth is that, beyond some reasonable compensation level, many people are motivated to a great degree simply by the feeling that they are genuinely being appreciated, that they are regarded with personal respect, and that the organization values their individual contribution. When managers and executives feel unappreciated, or even abused, it is easy for them to start dwelling on how mistreated they are. That is when they begin tuning up their résumés to start the process once again for an industrywide search for appreciation.

Appreciation means offering regular opportunities for personal contribution and recognition of the contributions. Yes, we can request a person's contributions in an appreciative manner, if we do so as a part of a mutual game planning, a type of give-and-take dialog where the ideas are *negotiated* and the final decision is made by the senior individual. Beyond that, it's the old business of giving credit where credit is due.

When an employee makes a mistake, allows an item to fall through the cracks, or just plain handles the situation in a manner other than you would, use the opportunity to *build* on the relationship, instead of to chip away at the relationship. Communicate to the employee that you recognize that the oversight or failure was at least in part contributed by the sheer magnitude of the job, the complexity of the task, or the demands of the particular situation. This is not to say that you should not communicate your disappointment with the failure, at least to a degree, but more to recognize that contracting places tremendous demands on the human system, and that the failure may be more related to the structure of the system than of the individual's lack of performance.

Beyond that, even if it is a performance failure, try to communicate that you know that the person is working hard, that his or her motivations are in the right place, and that you appreciate the approach that the person is taking to the job. Having provided all these cues, you might consider directly assisting the employee to perform a particular act, and/or using the opportunity to instruct the employee— not necessarily in the particular procedure, but in the underlying policies and reasons for the existence of the activity.

Above all, let the individual know that you genuinely appreciate the effort being put into the situation, that you know that the individual is stressed by his or her own recognition of the deficiency, and that you consider that recognition of the problem is one of the primary reasons why you appreciate the way that individual is handling the job.

Certainly it is true that an individual simply may not be right for the job, may not have the makeup to develop the right attitude, or may have some other problem associated with the job. These are criteria that you as a manager must be sensitive to and be prepared to take appropriate action on when necessary. If, however, your reconsideration of these issues leaves you with a determination that the individual either is the right person for the job or has enough potential to become the right person for the job, then the efforts to develop a mutual respect and a genuine relationship through appreciation will pay big dividends in genuine loyalty to you and the corporation during the times when you will need it most.

Management Reporting Systems

Related Topics

Computers

Daily Field Report

Documentation

Quality

The Zone

The Trees instead of the Forest

A fascination with all types of "accurate" data has fostered a whole new effort at all levels of business to focus on every nut and bolt. We organize our management information in reporting systems. Forms, faxes, computers, copiers, and even administrative assistants all exist because managers feel they must have instant information on every statistic, criterion, performance, and minute-to-minute activity.

Millions of dollars are spent on systems and procedures that use combinations of huge amounts of worker-hours and automated systems to dump mountains of cost and productivity data into central reporting systems. The information is collected and, at the very least, transmitted to managers who *should* be interested in the particular data.

If your operation is based more on direct labor and equipment than on the performance of subcontractors, generating *useful* information can increase your profitability. If, however, your system is not sophisticated enough to provide such reams of data, you may feel as though your organization is not as efficient as it should be.

On the other extreme, if your organization has developed to the point where labor and equipment productivity information is regularly documented, assembled, and transmitted to some central or other location, you may be wondering why all of this effort to secure such information has not resulted in any dramatic improvement in your levels of productivity—and ultimately your profitability. For example, some form of production report or other document is completed each day by a foreman or other individual, who needs to take significant time away from productive activity in order to complete the form, and the form is faxed or otherwise communicated to some clerk or manager. The process continues each day, but business in the field continues to go on as usual, and the additional administrative effort doesn't seem to be contributing to the regular improvement in—or even in the maintenance of—field productivity.

Over a period of time, such procedures steal increasing amounts of time away from otherwise productive individuals as they go on each day to complete increasingly complex reports. The reports can take on a life of their own, with the original reasons for them forgotten or at least diluted. The procedure seems to perpetuate itself. We find ourselves completing forms and preparing reports for their own sake.

Purpose and Procedure

When any new procedure is considered, it is important to begin with the *purpose* of the exercise, to identify the *goal* first: evaluation of productivity, cost control, or whatever. By all means, push on to design the procedure as the means to secure the relevant information of interest and to record the data in a *usable* form. But do not stop there. Think through and organize the information, and decide how often the information should be assembled and consolidated, who should be reviewing the information once it is generated, and what those people are going to do when they see situations that vary from the optimum. In other words, what are the appropriate management reactions, and what tangible information should trigger them?
Consider:

- How can the information assembly and reporting be streamlined?

- What is the best, fastest way to *consolidate* the information into relevant summaries?

- Once consolidated, how can the information be most efficiently assembled into a meaningful report for evaluation by human beings?

- Who is going to be evaluating the information?

- How often will this individual be evaluating the information?

- What response will be required by this individual when he or she observes the information varying from some standard, and requiring an action?

- How will that individual communicate the corrective action back to the offending source?

- What is the authority and accountability structure of the procedure?

Unless all of these things are thought through and provided for in detail, you will be doomed to the creation and maintenance of yet one more management information system that will drain huge amounts of time, energy, and effort. If you're not careful, it will drain these resources away from armies of key individuals in your organization with the result of generating a new truckload of data that has every appearance of being useful, but which will be in fact nothing more than one more weight that you will be chaining around the necks of the people in your organization who might otherwise be productive.

The 90-10 Rule

Remember the 90-10 rule of information. Revisit the introduction of this book if you need to. When designing the type and extent of information you need, consider the amount of effort required on a regular basis by whoever will generate the new data. You are guaranteed to discover yet again that you will get 80 to 90 percent of available information with 10 to 20 percent of the effort—if you *correctly* direct that effort. The reality again will be that securing the remaining 10 percent of information will usually require an extremely disproportionate amount of additional time—that other 90 percent.

Step back from the issue. Take a hard look, and ask yourself if spending that amount of energy to generate that little amount of information is essential to the effort. But do not stop there. Even if you answer honestly in the affirmative, go back to the list of questions in the previous subsection. Ask yourself *who is going to be using the information and how,* and how that information is going to be translated back to your troops. Look very closely, and the odds are you will see that the extra energy needed to generate this small amount of information will not be worth it, considering likely degrees of accuracy and the ultimate use of the information.

Master Services Agreement

No "Short Form"

An interesting approach that some take to construction agreements is to dispense with a comprehensive agreement for small contracts. They feel that the complete agreement somehow should not apply. Instead, a "short form" of the particular form of agreement is used—a small contract for a small scope of work.

As I see it, a major problem with this approach is that the cost to correct a problem on a construction site can multiply quickly, and much too often grow to dwarf the size of a small contract. In the face of such a problem, you may find yourself working under an oversimplified agreement that removed or otherwise watered down those rights and remedies that would have allowed you to resolve the issue. In your effort to avoid administrative, legal, and other costs associated with the issue's total and final resolution, you find yourself in a totally opposite situation. You have underestimated the potential for problems, and you have ignored all the improvements we have made in the construction agreements over the past 10 or 20 years. You will have squarely put yourself back into the old situations.

The major irony, of course, is that throughout it all you might actually *know* the proper language that you *could* have incorporated into your agreement, but did not for all the wrong reasons. To make it even worse, you actually *have* the appropriate language in your "long form" of the same agreement. It just doesn't make any sense.

The Master Services Agreement Approach

The situation that drives us to this absurd conduct is the idea that it seems inappropriate to have a very small subcontractor—say a pavement striping contractor—to execute a 22-page agreement in order to perform $1000 worth of work; it hardly seems worth the effort and the trouble.

Instead of using any "short form," use a master services agreement. The MSA form is simply a version of your complete standard subcontract form arranged in generic order. You and your subcontractor negotiate your entire relationship—in its complete detail—once. Your small subcontractor understands that, as a condition of performing the various small contracts with your firm, it is required to comply with all the terms of the complete agreement. Once the procedure has been followed, all that is necessary to effect that $1000 deal is to execute a one-page document that describes the scope of work. The document will refer to the particular master services agreement form currently in effect, thereby tying the one-page document to all the terms and conditions of the complete agreement. When the next $500, $1000, or $2000 deal comes along, all that is necessary is the execution of an additional one-page document performing the same function: defining the scope of work on the new project and incorporating all the terms of the master services agreement currently in effect.

Match Lines

Good or Bad Design Practice

Match lines in drawings and on plans are undeniably necessary in many large, complex projects. However, reducing the use of match lines minimizes the drafting time and design coordination necessary in document production. Moreover, divided plans are difficult to read, check, and coordinate. A match line provides one more possibility of an error or omission. Many design errors have been caused directly by match lines.

If match lines must be used, good design practice dictates that they should be placed precisely in the same location on every plan. If they are not, the plans will be even more confusing. This is true not only for the contractors who must work with the plans, but also for the various design professionals who must coordinate their designs. In contrast, match lines placed in varying locations throughout a set of design documents may be an indication of general carelessness on the part of the designer in the preparation of the plans.

Good Practice

Proper application of match lines requires that all plan orientations on all drawings be identical. The north arrow should be in the same place, and the building outline should be consistent on each drawing. It would be confusing to have different orientations on mechanical, electrical, structural, and architectural drawings.

If you accordingly should observe a more casual attitude on the part of the designers toward this most basic design procedure, you would be justified in becoming concerned, and even in expecting problems at other levels. Not only is it likely that errors will be directly caused by careless match line and orientation practices, but such a careless attitude toward design may be an indicator of other problems as well. In other words, if the designers have not properly accommodated one of the most basic of design considerations, it should not be a surprise to see other areas of design practice treated less than professionally as well.

Plan Review Procedure

The following simple steps may help in the identification of improper use of match lines in your **contract documents:**

1. If any match lines are present on the drawings, analyze the plans to determine if they were really necessary.

2. Compare the match lines of all floor and ceiling components of all drawings (including architectural, structural, mechanical structural, mechanical, electrical, site):
   - Are they in the same location every time?
   - Do they include the same information?
   - Is anything missing?
   - Are they complete and to the same extent on every plan?

3. Confirm that the north arrow is in the same place in each drawing (different locations may quickly identify changes in plan orientation).

4. Determine if plan orientations are the same for all drawings.

Negative answers to any of the foregoing will expose improper use of match lines or otherwise deficient drafting practices. On such determination, reserve time to perform a more detailed search of plans in order to expose other areas in which the design process may have similarly been compromised.

Unfortunately, if match line problems are exposed, the plans will be nearly certain to contain other flaws. It will therefore become critical to expose these problems as early as possible in order to minimize their impact.

Mediation

Description

The use of mediation as a **dispute resolution** procedure evolved as a resolution mechanism that won't bleed the parties dry with time, technicalities, and legal fees. It is an attempt to restore reason to the process under the guidance of an individual—the mediator. The mediator's job is to impart a sense of reality, pragmatism, and expediency. Theoretically, the mediator is someone who might have a fresh look and can add a new perspective that will bring the parties around to a meaningful compromise. Mediation is a special form of **negotiation.** Its success depends on the genuine neutrality of the mediator as an independent third party. Perhaps more important, if a mediation is to have any possibility of success, both parties must approach it with a clear understanding of the consequences of a lack of agreement and a genuine desire to reach an agreement and get it over with. Lacking this, mediation can unfortunately become just another delay to the ultimate resolution of the issue.

Mediation Evolution

Some years ago, it became apparent to the construction industry that conventional litigation carried with it serious problems that affected the expediency and economy in the resolution of construction disputes. Litigation was determined by naive juries, who need to consider extremely complicated issues—such as delay and interference—and who need education with even the most basic of construction concepts (such as retainage).

Because of problems inherent with litigation, arbitration became popular as the dispute resolution mechanism of choice—by both sides to a dispute. Originally, it was faster, and less expensive. In addition, the arbitrator or arbitration panel was selected because of its particular expertise, and was qualified to see through the complicated issues (theoretically) so that an equitable award could result.

Arbitration itself then began to develop as its own life form. Legalese has since compounded, and attorneys have complicated the process to the extent that it is now so close in appearance to a litiga-tion that the initial objectives of speed and cost have become blurred. And so, while it remains true that it is still quicker to actually begin an arbitration action than a litigation, the proceeding itself may wind up taking every bit as long, and be every bit as expensive.

With our industry's current fatigue over arbitration, we are now looking for yet another mechanism that might relieve us from the problems brought on by arbitration. And so one area that we now look to is mediation.

How It Works

As in arbitration, the parties must first agree to mediation as a means to attempt to resolve a particular dispute. After that, the parties must agree on the choice of the person who is to serve as the mediator, or at least agree on the method of choosing the particular individual. Generally, the mediation procedure is most often conducted along lines where the medi-ator would first meet with both parties, and then progress through a series of alternating individual meetings with the parties, interspersed with caucuses, and continue with still more meetings with both parties. In the individual meetings, the mediator is presumably using his or her skills as a facilitator in order to look for ways around deadlocks and other problems in a continuous attempt to direct the parties' attention to "rea-sonable" positions under the particular set of circumstances.

For mediation to have its maximum possibility of success, both par-ties must respect the opinion of the mediator. Beyond this, it is impor-tant that each side enter the mediation in good faith.

Potential Problems

Even if the parties are approaching mediation with absolute good faith, there are serious risks that should be considered, if there is to remain any significant possibility of avoiding arbitration or litigation. The first is that one or both of the parties, whether they will admit it or not, may be really interested in the mediation process as a fishing trip. While it is true that any actual statements used in a mediation are privileged, and technically cannot be used if the settlement **nego-tiation** as part of the mediation process ultimately breaks down and the matter winds up being pursued in litigation, a significant amount of information does change hands. Positions are tested and reactions gauged. The strength of an opponent's hand is gauged, and **docu-mentation** is even explored. Responses to positions and defenses are tried.

And so ultimately, if the mediation process leads one party to arrive at the conclusion that its position is indeed strong, the dispute can become a self-fulfilling prophecy. The mediation fishing trip might have disclosed enough sensitive information to substantially hurt one's position.

Nonbinding

A fundamental characteristic of mediation—as opposed to arbitration—is that the mediator has no explicit authority to decide the case in the event that a settlement cannot be agreed on between the parties. Because all communications between the parties and the mediator are privileged and confidential, the information cannot be used (officially) in any subsequent formal or trial proceeding. If the mediation fails and no award or other judgment is forthcoming from a mediator that will be binding on the parties, you may find yourself back at the beginning of the formal dispute resolution procedure.

Meeting Minutes

Related Topics

Agenda

Correspondence

Documentation

Job Meetings

Notice

Purpose

All meetings must at least be recorded, but that in itself is not nearly enough. If the meeting is conducted properly (see **job meetings** and special meetings):

- Each item is given its relevant place on the **agenda.**
- The *timing* of each item is controlled.
- Each issue is either completely resolved, or its specific resolution procedure and timetable are established.
- Ongoing items have definite steps determined for resolution, with those responsible named and resolution timetables confirmed.

The minutes themselves will:

- Organize the agenda.
- Establish the method of identification of issues and correlation to the rest of the project record.
- Keep everything *visible,* with people directly identified and *personally responsible* for specific actions.
- Display cause and effect of timely and untimely actions.
- Fulfill important notification responsibilities under the contract.

Action Rules

1. *Use a standard form.* Whether completed on a word processor or on forms made for the purpose, a standard layout gives these advantages:

- Prompts the recording of all relevant information while eliminating the risk of oversight. It will consistently display the project identification, meeting number, date, time, location, participants, distribution of the minutes, and any other regular information unique to the project.

■ Gets everyone used to the information display. It improves understanding of the issue identification and correlation features of the minutes, and minimizes the risk of people overlooking their responsibilities.

2. *Numerically identify each meeting.*   For regular **job meetings,** identify each meeting in numerical sequence. Even if it is a special meeting, call it Meeting No. S-1.

3. *Assign each item its own number, which will never change.* The third issue raised at Job Meeting No. 4 will be identified as 4.3. If you're conducting weekly job meetings and find yourself still considering item 4.3 under "Old Business" at Job Meeting No. 8, you automatically know that the thing is 4 weeks old. If you are a supervisor who does not attend regular meetings, simply reviewing any meeting minutes and comparing the item numbers with the job meeting number will give you an instant (and sometimes painfully clear) indication of the way things seem to be going.

4. *Use a title for each item.*   Keep it consistent each time it is mentioned. This will clarify the subject, speed research, and facilitate correlation with other topics.

5. *Include all appropriate references in the item title.*   If it is the subject of a change order, bulletin number, etc., keep these numbers in the description.

6. *Be concise, but complete.*   Use outline format wherever possible.

7. *Require definite action.*   Never leave an issue without a specific, step-by-step program that will resolve it, and identify *who* is responsible for the action. Assign times to each step.

8. *Name names.*   Do not say "The owner will respond." Instead say "Mr. XYZ stated ...." Let all see their names in lights—it will be harder to make excuses later.

9. *Insist on precise accuracy of all statements as they are recorded.* If you are not keeping the minutes yourself, keep precise notes. If the minutes either represent an issue inaccurately, or omit relevant discussion, highlight the correction at the next meeting. If it is not a regular job meeting, immediately send a written correction.

■ If this kind of problem persists, protest strongly. If you still do not get appropriate response, send a written notice that you reject the minutes as a misrepresentation of the facts, and will not allow the actual project record to be so compromised.

■ If you let everyone know that *accuracy* is your priority, it will follow you in improving the perception of legitimacy in everything you do. It will make your **scheduling, change order propos-als,** and other "statements of fact" more believable and approv-able.

10. *Include a "verification requirement" for all information con-tained in the minutes.*   The minutes are an important job record that will be used to substantiate every cause-effect issue. If their accuracy is questioned, their usefulness and effectiveness will be compromised. At worst, it may pervert the record in a manner that will better serve your opponent. Include as part of the standard form on every meeting record a statement to the effect that anyone noting any error or omis-sion in the document is to notify the writer by a particular date (the next meeting?), and that failure to do so constitutes acceptance of all information contained therein as it is represented. This will end many later arguments before they begin.

Negotiation

Contents

Related Topics

Nothing Has Changed

Doctor Chester Karrass made an interesting observation a number of years ago: despite the fact that humans have stepped on the moon and harnessed the atom, they are still bargaining as they did in ancient times. If a 5000-year-old Babylonian were to dress in a business suit and sit opposite us at a table, there is little reason to believe that person's methods would differ from ours.

Take a moment to consider this idea. It is as though time has stood still, as though the written word, printing press, computers, and the other string of technological advances have never been developed. Yes, we have spent a great amount of time, effort, and energy analyzing the reasons why, and applying psychology, and developing "persuasion theory," but if you carefully consider Karrass's observation, you can almost see yourself dealing with that Babylonian in tomorrow's **job meeting.**

Who Wins?

It has been said that in a successful negotiation, everybody wins. In actuality, however, this is very rarely the case. In truth, both parties do gain in the successful negotiation, but more often than not, one party gains more than the other. Losers make substantially larger concessions much more often than is necessary, while winners keep such concessions under better control.

Negotiation plays obvious and subtle roles in everyday affairs. Nearly every interaction we have with fellow employees, our boss, and the individuals in companies with whom we deal is in actuality a negotiation. Those who are successful in a process constantly win greater shares of money, consideration, and even appreciation. Some very capable individuals are routinely told precisely what to do, and chased around to confirm that they are doing their work, while others are being treated as thinking human beings and adults. Some individuals are intimidated by authority, whereas others calmly but firmly demand their share of power implicitly by their actions and their approach. Some managers accomplish things through force, intimidation, and one-upmanship; others get results through persuasion, **loyalty,** appreciation, and respect. A negotiation occurs whenever ideas are exchanged, behaviors are influenced, and resources are shifted.

The Bargaining Process

Negotiating power can be thought of in terms of certain bargaining processes. Relationships between the negotiators exist both in their simple interactions, but also—and often more important—in the negotiators' own interactions with the members of their own groups.

Various bargaining processes can be summarized as follows:

1. *Problem solving.* This is the process by which both parties work together to solve each other's problems, with the expectation that, if one negotiator sees the efforts by another to solve a problem, it is likely that a corresponding effort would be made in the other direction.

2. *Share bargaining.* This is the process by which negotiators share—or apportion—the settlement range of items between themselves. It is essentially dividing up a list of items. If one gets more, the other gets less.

3. *Personal bargaining.* This is the process by which negotiators make behavioral choices, applying their personal needs to the situation at hand. There is always a personal level to every negotiation; the difference is largely a matter of degree. Personal motivation can range from the need to simply be thought of as an intelligent professional, to a desire for monetary gains.

Negotiation Tips

Follow the guidelines below in order to keep your attention focused on your negotiation objectives. Do not give up more than you have to. Do not "split the difference" if you do not have to. Be a little unyielding, and you may be very surprised with the results.

1. Plan the negotiation. List every issue, and establish an achievement or aspiration level desired for each item.

2. Do not underestimate your own power. Look for all the suitable places where your power may not be apparent to either one of you.

3. Do not start negotiation without serious consideration of the limits to the other person's real power with respect to the specific situation. Try to understand if that individual genuinely believes his or her power position to be better than it actually is, or if it is a front. Look for the kinks in the armor, and have your plan designed to penetrate.

4. Look for a better deal for both parties. Try to move your negotiation from competition and competitiveness to cooperation.

5. Approve or *tentatively* agree on each issue in sequence with "conditional" cooperation. Do not start with a chip on your shoulder. Be positive and considerate. Be clear that your agreement on an issue is contingent to your ultimate agreement in total.

6. Do not discuss an issue or decide on it unless you are thoroughly prepared.

7. Do not be afraid of **deadlock** or become too pessimistic if you are far apart on an issue. Calm down, take a breath, and take the time to explore possibilities. Move on to other items, specifically intending to revisit the deadlock later with a clearer head.

8. Understand all objectives by all parties. Are they all business, or are some personal? Are they coming from your opponent or from somewhere else within the opponent's organization?

9. Practice. Dry-run the negotiation at your earliest opportunity. Take your opponent's position in a devil's advocate role. List every conceivable objective or point of view, and prepare your responses and approach beforehand. Refer to **change orders, handling rejections** for related discussion.

10. Understand that you are coming together in a negotiation because both parties presumably *want* to make a deal. Leaving the deal unresolved leads to uncomfortable problems for both organizations. Ultimately, it may be your opponent who wants the deal resolved even more than you do.

11. Train yourself to get something from every concession.

12. Believe that a 50-50 split is not always reasonable. If someone said to you, "Let's split the difference," consider responding with, "I can't afford to." Another version might be to reintroduce previ-

ous **concessions** into the total to be considered before splitting. It might be a way to maximize the total value, and thereby effectively move the split more to one side.

13. If the negotiation moves in an unfavorable or unexpected direction, consider yourself free to revisit earlier items that otherwise might have been considered to be resolved. Be clear that there is no final agreement on any component, without final agreement on the total.

Nepotism

Contents

Related Topics

Integrity

Loyalty

Sabotage

Controlling the Evils

One writer has provided an entire chapter on the subject as follows: "It happens."

The hiring of family members by higher management to work within the business does not necessarily have to be detrimental to the preservation of authority and accountability. In such cases, it's best for everyone at all levels to avoid wasting energy complaining about it, and otherwise wishing it were not so, and instead acknowledge the event and treat the issue directly with those involved, doing your best to keep it all on a professional level.

If, for example, a nephew is hired by an uncle in top management, it should be made clear to the nephew that his particular supervisor is his "boss." It is up to the uncle to get the situation off to a good start. Beyond this, however, the nephew's supervisor would do well to look for an early opportunity to politely and professionally openly address the situation, and clarify to both the uncle and nephew how he views the situation. After all, it is a business, and work needs to be accomplished. The supervisor should look for ways to form a three-member group (the uncle, nephew, and supervisor). The supervisor can then use the situation to demonstrate a concern to "reasonably" manage the situation to the benefit of the parties and the company, in a way that will minimize the appearance of favoritism to the rank and file.

Suggestions for the Supervisor

1. Make a point of distributing the workload on a professional basis to all subordinates. If another employee is dissatisfied, the supervisor should maintain his or her position and enforce equitable assignments.

2. The only appearances that the supervisor should be concerned with is that the supervisor is genuinely distributing the workload according to needs and talent—not any favoritism.

3. If the nephew shows an aptitude in a particular area that could lead to a promotion or other changes in responsibility, consider waiting a short time before making any such formal changes. It

might be better to confirm that the aptitude is as real as it initially appears.

4. If aptitude or discipline does become a problem, be sure that every effort is made to professionally bring the situation to the employee's attention. Keep track of your efforts. If the situation does not improve, go first to the "uncle," using clear examples of specific problems that are created. Avoid generalities at all costs. Ask the *uncle* to suggest the next move.

5. If in such a case the uncle is not inclined to assist in the resolution of the problem, you might need to go to a higher authority for assistance or specific recommendations. After that, it is up to the supervisor or to the higher levels of the management so appealed.

Never Say These Things

Star Performance

Consistently avoiding any of the following kinds of statements or actions will help you go a long way toward success in business. These are more serious than they might first appear.

Never say these things:

1. "What do I do next?" Be a troubleshooter. When you run into a problem, do not immediately run to your boss for the answer. Do your best to think of at least one or two solutions before you bring that problem to your boss. Your boss may come up with a third or fourth, or may modify one of yours, but you will be seen as what you are: a problem solver and a doer.

2. "Everything's OK" (when it isn't). Never withhold bad news. Advise everyone who works with you or for you that you have a "no-**surprise** rule." Be clear to your peers and to your subordinates that you do not withhold bad news and that, withholding bad news is absolutely the worst thing that any of them can do.

3. "They didn't get back to me." There are all kinds of versions of this statement. Too many people feel as if the act of asking someone to take care of a problem ensures that it will be taken care of. Be part of the solution instead of the problem. Take initiative. Follow up. Think on the fax machine; confirm all your requests for information on performance—both internally and externally. Make it happen.

4. "No one ever told me." If you make this kind of language a habit in talking to your supervisors, then you'll be making a very clear statement about the way you work, and the level of initiative that you are applying to your position. You are telling your boss that essentially you operate in a tunnel, oblivious to any information originating off the edge of your desk.

5. "I didn't have time." The variation: "I am (was) too busy." Occasionally, this remark is only a nail in the keg. But make statements like these routinely and you might find yourself with plenty of time to be writing your resume.

6. "I didn't think to ask." This type of statement indicates that you are not taking the time or initiative to look beyond an immediate reaction to an ultimate result. It demonstrates lack of foresight, or of the ability or willingness to understand or appreciate the details of more complex relationships.

Become a Doer

Lose this type of language, and you will immediately be perceived as more a doer than a spectator. Forcing yourself to simply stop making these kinds of statements, will also force you to amazingly come up with the right action, instead. You will really *become* a doer, well beyond merely creating the impression of one.

"No Damages for Delay"

Related Topics

Delay

Exculpatory Clauses

Force Majeure

Implied Warranty

Basic Idea

Contractors whose progress is delayed are generally entitled to damages associated with the delay, unless their contract specifically contains an enforceable "no damages for delay" clause. Such a clause would be included by an owner in a contract usually to protect against extreme cases of construction delay and resulting delay claims.

Types

The type and substance of "no damages for delay" clauses vary considerably. Such clauses may specifically delineate the kinds of delay which will not entitle the contractor to recover for related costs, or the clause might simply state that the contractor is not entitled to any monetary compensation for delay, no matter what the cost.

The clause might be incorporated into a paragraph identified clearly as a "no damages for delay" clause. Such a clause may again either describe in detail those specific instances of delay that would otherwise justify a claim, such as act, omission, neglect, or fault of the owner, or damage by fire or other casualty.

Recognizing a "No Damages for Delay" Clause

The "no damages for delay" clause may be incorporated into an article of a general contract otherwise designed to deal with time extensions. The language precluding recovery for damages might be tacked onto the language allowing for a particular time extension.

In addition to the various methods of positively providing for "no damages for delay," a clause may be simply phrased in a negative form. In these cases, the language might highlight the entitlement of a time extension, but then note that such time extension if granted would be the contractor's "sole" or "exclusive" remedy. The presence of these words should send up a red flag to focus your attention on the actual meaning of the clause.

Finally, a clause that outlines the costs which a contract would cover in the event of project delay, or that describes a specifically required response "both in content and time" on behalf of a contractor in the case of any project delay, may cause a "no damages for delay" situation when the contractor fails to act within those requirements.

Enforceability

While such clauses are generally considered to be enforceable, court-created exceptions have provided some basis for recovery in certain situations. In addition, these arguments may satisfy an arbitration panel by the same logic. They include:

1. Delays of such a nature that were not or could not have been contemplated by the parties in preparation of the contract.
2. A delay of such a duration as to effectively amount to an abandonment of the contract.
3. A delay as a result of bad faith, arbitrary action, negligence, or fraud.
4. A delay as a result of "active interference" on the part of the owner or design professional with the work of the contractor. Refer to **implied warranty** for related discussion.

Although these exceptions are fairly well recognized, there appears to be a trend by the courts in recognizing a certain level of sophistication of the entities involved in a construction contract. Because of this recognition, such courts are therefore tending to hold both parties to the letter of their contract language. This trend has resulted in a more restricted application of the sections to the "no damages for delay" principle.

One Remedy

One approach that might in certain circumstances allow a contractor to submit for recovery of "delay" costs, despite the "no damages for delay" clause, is to look for ways to reclassify or redefine the category of the particular cost. Is there a way, for example, to categorize certain costs as direct job costs, instead of delay costs? Can other costs be more clearly categorized as costs associated with the performance of a specific activity instead of delay costs?

This approach certainly does not work every time and in every instance, but it can remove at least certain cost amounts out of the delay category and into other categories. To the extent that this approach succeeds, it can remove such costs from the consideration of the enforceability of the "no damages for delay" clause.

Notice

Concept

In a modern construction contract, there will be literally dozens of references to numerous kinds of "notice" requirements related to almost anything. Most commonly, the more complicated notice provisions will be those relating to changes and claims, but notice can apply to other items as well.

In some contracts and general conditions, the notice network can be extremely complicated. It can require an excruciating amount of review to understand the matrix of conditions that need different kinds of notice, and it can add still further sets of circumstances. In certain forms of agreement, the whole thing seems to have gotten way out of control.

Actual or Constructive?

It is not necessarily the date of the first formal **correspondence** that establishes the effective notification date. Notification has in fact been achieved if there has been an understanding in the mind of the recipient. The purpose then of "written" notification is simply to remove doubt as to when this understanding had actually been achieved. This requirement can be further qualified as the date when such understanding *should* have been achieved, even if it has not actually been achieved because of the recipient's neglect, oversight, or other reason.

Notification, therefore, can sometimes be said to have occurred in a number of types of communications including:

- Telephone or other conversations
- **Job meetings**
- Other letters and communications
- Faxes and **RFIs (requests for information)**
- Shop drawings
- Progress **scheduling** distributions

Notice can therefore be *actual*—formal written notification as strictly required by any contract language, or *constructive*—the result of an event, other information, or any circumstance by which the recipient has achieved the understanding as described above.

Action Rules

It is not a good feeling to have lost a legitimate issue on technical notification grounds; don't put yourself or your company into that position. When in doubt, get *some* kind of notification confirmed.

Be aware that notice can be complicated, and the need for some kind of notice should almost be routine. Conduct all of your activities with a profound respect for the notice requirement. Be aware of your contractual notice requirements for *this* contract. Refer to **contract versus contact** for additional discussion in this regard.

Consider the following in your routine conduct on every project regarding notice:

1. *Always establish the earliest possible legitimate date of any notice or "awareness."* If the issue is discussed in a **job meeting** or in **telephone negotiations,** for example, refer back to it in the first part of any written notification. "Confirming our conversation of (date)," or "In accordance with the discussion at the (date) job meeting," or something similar will usually be enough.

2. *Notify everyone who might possibly require it.* Do this either directly or by copy of your written notification.

3. *Specifically name the individuals involved in the prior notification.* "Confirming my conversation with your office," is much too weak. Name names. Let each individual see his/her name in lights, and see that those lights have been distributed.

4. *Get into the regular habit of confirming all potentially significant conversations and discussions immediately.* Any piece of information that has any potential to affect the project should be recorded in a manner that corresponds to the level of potential effect. Even if a seemingly insignificant item begins as a plain note in a file, it can form the basis of later formal notification if one should become necessary.

5. Be concise, but be clear.

Refer to **correspondence** and **documentation** for related discussion.

If you are doing *your* work properly, you should have a minimum of problems with regular distribution of your own work product. Items like **change order** logs, **RFI** logs, construction **scheduling** revision notes, and so on can be distributed as regular, routine information, while you regularly perform actual or constructive notification to all parties involved. To the extent that you can distribute these kinds of communications routinely, you may find yourself consistently in the favorable position of always being in compliance with every conceivable notice requirement that might be thrown at you.

Notice can be a funny thing. If you strictly follow an attorney's advice, the language in your letters will give your opponent the impression that your primary objective is a legal setup. At the other extreme, if you fear offending the owner or design professionals to the point that you water your communications down, you can wind up maintaining your good relations right through your significant job losses.

The "art of the notice," then, will rely on your ability to formulate effective communications that are courteous, but also clearly protect your interest. If done properly, you can be respected for your professionalism. If such courteous, justified communications do not then produce the desired result, you might then be able to legitimately take blunt, decisive action. In these cases, it might actually work out that you can still manage to be admired as a fighter, and not be criticized as an opportunist.

If, on the other hand, a "hardball" approach has begun too early in job communications and without any prior justification (without having been abused at least once by your opponent), using strong statements peppered with "legalese" may prematurely cause you to appear more frivolous than serious. If this should happen, it will be a difficult first impression to change.

Even so, your particular contract may have very precise—and very dramatic—notice requirements. An example might be that your contract specifically requires notice by certified mail, return receipt requested. In such a case, you may not be technically complying with the requirement if you fear shocking or offending, and therefore ignore the certified requirement, and so you must decide if an alternative treatment may be possible.

The point is, know your contract. Don't lose on an issue through failure to comply with some simple technical requirement. Use the situation to demonstrate to your client that you are trying to act in a responsible, businesslike manner, but it is the *contract* that is forcing you into the current posture.

Old Age (Specifications)

Concepts

Specification age becomes an issue in the design development process if a project is left to sit for any appreciable amount of time. It is a problem associated with **defective specifications** and compounded by the **cut-and-paste** procedure described in this book, and becomes an issue on a project more often than it really should.

Origins

If a specification's age (or a portion of it) becomes a problem, it will usually be on a public project. This is because public projects are subject to the winds and tides of political funding. It is not uncommon for a state or federal project to be shelved for two, three, or more years while it waits for the political climate that will allow it to proceed.

In the meantime products change. Specified items become unavailable. The configuration of specified products will become different. New, superior, and more economical products may become desirable.

The project time on the shelf increases the possibility that project priorities might change. The agency originally controlling the project might have a different chief. People in the chain of command might have different authorities. Even if the people who designed the project in the architect's office are still working in the same office, their responsibilities and personal priorities might have changed. Their preferences similarly will be subject to "development." At worst, the original design professional may be out of the picture altogether.

The net effect of all this is that the original project concept might become watered down. The reasons for certain design considerations might be lost; accountability for the design's success becomes defused; motivations for decisive action necessary to keep on schedule may become compromised.

Pass-Through Clause

Prime Contract Incorporation

The pass-through clause is to a general contractor perhaps the most important clause in the entire agreement between it and its subvendors. Sometimes referred to as the *conduit* or *flow-down* clause, the provision incorporates into each subcontract by reference all the rights and responsibilities of the general contractor to the owner as they relate to the work of the respective subcontract.

For example, the general conditions may make the "contractor" responsible to provide "all scaffolding, hoisting equipment, etc., as may be necessary to perform the work." The pass-through clause will narrow this description to mean, for example, that the plumbing subcontractor provides all these items as necessary to complete the plumbing work, the plaster subcontractor provides these items as necessary for the plasterwork, and so on.

The authority of the pass-through is further emphasized within each individual specification section that references the general conditions, supplementary general conditions, etc., to be incorporated into the requirements of the respective technical specification section. These references thereby bring all those requirements to bear directly on the work of that particular bid package.

Application

The application of a pass-through clause can be very straightforward. As you read any particular specification requirement, simply insert the name of the subtrade being considered wherever the word *contractor* appears, simultaneously inserting the words *general contractor* wherever the word *owner* appears, and read the clause in that context.

For example: the general conditions may require that "The contractor will remove all rubbish," and "In a case of a dispute, the owner may remove the rubbish and charge the cost to the contractor." The pass-through clause will translate the same clause as it relates to the millwork subcontractor as "The millwork subcontractor will remove all (millwork) rubbish," and "In the case of a dispute, the general contractor may remove the rubbish and charge the cost to the millwork subcontractor."

Exceptions

If the words *general contractor* or *prime contractor* have been used in the original specification between the owner and general contractor instead of the word *contractor,* proceed with caution. They may have been put there as a specific indicator of just what they say—as an intentional modification of the pass-through relationship.

For example, if the *general* contractor has been specifically called on to furnish and remove scaffolding "for use by all trades" in a certain area, it may have been precisely specified this way in order to avoid the extra time and expense that would be incurred if several different trades were required to erect and remove scaffolding in the same area.

Be aware of sudden changes of language, and keep your application of the pass-through correct.

Patent Errors

Description

A patent error (or patent ambiguity) is an obvious defect or error in the document. This is to be distinguished from a **latent defect** (or latent ambiguity), which is a defect that could not be readily detected by a reasonable, competent contractor.

A patent error is generally considered to be one so obvious or glaring that a competent contracting professional should have undeniably discovered it through its reasonable review of the documents prior to bid.

For example, it is likely in a mason contractor's experience that every cavity wall that it ever constructed had some kind of ties between the brick veneer face and the block backup as an integral component of the design. If the design detail on this project, however, does not specifically indicate ties, the defect might be considered to be so obvious to any experienced mason contractor that it would be incumbent on that contractor to bring it to the attention of the owner. Note that in this black-and-white example the error is so obvious—or *patent*—that the point should be clear. In reality, the definition of what qualifies as "obvious," "glaring," or "patent" is the fertile gray area that resists any easy definition. In such cases, the idea of **trade practice** may become relevant.

Duty to Disclose

Wherever it can be demonstrated that a contractor has reason to know of an error that can be considered patent, that contractor has a clear duty to bring them to the attention to the owner on discovery. The first intention of this responsibility is to hopefully identify such patent errors and to bring them to the owner's attention prior to bid. If the contractor is competent, and has in fact performed its reasonable review of the documents, the discovery of such patent errors can be considered to be a reasonable expectation on the part of the owner.

If, however, a patent error is discovered by the contractor after the bid—or after the contract is awarded—it becomes a difficult issue for the contractor indeed. In such a case, the only way that a contractor would be entitled to compensation for the error would be to demonstrate that some other reasonable **interpretation** was available to it at the time of bid. If there is no such other reasonable interpretation, the contractor might just find itself being responsible for the patent error.

Pay-When-Paid

Contents	Related Topics
Description	Agreements versus Understandings
Risk of Nonpayment	
Legal Interpretation	
Sample Language	
Conclusion	

Description

There is probably no other clause in any subcontract that is more dear to the heart of a general contractor. Simply put, a basic "pay-when-paid" provision is *intended* to ensure that the general contractor will have no obligation to pay the subcontractor until the general contractor has received payment from the owner specifically for the work of the subcontractor. *Intended* is highlighted for good reason.

Risk of Nonpayment

If strictly left to the general contractor (and as basic pay-when-paid language may first appear to indicate), a pay-when-paid clause would completely require that each subcontractor on a project be responsible for *directly assuming the risk of nonpayment* of the owner. On its surface, the clause appears to mean what it says, thereby leaving the subcontractor holding an empty bag in the event of nonpayment by the owner. Moreover, it further appears that with the presence of such a clause, the subcontractor is left in its unenviable position even if the reason for nonpayment in actuality has nothing to do with the subcontractor.

The general contractor, then, appears to be motivated by the need to control the risk of nonpayment by the owner. The attitude is simply that, just as the general contractor is left to determine for its own the level of risk that it is willing to assume in choosing the parties and circumstances of doing business, so the general contractor should be able to make it clear that it expects the individual subcontractors to make the same determination for themselves. As businesspeople in their own right, the subcontractors should be put on notice that they are specifically assuming such risk of nonpayment. They can then decide for themselves whether or not they are willing to assume that risk under the particular set of circumstances.

The subcontractor's perspective, however, may be a little different. From the sub's viewpoint, there are just too many variables that are outside the subcontractor's control that can result in nonpayment. Nonperformance by the general contractor, the subcontractor, or the design professionals can cause or contribute to nonpayment. Because from the subcontractor's standpoint these risks are so extensive and varied, the sub might argue that no competent businessperson could ever agree to subcontract on a project under these conditions.

For this reason, the sub argues that the inequitable application of pay-when-paid in all circumstances of nonpayment cannot be within the contemplation of a "reasonable" expectation with respect to contract performances.

In the cases of the simplest versions of a pay-when-paid clause, state legislatures have fairly consistently supported—to many general contractors' surprise—this idea that a subcontractor cannot be expected to assume the same level of risk of nonpayment as a general contractor. To general contractors, the basic language appears to be clear, that the subcontractor is entitled to payment only after the general contractor receives it. To the majority of courts, however, it is not so clear. Surprised?

Legal Interpretation

In dealing with this subject, a majority of courts have determined that such a provision in an agreement between a general contractor and a subcontractor serves only to establish a time *and not a condition* for payment. These courts reason that the clause only serves to give a general contractor a "reasonable" period of time to collect funds from the owner before paying the subs. The ultimate obligation of the GC in the face of unsuccessful collection efforts remains the subject of intense scrutiny. And so pay-when-paid, in its historical representation, no longer means what most general contractors expect.

For the general contractor, however, all is not lost. If the intention of the contractor-subcontractor agreement is to specifically require the subcontractor to assume the risk of nonpayment as described earlier, that clearly expressed intention can be communicated directly in the agreement. The more clearly the GC's clause provides express and unequivocal language that the subcontractor assume exclusive risk of nonpayment—and that the general contractor is under no obligation whatsoever to pay the sub any sum of money which is unpaid by the owner for any reason whatsoever—the more evident the true intent of the parties will become. Remove the subjectivity and the general basis for the liberal interpretation, and the pay-when-paid intent can be restored to the understanding of the agreement. The subcontractor will accordingly have a much more difficult battle in arguing applicability. Refer to **agreements versus understandings** for related discussion.

Sample Language

Review this entire issue closely with your attorney. If you are a general contractor, identify the specific language that preserves the intent of the provision. If you are a subcontractor, know what the new language looks like, and be able to recognize it for what it actually is—the genuine assumption of nonpayment by the owner. In either case, sample language may appear to be along the following lines:

> Subcontractor agrees that for payment of all work performed, it relies exclusively on the payment ability of the owner and not that of the general contractor, and therefore agrees that payment by the owner to the general contractor for work performed by the subcontractor is a condition precedent to any payment obligation of the general contractor to the subcontractor whatsoever.

Such a clause might go on to emphasize and clarify by adding:

> If the owner has not paid the general contractor for any reason whatsoever, including the owner's financial inability or for any reason not related to subcontractor, subcontractor agrees that the general contractor shall not be liable for payment to the subcontractor. Subcontractor agrees that it exclusively assumes the risk of nonpayment by the owner, and further agrees that liability of the surety on the general contractor's payment bond, if any, is subject to the same conditions precedent.

Conclusion

If you are a GC, know the specific language that is required to leave you with a clear, enforceable contract provision. If you are a subcontractor, understand what the new pay-when-paid language says. Give yourself the ability to negotiate your position, or at the least clearly understand the new levels of risks you may be assuming.

It has been the action by the legislatures that has caused the reaction in the general contracting community. Pay-when-paid has been given new attention and very specific language that shores up the idea that the subcontractor unequivocally and exclusively assumes the complete risk of nonpayment from the owner—for *any* cause.

If you are a general contractor, don't be overly comfortable with the fact that your attorney has drafted you a new pay-when-paid provision. While it is true that such provisions are often construed to constitute a barter with sub's right to payment if—and only if—they are specifically required as a *condition precedent* to the general contractor's obligation to pay the sub, courts have consistently demonstrated a strong reluctance to actually apply this condition. Instead the majority of the courts still seem to interject an unusually high standard to the final dtermination as to whether *"pay-when-paid"* applies to a subcontractor as *"pay-if-paid."* In the absence of *very* strong, clear, and even redundant *pay-if-paid* language in the body of the subcontract document, the courts still look for every opportunity to interpret the subcontract in a way that will require the GC to pay the subcontractor, even in the face of nonpayment by the owner to the GC.

"Performance" and "Procedure" Specifications

Performance Specifications

A *performance specification* is one that describes that ultimate *function* to be achieved, as a result of an installed product's ultimate performance. It specifically leaves the means and the method of achieving such a function completely up to the contractor. It describes the performance and characteristics on completion of a component or a system, without indicating the precise materials to be used in their achievement, or the relationship with contiguous work.

Consider foundation insulation as an example. A performance specification would not concern itself with the particular material, its dimensions, its shape, and compositions. It would simply describe the installed performance in terms of what is to be achieved. In terms of thermal properties, for example, it might provide that the perimeter insulation "have $K = 0.20$ at 75°F with a minimum compressive strength of 20 lb/ft."

Such a performance specification leaves it up to the contractor to determine the materials and methods to be used to achieve the performance objective, and to install whatever is necessary to meet the stated design criteria. Because ultimate performance is the design objective, the particular material selected is not necessarily of any consequence, given the proper level of quality.

Note, in this type of situation, that it is the *contractor* who bears the risk of selecting the materials that will meet the stated objective of the performance specification. If the means and the methods so selected by the contractor do not live up to the design criteria, the contractor may indeed find itself responsible to correct the problem. Refer, however, to **defective specifications** and **implied warranty** for important related discussion.

Procedure Specifications

A *procedure specification* explicitly describes the material to be used and its physical relationship with remaining and contiguous construction. It details the properties, qualities, composition, and assembly of all components. It provides the "how" and "what," and leaves the performance of the specification as an explicit instruction to the contractor on the materials to be used.

Consider foundation insulation again as an example of how a procedure specification would be applied. In contrast to the previous description, it might read: "excreted closed-cell polystyrene board as manufactured by XYZ Corp., 2 in thick × 24 in wide."

The procedure specification leaves no question as to specific material to be used. If, however, such a procedure specification does not live up to the designer's explicit or implicit performance criteria, the procedure specification will keep the liability for such a problem with the designer.

Application

There is nothing inherently wrong with either type of specification. On the one hand, performance specifications may shift the design risk onto the contractor, but they decrease the designer's control over the design. On the other hand, a typical contract will contain a much larger percentage of procedure specifications. Performance realities or product descriptions may, however, weave performance requirements in with a specific product's procedure requirements. Because of this, there is often a risk of duplication in the product specifications which accordingly can become an interface of possible inconsistency or other defects in the documents.

Performance specifications are commonly used in the procurement of mechanical and electrical equipment. In such a case, for example, the performance characteristics can be readily measured and tested. Procedure specifications must be correct in every respect in order to avoid problems with the design. The sufficiency of the architect's design must be relied on by the contractor in order to achieve the intended result. If the procedure specifications are properly followed, the risk of the design success remains with the designer.

Conflicts

On occasion, a product is specifically described *and* performance requirements are indicated. In such a case, the contractor is probably secure in its belief that it is performing its obligations by procuring and installing the exact material detailed. There should be no further duty (aside from the **duty to inquire** or to disclose **patent errors**) on the part of the contractor to be sure that the precisely described materials also meet the performance requirements listed. That is more of a design **coordination** issue that should be more rightly left to the designer.

When a difficulty between the performance and the procedure specification arises, it can lead to a number of responses on the part of the owner and designer. Understand the rights regarding **ambiguities** and **interpretation—right to choose** to position yourself for your best response.

Personal Guarantee

Contents

Uneven Approach
Rebalance the Equity
Ask
Practical Effect

Related Topics

Breach of Contract
"Conspicuous" Contracts
Indemnification Clauses

Uneven Approach

The approaches in the construction industry to effectively securing personal guarantees—or their equivalent—from general contractors and subcontractors has spread in two divergent directions almost unnoticed. It is widely accepted that a general contractor will provide some level of personal guarantee in many cases—most often through the payment performance bonds provided to the owner for a construction contract. In most of these cases, those bonds are secured by personal guarantees on the part of the general contractor.

It is correspondingly true—particularly for major subcontracts—that a number of subcontracts are similarly guaranteed through their payment performance bonds provided to the general contractor. In terms of the sheer number of subcontracts let out by a typical general contractor's office, however, the number of subcontracts incorporating subcontractor payment performance bonds is usually very small relative to the number of subcontracts that do not provide similar security. And general contractors go on subcontracting over and over again without even so much as asking for a personal guarantee because for some reason most of us have come to believe that to require such a request is somehow "unreasonable."

Rebalance the Equity

As either a technical matter (through its bonds to the owner) or a practical matter, the fact remains that the general contractor is likely to have provided a personal guarantee or its effective equivalent to the owner. If a subcontractor accordingly refuses to provide a similar kind of hard security for its performance, the general contractor should look on the act not as a prudent businessperson's use of the "corporate shield," but as an unreasonable avoidance of the same kind of commitment that the general contractor has made.

Ask

If you are a general contractor, include a paragraph in your standard subcontract form that requires the individual executing the subcontract to personally guarantee its compliance with the terms of the subcontract. Yes, it is certainly true that, on first review of the subcontract, the individual will undoubtedly object to the incorporation of that language. If you can manage at that point to have a meaningful discussion regarding the actual character of equivalent personal guarantee that the general contractor is similarly providing to the arrangement, you may to your own surprise find that the subcontractor is reconsidering the situation. No, you will not get a personal guarantee every time—or even most of the time. If, however, you take this approach in every subcontract as a standard application, and you take the effort to explain the situation, all the while acting empathetically in your belief in the equity of the requirement, you may find yourself surprised by the number of times that you will actually succeed in having your subcontractor provide you with a personal guarantee.

If you don't ask for it, you'll definitely not get it. If you ask every time, you'll get it some of the time.

Practical Effect

As a general contractor or a manager of a construction contract, your objective in securing a personal signature really should not be to pursue a small subcontractor individually and secure damages. Often this ultimate act may not prove to be economically viable compared to other courses of action. The real reason behind securing a personal signature is to increase your odds of focusing the subcontractor's attention on its genuine responsibilities. You may be in a better position to minimize performance problems, enforce compliance with the subcontract, and settle payment/performance issues between you and your subcontractor much more quickly, when that subcontractor realizes the "personal" nature of the relationship.

Photographs, Preconstruction

Need

Film is absolutely the cheapest investment any contractor can make. This is a point that would not be argued by any contractor who has ever received a phone call from a property owner a quarter mile from the site claiming that the crack in the sidewalk in front of the house was caused by a concrete truck on its way to your job site.

Since it is impossible to tell prior to the start of any work where your problems may eventually lie, it is imperative that a thorough photo record be made of the site, as well as all surrounding areas and approaches within a reasonable distance.

Procedure

1. Use a 35-mm camera of good quality.

   - This will let you select specific photos at a later date and maintain acceptable quality in enlargements.
   - Auto focus is available on many cameras. While not required, it is highly desirable.
   - Many cameras now have either as a standard feature or as an option an ability to place the date of exposure in the corner on the face of the photograph. This feature should be used if at all possible.
   - Auto flash systems are available for little or no additional cost above conventional flashes. Although not required, they save time and guarantee correct exposure.

2. Organize your approach. Split your photo sets between:

   - The site itself (within the contract limit lines)
   - All property immediately adjacent to the site
   - All approach routes (roads and sidewalks) to the site

3. Keep each area as a distinct set.

   - Start in a logical place, and proceed methodically through the entire area. Do the entire site first, then photocopy every property adjacent to the site. Pay particular attention to areas along the property lines until all physical construction (buildings, parking area, fences, etc.) has been completed.

- Make particular note of all existing damage: cracks, settlement, damaged surfaces and finishes, etc.

4. Secure permission for complete photo sets. Wherever there is any existing building or structure that might possibly be affected by any construction operation (such as blasting, pile driving, or dewatering), contact the owners of those properties to secure permission for detailed preconstruction photo surveys of the complete properties. If such permission is obtained, photo-survey each entire premises. If permission is not obtained, photograph as many views and features as possible from outside the property line. In any event, pay particular attention to all existing apparent damage, such as foundation cracks or badly maintained landscaping and grounds, and settlement for all the structures.

5. When in doubt, shoot. Film is the least expensive part of the project documentation but will have the most dramatic effect on settling disputes and saving huge dollars. Never skimp on film and photos. Keep your priority on ensuring the most comprehensive photo survey possible.

6. Identify and date the photo survey. Note your photo-taking activities on your **daily field report,** and include a copy of the field reports in the photo survey record file. Include any other narratives or other appropriate descriptions to make your photo survey file complete.

7. Have all photographs developed immediately. Do not leave undeveloped films in their cans as a photo record. Not only are they cumbersome to deal with and difficult to file properly, but you will not be able to research the file. There is also no guarantee the photos all came out (or that they are not of some stranger's vacation).

8. File correctly. Forward all developed photos with the field reports and other relevant **documentation** to be filed permanently in your home office project files.

Refer to **video, preconstruction** and **photographs, progress** for additional related discussions.

Photographs, Progress

Need

The job photo record should begin with the preconstruction photograph survey and the preconstruction video. Ongoing construction photographs should then become a reflex on the part of the project manager, project engineer, site superintendent, and any other company individual regularly visiting the job site. These construction photos are divided into regular progress photographs and those required for special situations.

There should *always* be a camera on site and ready. Whenever there is any situation involving *any* question or the potential for **change orders,** problems, **questions,** etc., taking a photo of the area before *any further discussion*—and certainly before the area becomes further disturbed—must become the habit of the entire field staff. The film will always be the least expensive but most powerful agent of any **negotiation,** resolution, and settlement effort.

Resist the temptation to use wide-angle lenses in all photographs. While they do make it easier to get more into an individual photo, they distort shapes, relative sizes, and perspectives. They accordingly move the representation a notch further away from the actual reality. Remember that the objective is to provide an accurate record. Use lenses with normal focal length, and your photos will remain a truer representation of reality.

Procedure

Regular progress photos may or may not be required by the owner or company's client. If they are, the number of views, sizes of prints, and other criteria might be specified. If progress photos are not a client requirement, arrange for *regular* progress photos anyway, as a routine company procedure. In this effort:

1. Set aside a regular day each week to conduct the photo record. Use the first Monday or first Wednesday or any other convenient day. This will help to establish an important routine that would be easier to monitor.

2. Use a 35-mm camera of good quality. Auto focus and auto flash systems are highly desirable but not necessary. If at all possible use a camera that automatically dates the film.

3. Note the photo effort on the daily field report and any other regular project reporting.

4. Generally follow the guidelines in **photographs, preconstruction.** There should be no need for the level of detail of the preconstruction set, because the regular photos are intended to show the general state of progress and, although they might stress potential problem areas, they may not necessarily be aimed at catching specific issues. That approach will be provided by special photographs (see **photographs, special**).

5. Consider supplementing the photo set with a regular progress video. As with the preconstruction effort, the video is not a substitute, but will be a thorough record of the entire project.

6. Identify and date each regular survey. Include a copy of the **daily field report** that records the photo effort.

7. Have each photo set developed immediately and sent to the central office for filing.

Photographs, Special

Contents	Related Topics
Need	Documentation
Procedure	Photographs, Preconstruction
	Photographs, Progress
	Video, Preconstruction

Need

"Before–during–after" photos are necessary throughout each situation involving actual or *potential:*

- **Change orders**
- Claims
- **Backcharges**
- Insurance claims
- **Surprise** du jour
- Any other special or *potentially* special situation

In these kinds of events, fast action is necessary to gain the maximum advantage possible. A "preconstruction" photo or series of photos will be the best record to confirm the actual state of affairs prior to a changed work sequence.

Procedure

If the duration of the anticipated construction sequence or activity is relatively long, progress photos of the specific sequence should be taken.

An instant camera may prove to be a valuable *addition* to the project photo effort. If used, however, it is to be considered as a supplement, and should only become a substitute for better quality photos in the simplest of situations (such as a cleanup backcharge). The principle advantages of instant pictures is that they immediately display the specific information that has been recorded in the photo. It is therefore immediately evident if your photos indicate everything intended, or if additional photos (perhaps from other angles or positions) will be necessary for a clear and complete display. This may be particularly important if conditions are likely to change quickly, leaving little time for conventional photos to be reviewed. Even so, 1-hour developing service is becoming widely available, so don't give up 35-mm quality too easily.

Follow the procedure outlined in **photographs, preconstruction** and **photographs, progress** for the individual steps required to improve the odds of acceptable photographic results.

Power of the Standard Form

Legitimacy

If we sit together, and I write a contract word-for-word in front of you, you will question every mark on the paper, be very concerned about my intent, and have some level of objection to nearly every statement. If, on the other hand, I present you with a standard form contract, it is very likely that you will sign it after an effort ranging from specific consideration of certain obvious provisions—like payment terms—to possibly little more than a superficial consideration of the balance of the terms. Why?

People get hypnotized by forms. There is an implicit assumption that the terms of the standard form have been worked out over a period of time and are there because they have a track record of working. Under such an impression, it is easy to consider the idea that such terms are "reasonable." It's nonsense.

People hesitate to mark up neat, expensive-looking, preprinted forms. This effect is not so significant if this issue has been discussed openly with a person, but if not, it works consistently on a subliminal level. The effect seems to be more pronounced the larger and more bureaucratic-appearing the organization that is presenting the form. After all, "standard procedure" is standard procedure. Isn't it? No.

Don't Buy It

If someone is presenting you with a standard form, look past it. See through the language, and understand its meaning. Force yourself to wade through all the **detail.** Don't hesitate for a moment to rewrite the entire thing, if that's what the situation demands. Don't get hypnotized, and stay focused on the *result.*

Use the Power

If, on the other hand, it is you who are preparing the particular form, use the power for your own advantage. Always have your contracts printed in "standard" form, even if it's a one-shot deal. Make it at least appear that it's business as usual, and that the terms and conditions are tried and true. Have your **RFIs (requests for informa-**

tion) fitted to a standard format as well. People tend to fill out *all* the information on a form, even if it's irrelevant. Similarly, it's surprising the degree of sensitive information that people will volunteer if it is asked for within the body of a "standard" document.

Don't Misuse Your Word Processor

The good news is that sophisticated word-processing software, combined with inexpensive high-quality printing technology, has made the creation of a preprinted document fast and inexpensive.

The bad news is the sheep's clothing. In our effort to appear professional, to produce neat contracts, and even to speed along preparation of the documents, many of us have fallen into the habit of regularly modifying our standard form agreements in the word-processing program for the particular negotiated deal. The result is a document that is clean and neat, and incorporates a small or large amount of custom language.

The serious problems that are buried deep within the neatly appearing form are as follows:

- You risk unwittingly modifying your standard form. With the exception of those instances where a lock has actually been placed in the document that prevents modification without authorization, it's almost a guarantee that somewhere along the line, your standard form of agreement will become altered. When this happens, that portion of all that hard work that went into drafting your agreement in the first place will be lost. To compound the sin, no one in your organization will even realize that the language has been modified.

- It is impossible for your project people to use a negotiated contract to manage the work. Sooner or later, all your people understand what the standard form language is in your agreements. If you modify the agreement neatly in a word-processed package, adding or deleting a single word (the word *not,* for example) changes the meaning of an entire clause. Finding language that might be added (for someone who's really familiar with the standard form) would be a challenge, but identifying language that has been deleted is truly a Herculean task.

And so, if you allow this procedure, you will allow a condition where virtually every single contract form on every one of your projects cannot be assumed to be standard in any way. For your people to truly know where they are with respect to the particular deal, they would have to place it next to a standard form, and compare each line almost word-for-word in an attempt to discover where the home office altered the standard deal.

In contrast, determine now that your standard form will be printed, and left intact, as it is. Minor modification should be done directly on the form by strikeouts and initials. Numerous modifications, or major changes, can be cataloged on an attachment to the standard form. In either case, every modification from your standard language is dramatized and clearly called attention to. Your project people have no trouble understanding where your standard deals have been modified. You'll regain control of your contracts by managing the individual requirements unique to each deal, instead of having your people regularly being slammed by opponent after opponent who knows what their deal is much better than your own people do. This is a *major* consideration, not to be overlooked, and not to be taken lightly.

Proprietary Specifications

Limiting Competition

A proprietary specification is one that intentionally limits competition. It specifies a single or just a few products to fulfill a particular specification requirement. In such a condition, there are no openly allowed alternative sources of supply, nor are there any requirements (or allowances) for any products to be provided as "equal" to that specified.

Public versus Private Contracts

On private contracts, owners have the right to specify exactly what they want if they're willing to pay for it. Although there still may be formal and informal procedures to consider (refer to **"Equals" and "Substitutions"** for related discussion), there is usually no obligation on the part of the owner to provide for fair competition among competing products for a particular specification.

On public contracts, however, the owner *does* have such a responsibility. Specifications in public arenas are supposed to be written with the clear intention to encourage competition, and to allow as many legitimate vendors as possible access to compete in the project's "market." To this end, each product description should name at least three "acceptable" sources of supply and/or manufacture, and/or should add the words "or equal" to the list of acceptable named sources. In the case where this language treatment has not been complied with, public policy, state statute, or federal regulations may provide the needed basis to provide for appropriate competition.

Hidden Agendas

Although a specification may appear on the surface to comply with the requirements of a properly competitive specification by naming several alternative sources of supply and by using the words "or equal," the difficulty may lie in the fact that except in the most simple product descriptions (like a steel stud, for example), it is actually rare to find two products that are in fact manufactured precisely the same, or have the same list of technical specifications or performance features.

The problem is compounded with the complexity of those product descriptions. A Douglas fir stud is a Douglas fir stud, but carpets will have two dozen or so technical criteria, with no two carpets ever having precisely the same list. The problem may be even worse for mechanical equipment; heating, ventilating, and air-conditioning (HVAC) control systems; and computer systems.

Specifications for these kinds of items might therefore *appear* to provide for sufficient competition, but the product description itself actually creates a proprietary specification. In such a case, you might ultimately find yourself in a situation where you have based your bid on your reasonable anticipation of the use of an "equal," but now find yourself being forced to use the specified item strictly because of some obscure performance criteria buried deep in the "specified" manufacturer's brochure. Refer to **strange specifications** for important related discussion.

One Way Out

If you find yourself with a proposed product that is being rejected because it does not precisely match up to a long list of technical items, performance criteria, or just plain "goodies," the specification itself might be considered to be unnecessarily restrictive and to illegally limit competition. Beyond this, the problem might simply boil down to the designer's placement of an inappropriately large amount of weight on some technical criterion that does not really go to the essence of the product's function, appearance, performance, operation, or use. Refer to **"equals" and "substitutions"** for important related discussion.

Punchlist

The Real Definition

Whether a majority of the work on a given contract is self-performed or subcontracted, too many companies have allowed the definition of *punchlist* to degenerate. It now seems to mean a list of jobs or items of work that are clearly incomplete when the responsible trade is allowed to leave the area or the jobsite. The word *punchlist* should be reserved for a list of items of work that have actually been performed, but require some *small* degree of adjustment or correction in order to meet the standard of quality specified in a contract.

It seems now that every trade and every worker no longer approaches any given project or activity with the idea that they are going to finish it once and completely before they leave the site. Each task is approached almost with the *anticipation* that the trades person is going to leave the item of work incomplete to some degree—that it is a punchlist item. To compound the problem, superintendents, supervisors, and managers on so many levels have almost been conditioned to accept this approach as the industry's routine. And so in the final analysis, it is the *tolerance* by these supervisory individuals that perpetuates the situation, and results in punchlists that are longer than the original list of work items included in the contract.

As managers, we need to redefine *punchlist* for what it is intended to be: a list of *completed* items that require certain adjustments or minor corrections to bring them into compliance with the quality level specified in the contract. It must not be allowed to continue to be defined as "that list of incomplete items of work that project supervision allowed to remain without being completed, and which got by the design professionals prior to their approving final payment."

The Real Costs

If you have subcontracted an item of work, you presumably have bought the item at least as completely as your client has bought it from you. (Refer to **pass-through clause** for related discussion.) You

283

are entitled to the same level of performance, and you remain completely responsible for its acceptable performance to your own client. It accordingly makes absolutely no sense at all for you to allow your own supervisory people to allow any subtrade to leave a project site without having positively confirmed for yourself that the particular subcontractor has in fact complied with 100 percent of the items of work required. To the extent that such incompletion is allowed, that is the extent that your own supervisors are blatantly failing in the performance of their own duties.

If you perform any items of work with your own force, ask yourself if it makes any sense at all to remobilize your entire crew to return to the site to perform an item of work that doesn't even compensate for the gasoline burned in the crew truck that day.

Incomplete punchlist items do much more than increase liabilities disproportionately, at huge costs to the final completion of work items, and extend the period of final completion. Delaying the completion of several thousands of dollars worth of work *will* delay the release of the retainage amount of the entire project, confuse guarantee periods, and require a continuous stream of diversion of your own company's resources (supervision, labor, equipment, etc.) to return to a project for odds and ends. It can chip away at your company's reputation for ability to fulfill its contractual commitments. Companies do not usually add up all these costs because, frankly, they do not want to know.

Containment

Get control of your own punchlist situation from the top down. Clearly communicate to your own supervision that your own company has bought nothing less than 100 percent of the specified product, in all its detail, and you expect nothing less in return for your own contract commitment. Point out to your own people the specific liabilities incurred by you to your own client for performing less than 100 percent of the respective items of work, in all its detail. Following that, advise your own supervisory people that you unmistakably will consider their willingness to follow through on the organization, coordination, and completion of work by subvendors and your own crews as a very specific and obvious criterion by which their own performance will be measured. Make your expectations clear.

Next, treat the punchlist compliance in your own subcontracts as profoundly as the issue demands. Include the definition of *punchlist,* which specifies that the terms apply only to the adjustment and/or correction of completed items, and does not apply to items of work that have not been completed. Further, clarify that if such a punchlist does include items of incomplete work, the respective subcontract would not be termed substantially complete until such items of work are completed. From that point, add a requirement that all punchlist items must be finally complete and ready for final inspection within a certain number of days after receipt of the punchlist.

However noble all this subcontract language may be, it will then be necessary to add some weight behind the requirement. Consider including in your punchlist clause a cost per day that will be charged against the subcontractor's account for every day that the punchlist work remains incomplete beyond the original punchlist completion period. You can note that the per-day cost is to partially defray the added expense for your continued involvement with the project, including among other things ongoing supervision and paperwork.

Enforcement

Having notified your own people of your expectations, and included appropriate language and clear requirements in your own subcontract, you have made it clear to the world what your expectations are and what the remedy is for anyone's failure to comply. But do not stop there. In every case of every abuse, be completely intolerant. You now have the right to be impatient with your own people's inability to enforce completion of the work, and have the contractual basis to prepare and present an immediate **backcharge** to every offending sub.

Follow up and follow through, and you will find yourself with projects that finish within a reasonable amount of time more consistently. You will also find yourself cashing more "final payment" checks in reasonable periods of time, as well.

Quality

Contents	Related Topics
Confusion	Agreements versus Understandings
Clarifying the Concept	Contract versus Contact
Do It Right the First Time	Cut-and-Paste
	The Zone

Confusion

Quality, like *reasonable,* is another one of those words in our language that has been so overused that it has all but lost its meaning. At the outset, the word *quality* is immediately and intuitively changed to the words *high quality.* From that point, understanding gets much worse.

Somehow, the concept of quality has over time taken on increasingly subjective attributes that have become less and less tangible. And so in most cases, the word *quality* has been lifted out of the realm of specific definition, and left to be expressed in words such as *bright, shiny, hard,* and *straight.* From that point, the quality is associated (and almost interchangeable) with expense. And so marble is quality, whereas vinyl tile is not.

Clarifying the Concept

The true concept of quality is really not vague, subjective, or intangible. Words like *smooth,* or even *satisfactory* do much more to confuse than to clarify. To the contrary, the idea of quality should be very specific. The measure of the highest quality is simply meeting or exceeding the stated requirements, to do so the first time, and to do so in every situation. If the stated requirements are unclear or otherwise inappropriate, they must be officially changed. The new, clearly represented requirements can then be met completely and measurably.

If, for example, all the requirements of a Rolls Royce are met, it is a quality vehicle. If on the other end of the parking lot all the requirements of a scooter are met, it also is a quality vehicle. It has nothing to do with luxury. Luxury, or its absence, is spelled out in the vehicle's stated specific requirements. If each conforms strictly to its stated, measurable requirements, both are of high quality.

Construction specifications generate their own quality problems by using unclear words and requirements that are not subject to any degree of measurement. Using words like *flat,* or *reasonable promptness,* is not specifying quality, since there is no specific requirement that can be clearly met without significant interpretation (and probably argument). Performance relevant to the requirement cannot be properly measured or evaluated. Those kinds of specifications must instead be changed to read "flat to within 1/8 in in 10 ft in any direction," and "within 10 work days." Make the requirements tangible and specific, so that the relative performance can be measured, and you have a quality specification.

Do It Right the First Time

Yes, it is a cliché, but it is one that bears repeating because it is not given enough genuine attention. This is the place for my speech. We are in an incredibly time-squeezed business. No, there is never enough time to do the job right. There always seems to be, however, enough time to do it again—and possibly a third time—but only after we've had the time to argue about it, be humiliated about it, and create some other damage further down the line. The failure to accomplish tasks correctly, completely, and on time and to do them just once causes continual disruptions, creates those incessant fires, and protracts those arguments, delays, rework, and all the other problems that explode budgets, destroy schedules, set the company back, and put people's careers on hold.

Get focused. Be task-oriented. Get in **the zone,** and do it right the first time.

Questions

Road to Understanding

The most direct route to understanding is a good question. A problem most of us have is that we usually think of our best questions in the car as we travel back to the office, after we have dealt with the particular issue.

Many of us do not ask questions because we do not want to appear ignorant. There seems, however, to be an inverse correlation between the number of individuals in a room and the amount of genuine understanding of an issue. In other words, as the number of people in the trailer during the **job meeting** increases, the aggregate understanding of an issue by the group plummets.

If you are not intimidated by asking a question, it is all but assured that if you ask it, you will discover that *several* other people in your immediate vicinity would suddenly like the answer to the same question. It is a very predictable response.

Don't waste time with the idea that your intelligence might be questioned. If you need to understand the issue and deal with it effectively and responsibly from your end, ask as many questions as it takes, and as many times as you need to get the answers that will allow you to proceed in the best interest of you and your company.

Dos and Don'ts

1. Get your questions ready in advance, to the extent that you can.

2. Don't ask questions that pry into the other person's affairs.

3. Ask questions innocently. Encourage communication, and complete answers.

4. Ask questions even if you feel that they may be evaded. This in itself may be an answer.

5. Ask a few questions to which you already have the answer. This will help you calibrate the accuracy and credibility of the other person's answers.

6. Don't ask antagonistic questions unless you want a fight.

7. Don't cancel your teammate's question by asking another question before his or hers has been answered.

8. Don't pick any time to ask a question. Wait for the right time.

9. Don't ask questions that show doubt of the honesty of the other person. Calling a person a liar won't make him or her honest.

10. Don't stop listening in anticipation of asking a question. Write down your question and wait.

Remedies

Need for Clarity

Remedies to contract breaches that are clear and reasonable and fit the breach are usually defined only for those breaches that are the most serious.

Typically, we and our attorneys draft our agreements in increasingly excruciating detail. We go into each clause, subclause, article, and paragraph to define first the major responsibilities and then all the tiny details that will eventually make up the sum total of all the specific obligations.

Near the end of the agreement, our attorney has dutifully included a provision to the effect that any violation in the performance defined in the agreement will be considered a breach. The agreement will then follow with the "remedy" that any breach will be grounds for *termination*.

"Remedies" That Are Not

And so, by the letter of our agreements, we describe conditions where

- "Shop drawings must be submitted within 10 days."
- "Certified payroll reports must be submitted with each application for payment."
- "The party must accelerate its work as directed."
- "The party will proceed with work that is the subject of the dispute."
- "The party agrees to complete its punchlist within 5 days of being notified, and further agrees to provide all documents in form and content as prescribed."

The problem, however, is that we routinely fail to provide the immediate counterpart to each of these requirements in the agreement. We fail to include an immediate, reasonable, and clear result that is tied directly to the breach. And so our contracts would provide a "remedy" of termination for a party delivering shop drawings within

15 days (instead of 10 as required). If the punchlist is completed within 20 days instead of the 5 provided in the agreement, our contract will provide us with the "remedy" of termination.

To make things even worse, when we decide that we would actually wish to pursue our termination option, we are told by our attorneys that the particular breach is not "material," or that it is in some "gray area." In such cases, all we have managed to do is write another check for legal fees while our issues on the projects remain unresolved.

And so it is not even sufficient to define an act as a breach; it must be a material breach. If it wasn't all so very serious, it would just be plain silly.

Punishment to Fit the Crime

For every contract provision for which you specify a requirement, follow through with a direct consideration of the specific result that would occur for failure in performance. Look for ways to design the result to apply to incremental failures.

For example, if your contract provides that the punchlist work will be complete within 5 days of notification, follow with language, for example, that failure to complete that punchlist within the prescribed time period will result in a $150 per day management fee commencing on the sixth day, and continuing until the work of the punchlist is finally complete. The punishment fits the crime.

As an additional example, include a provision that stipulates that for each day that a submittal is late, or acceleration is refused, or certain other conditions persist, that day is on the project's critical path, and it is therefore subject to all costs and damages associated with the corresponding extension of the project's end date.

Still another example: If submittals are not given to you in proper form and content, you will withhold $50 per document from any current payment applications until such documents are delivered.

Make each punishment fit each crime, and give yourself the power to enforce the individual contract provisions.

Representatives

Contents

Related Topics

Authorized Individuals

In construction agreements, clauses typically refer to one party or the other or its "authorized representative." While it might be obvious that the individual actually executing the agreement has the authority to make ongoing operating decisions, it is usually not so clear, at least initially, in the field.

We have finely detailed written agreements which are changed by the constructive actions of the parties. Someone on some level of the totem pole directed or allowed some change, for which you eventually submitted your payment application—and actually received payment. Such a sequence of events may not only have constructively determined the actual mechanism of your contract administration, but may also have served to confirm the actual limits of **authority** of certain individuals in the administration of the contract.

And so you begin to believe after a certain number of transactions on the job site that you now know how your contract *really* works on this site. And so you continue to perform additional change work with at least a certain amount in the idea that the individual authorizing you to proceed had at least the implicit authority to do so.

And then comes your **surprise.** Someone from the elevated end of the totem pole advises you that the individual with whom you are dealing suddenly has—or has never had—any authority to be dealing with you in that capacity. The new change may be beyond his or her original limit.

Preconfirmation

Do your best to avoid these kinds of problems when you have the opportunity to exert some influence on the process: before you execute the agreement.

Consider including, either directly in your own contract form or as a separate exhibit attached to your contract, a schedule which clearly includes the names of the particular individuals who will be participating in the project administration at the various levels, along with their particular responsibilities and levels of authority. Along with each name, include the title, a brief remark as to the performance responsibilities of the individual, and a monetary limit of that individual's decision-making capacity.

Later on, at the jobsite, when you are faced with a situation in which an individual is giving you a directive for which you've got some concern, you might now find yourself with a legitimate fallback position. Your *representative assignment sheet* might provide you with a written confirmation that you in fact should not be taking orders from that particular individual with respect to the issue in question.

Use the procedure to be aware of precisely who you are dealing with, their specific designed responsibilities, and their absolute levels of authority.

RFI (Request for Information)

Description

The *request for information* (RFI) is a form and procedure that has become generally accepted within the industry. Used most effectively, the RFI can be more than a request for information; it can also be a request for confirmation of a clarification or directive or the actual confirmation of such a clarification or direction itself.

It is probably a good idea to instruct your people with the idea of using an RFI form instead of any other memorandum or fax form that you might have. It's a simple matter to design your RFI form as a self-fax document, by simply providing a checkbox or something similar near the top of a form that highlights the fax option, along with a space to insert the fax number of the addressee.

"Think on an RFI"

Further instruct your people to "think on an RFI form." You might begin with the idea that the only purpose of actually having a conversation with an individual is to allow you to begin the RFI with "Confirming our conversation of...." (Refer to **notice** and **documentation** for important related discussion.)

Have every member of your project staff develop a habit that, in every instance in which a **surprise** is discovered, and a change in program—to any degree—is necessary, they begin documenting the issue directly on your RFI form as they dial the number to the design professional's office, or while they are on hold waiting for the individual to respond to a question. By the time they are only beginning the discussion, their RFI should already have begun with "Confirming our conversation of ...." They should already have the description of the problem written down, and be ready to write down either the direction they are about to receive, or the confirmation of the commitment that they have been able to secure from the designer to address the issue and respond.

RFI Format

The request for information becomes a crucial element in a complete project record. Learn to express your thoughts on the RFI, and your project **documentation** will improve dramatically.

The RFI should be used in all cases regarding any clarification of information coming from the owner or design professionals. It is a good idea to establish some kind of numbering system, in order that a positive correlation can be achieved between RFI numbers and ultimate **change orders.**

The RFI form should be designed so that the first portion of the form is clearly dedicated to a description of the issues. When providing such a description, be specific; refer to plan details, specification section numbers, etc. Name names; include dates. It is also helpful in the first portion of the RFI to include some prompt that will help you identify particular work that was either stopped or otherwise affected by the subject of the RFI, and whether the crews were able to move to other work.

The second portion of the RFI should be designed first to confirm that the portion of the RFI is either a confirmation of a verbal directive, or a request for direction, clarification, or interpretation. Beyond the basic area to simply write the facts, the RFI might be designed to include checkboxes that note, for example, (1) whether the directive was given in a telephone conversation or site visit, (2) the day and time of such direction, and (3) whether the direction by itself is complete or supplemental drawings or other instruction are forthcoming. If, instead of confirming some direction received, your RFI is requesting direction, arrange some prompt on your form that will help you secure a commitment from your addressee with respect to the type of response forthcoming, the form of response (drawings, instructions), and the day you expect to receive the response.

End your RFI form with a signature block that confirms either your representation of some verbal direction or the commitments made with respect to when and how the direction will be delivered. It is also a good idea to clearly note the distribution on the RFI form, including the owner if your RFI is addressed to the design professional and the design professional if your RFI is addressed to the owner.

Use of the RFI

In using the RFI form as your notepad during your conversations with the designer, do your best to actually confirm the answer to your questions as soon as possible. To the extent that you can secure an answer now, you will be able to minimize interference with your work. In such cases, the form will then be used as confirmation of the direction that you've managed to guide.

If you are unable to confirm your direction immediately, be sure to fax the form with a written statement of the issue to the responsible party, noting the critical nature of the required response date. Mailing a copy of the RFI form is a great way to refresh the attention needed with a repeat written notice to your addressee one or two days later. For emphasis, you might also consider sending a confirmation copy of the RFI via Express Mail or other next-day delivery service. Do whatever it takes to get the form into the hands of the other party immediately. Stress the urgency of a quick yet *complete* response.

Sabotage

Contents

Related Topics

Forms

Unfortunately, there may be more sabotage going on in a given company to varying degrees than any manager would care to admit. The obvious form, at the physical level, is damage to property, which may fall into such categories as *accidents* or *vandalism.*

On the administrative side, too, there are so many opportunities for a disgruntled employee to allow, or even set up, enormous problems for the company, that, if you consider the issue carefully, it's difficult not to become paranoid.

Physical Protections

In order to keep incidents of accidents, vandalism, or downright *sabotage* under control, consider giving attention to as many of the following items as you can:

1. Have supervisors physically present throughout as many activities as possible.

2. Be sure burglar alarms are installed, operating, and tested regularly.

3. Be sure that all fire protection systems are operating and tested regularly.

4. Ensure that passes and badges are returned to the company by all ex-employees.

5. Have a system of definite controls for all keys to all company facilities.

6. Maintain housekeeping procedures in ways that prevent the accumulation of trash and flammable materials.

7. Analyze every production mishap. Determine the cause, and implement the specific solution.

8. Have every guard report every suspicious activity.

9. Secure all parking lots and outside areas.

10. Restrict all computer areas, keep all file cabinets locked, and ensure that all project records are under tight control.

11. Drug-test every applicant for employment. Check with your human resources department and attorney to determine what your rights are for periodic drug testing of current employees.

12. Perform background checks on all applicants.

13. During collective bargaining periods, consider adding guards and stepping up normal security procedures.

14. Be sure that all phone numbers for the police, fire, and other emergency services are posted and readily available in all areas that may require it.

Administrative Precautions

If an employee such as a project manager, project engineer, site superintendent, or production foreman is determined to hurt the company, his or her ability to do so will be directly related to the lack of communication, reporting procedures, **scheduling, documentation,** and **management reporting systems** in place throughout the organization.

The extent that employees are given autonomous control—either formally or informally, over an entire project or a portion thereof—will be the extent of opportunity for sabotage that can go on for a protracted period of time virtually undetected.

To make it all worse, the fact remains that, although the resulting problems will certainly become apparent, whether or not it was deliberate sabotage or simply bad management may be in question. As a result, the risk of getting caught for sabotage in this category might be considered to be low indeed. Refer to **spying** for important related discussion.

As a manager, be aware of the risk. If all the practical and economic reasons for establishing and maintaining effective management control systems are not enough by themselves, add the black cloud of potential sabotage to the equation, and you might be looking at your management control system with newfound respect.

Longer-Range Solutions

Most companies are vulnerable to an employee who is determined to commit sabotage. At best, management can reduce the opportunity for sabotage by such an individual through use of some of the actions suggested above, but long-range solutions require more effort. Given consistent, relentless application, these longer-range approaches can significantly reduce the number of potential saboteurs:

1. If you don't already have an employee manual, develop one that describes the policies of your organization. Whether the manual is distributed only to supervisors or to the entire operation, it can contain a strong admonition that any employee who is caught damaging company property deliberately is subject to immediate dismissal. Similarly, it can state that any manager, supervisor, or person in position of similar capacity found to have acted (or failed to act) in ways that cause damage to property, equipment, or construction projects will be considered to have performed that act deliberately and is also subject to immediate dismissal. Such actions/inactions include failure to remove and replace defective work and knowingly causing or allowing defective work to proceed.

2. In larger companies, it might be possible to have all employees wear badges that indicate their employee ID numbers and other relevant information. Different color badges might be used to indicate which department or production center they report to. Supervisors and foremen might thus be able to determine who is loitering or is otherwise in areas where they should not be. Maintenance supervisors, for example, could report personnel who are found trespassing in computer rooms, file areas, physical plant areas, and unauthorized areas of job sites.

3. No matter how small, all fires should be reported to the local fire department. Company management should request a copy of the fire marshal's report in order to ascertain the cause of the fire. Even if an employee cannot be immediately identified as a cause, the fire marshal's office may be able to incorporate this information with information regarding other area fires.

4. Acts of destruction to the premises should be reported to the police for the same reasons described above for fire. Often, the police will then cooperate by patrolling the area more frequently.

5. If you are able to confirm that either physical or management sabotage has occurred, and you are able to establish factual evidence, strongly consider pursuing civil and criminal penalties. Be sure to make the pursuit of these remedies as visible and as widely known as possible. Pursue the case not only because it is moral to do so, but also to turn your problem into an opportunity to display to the remainder of the organization that your company takes these things extremely seriously, and will act decisively. Communicate to the entire company that there *is* significant risk to any other potential saboteurs.

Safety

Accident or "Act of God"?

The idea of an *accident* is often confused with the term *act of God*. The difference, however, should be clear; while floods and earthquakes cannot be prevented by any businessperson, workplace accidents for the most part *can* be prevented.

No one wants an accident to happen. Even beyond simple humanitarian concern, a serious accident or death of an employee can cause the loss of profit, and in some cases, the entire business.

There are reasons why accidents happen. It may take some thought, but once you know the cause, it is possible to develop a solution. Once basic facts are confirmed, you might need to develop the answer yourself, but more likely, you might be able to secure the answer from others who have it already.

Accident Prevention Program

Beyond the technical Occupational Safety and Health Administration (OSHA) requirements for an accident prevention program specifically required for our business, we need to concern ourselves more specifically with those types of accidents that could happen in our particular workplaces. Even in the same industry, we conduct our businesses in ways that differ to small or large degrees. These differences correspondingly result in workplace conditions that vary as well.

While these details do vary, there are basic policies and practices that can generally define an effective accident prevention program. Such a program can include the following ideas:

1. Top management assumes the leadership role.

2. Responsibility for safety and health activities is clearly assigned.

3. Possible causes of accidents are identified, and either eliminated or reasonably controlled.

4. Appropriate company-wide safety and health training is initiated and maintained.

5. A documentation—accident record—system is initiated and maintained.

6. A medical and first aid system is established and is kept ready for use.

7. There is continued effort throughout the organization to develop jobsite awareness and acknowledgment of the safety and health responsibility of every company employee.

Regardless of the size or complexity of your organization, each of these elements should be employed to the degree necessary to prevent workplace accidents and possible injuries and illnesses.

Begin considering the probable hazards in your methods, processes, and practices. Know which standards apply to your business.

Safety Implementation Checklist

Technical assistance in providing for safety in your business is available to you through your insurance carrier; the local safety council; local, state, and federal agencies, including the state consultation programs; and OSHA area offices. These organizations provide lists of individuals available for specific consulting, checklists that you can use to perform various kinds of factual self-inspection, and training aids in virtually every category.

The implementation list that follows provides an idea of the appropriate level of initiative that you should apply to various safety concerns. In every case, consult with current OSHA requirements at a minimum.

1. Is the required OSHA workplace poster displayed in your place of business as required where all employees are likely to see it?

2. Are you aware of the requirement to report all workplace fatalities and any serious accidents to a federal or state OSHA office within 48 hours?

3. Are workplace injury and illness records being kept as required by OSHA?

4. Are you aware that the OSHA annual summary of workplace injuries and illnesses must be posted by February 1, and must remain posted until March 1?

5. Are you aware that employers with 10 or fewer employees are exempt from OSHA record keeping requirements, unless they are part of an official survey and have received special instructions about records?

6. Do you demonstrate an active interest in safety and health matters? Have you defined a policy for your business and communicated it to all employees?

7. Have you established a safety committee or other group that encourages participation of employees in safety and health activities?

8. Does that safety committee or group meet regularly and produce written reports of its activities?

9. Does your organization provide some level of safety and health training for all employees requiring such training? Is it documented?

10. Is one person clearly in charge of safety and health activities?

11. Do all employees know what to do in various types of emergencies?

12. Are emergency phone numbers posted?

13. Is there a procedure in place for handling employee complaints regarding safety and health?

Sources of Help

The following are just a few of the organizations available to assist you to any degree in the development and implementation of your own safety program:

- Your local OSHA office
- Workers' compensation carriers, and other insurance companies
- Trade associations and employer groups
- Trade unions and employee groups
- The National Safety Council and its local chapters
- American National Red Cross (for specific medical consultation)
- Your local library

Schedule as Evidence

Schedule Objectives

The primary objective of any construction schedule is its use as a management tool that facilitates organizing and directing the work in a complete and coordinated manner. The project should be planned to be completed in the shortest possible time consistent with the material, equipment, and personnel constraints, thereby providing a good profit for your organization.

Over the years, courts and arbitration panels have considered construction schedules from two fundamental points of view. The first is that schedules are a catalog of firm commitments. They represent a list of precise milestones and completion priorities that must be achieved by the contractor as so planned and notified, if the contractor is to be considered to be in compliance with the contract. There is a tendency among those with this perspective that changes to the program may be more likely a result of poor planning on the part of the contractor than reaction to the various influences that impact the plan. The reality of the industry, and of the plain logistics of construction, however, has seriously weakened any support for this perspective. It simply is not based on the reality of the business.

The second perspective given to schedules is tempered with the idea that schedules should be fluid. Contemporary contracting recognizes that the scheduling effort must begin with a competent and realistic plan that accurately reflects the procedure intended by the contractor to achieve the requirements of the contract. From there, it recognizes that schedules are not static, that minute-by-minute progression of daily events exerts repeated and continuing influences that will dramatically affect even the best-laid plans. As a simple test of the legitimacy of this concept, ask anyone to identify a single project that was built precisely according to its original plan.

And so we finally recognize that changes in our industry are a normal part of the process. Every construction professional knows that, in all probability, there will be continuing changes occurring on the project that will affect not just its final duration, but also the individual planned sequences that need to be accomplished in order.

A good schedule will provide significant visible comparisons and convincing proof of damages, including those related to **delay, acceleration,** suspension of work, inefficiencies, disruption, and interferences.

Presentable Evidence

The suggestions below catalog a basis for maintaining your schedules as presentable evidence in litigation and arbitration arenas. Ironically, following the suggestions, by establishing good records, clear accountability, and cost-effective presentation, will help you improve your management and communication abilities to the point where you might find yourself becoming better at keeping yourself out of difficulty. If not, the ideas that follow will help ensure that your schedule will be useful and "admittable" when you must go to war:

1. *The schedule must be the one that was actually used to build the project.* Even if a schedule substantially different from the one under consideration was formally submitted and approved by the owner and design professionals, the schedule that was actually used and depended on by the various trades will generally be considered to be the legitimate document.

2. *The schedule must be periodically revised.* Because changes to, or corrections of, a schedule are inevitable, the schedule must be updated periodically to maintain a current and accurate representation of reality. The revisions must be founded on and confirmed by the project record **documentation.**

3. *The periodic updates must show all positive and negative influences by all parties.* The effects of certain parties must not be singled out nor must those of others be absent for convenience. If, for example, every update seems to indicate only those delays caused by the owner, and fails to delineate other known problems caused by other parties, it wouldn't be very difficult for your opponent to demonstrate the bias that has been built into the document. Failure to recognize all significant events will bring into question the validity of the entire schedule presentation.

4. *The schedule must include realistic construction logic and activity durations.* The professional ability and the level of competence of the planning and scheduling team should be demonstrated. Illogical sequences, or the lack of consideration of critical variables, will otherwise only demonstrate that the constraints in the schedule were not realistic to begin with.

5. *The schedule must fairly represent the actual method intended to build the project.* If, for example, the schedule had been prepared

primarily to cater to progress payments, or was otherwise unrelated to actual intended sequences of construction, it will become clear that, as a tool for managing the project, its value is marginal at best.

6. *The schedule updates and analysis must be realistic in perspective.* An overly aggressive computation of damages might only hurt the validity of the entire analysis. Direct cause-effect relationships must be demonstrated, along with realistic methods of quantifying the individual components of a problem. Keep it realistic, documented, and supported, and it will stand a greater chance of prevailing in your argument.

Schedule of Values

Invoice Mechanism

If you're a general contractor on a sizable private project or any public project, you will be required to submit a schedule of values to the owner. If you are a major subcontractor, you will most likely be required to submit a breakdown of your work for the general contractor to include in the general schedule of values to the owner.

In any case, the contract clause requiring a schedule of values will read something like this:

> ... as a basis for estimating partial payments, the contractor shall furnish ... a certified schedule of values, broken down into quantities and unit costs for the various parts of the work ... aggregating the total sum of the contract. ... The application for payment shall correspond with the approved schedule.

The preparation of a schedule of values can be tedious, but your awareness of key considerations can improve your cash flow for the life of the project.

Whether or not contractually required, a schedule of values is an itemized breakdown of the components of the work that add up, at least generally, to the total project (or subcontract scope of work). It is the vehicle used for partial payment invoicing purposes; presumably it is designed to provide some basis for evaluating the proportionate values of individual work items put in place during a particular payment period.

Payment Invoicing Only

If you indicate 5000 lf of pipe in the schedule, and 4000 lf are actually used on the project, or if you inadvertently include a duplicate of the item on the billing schedule, will you get asked for a credit? The answer depends on the owner (or general contractor if you are a subcontractor). When such an error surfaces and the other party is trying to use it to its advantage, you face an uphill battle, but there is a precaution that can be used to significantly strengthen your position.

When you submit your next schedule of values, include a statement similar to this:

> Attached is the schedule of values for the project, submitted in accordance with (insert the appropriate specification reference) to be used as a basis for estimating partial payments only, and in no way to be used as any basis for adjustment in the contract price.

This is a simple but powerful punch that will go a long way in ending arguments before they begin. If the language is objected to for any reason, contact the approving authority to explain its meaning. Illustrate that it protects *both* sides of the contract from unjust profit because of clerical or other errors. Refer to **agreements versus understandings** for related discussion.

Have a form letter made in your office, and be sure that no schedule goes out without such a statement of clarification.

Level of Detail

Often, contractors and subcontractors resist providing a level of **detail** in their billing breakdown, believing that such detail will somehow disclose unit pricing or other criteria which will come back to haunt the contractor.

Because it can be such a tedious assignment, there can be a temptation to keep the schedule of values as short and as uncomplicated as you can get away with. It is a worthy goal as far as paper volume is concerned, but be careful; it can work against you.

The first irony with this approach is that any item left as a large component of the schedule of values would eventually need to be explained in an increased level of detail in order to justify any significant billings against that item. This adds time to the process, injects subjectivity, introduces a new negotiation where one should not have been necessary, and raises eyebrows on the part of the approving authority.

The second problem is simply that if it is not broken down into detail sufficient for the owner, it will stand a good chance of getting kicked back for correction and resubmission. The worst part of it all is not that you'll need to go back and work on it, but that it will delay approval of your first application for payment.

If, on the other hand, that item had originally been broken down in complete detail in a submitted and approved schedule of values, there is a preagreement on the basis of payment, there is no subjectivity involved, there is no negotiation required, and invoice approval is reduced to arithmetic.

If possible, review your first submission with the owner *before* you formally submit it. A few minor corrections informally agreed on can save you weeks to months on your first progress payment.

Peanuts Are Filling

The second major consideration is that it has been proven over and over again that it's easier to maximize your price, payment, or whatever when you're reviewing a large number of items with small relative dollar values, than if you're considering a few large items.

On one project, there was "sitework" with an established total value of $450,000. You can imagine the difficulty the contractor encountered in substantiating an invoice for $320,000 for one sitework item. And so the detail work needed to be done anyway. The only way to avoid such a difficulty, of course, is to have a separate, "unofficial" breakdown of all items, their quantities, and so on, in order to allow review by the approving authority.

On the other extreme, a detailed breakdown can be pushed too far, beyond the point of reason. But even in this situation, you find yourself reviewing such a large number of very *small* values, that payment maximization genuinely becomes almost a by-product of the payment review process. It exemplifies the idea that "peanuts are filling."

Lump Sum or Unit Price Contract

Unless a particular agreement under which you are working is specifically designated as one being a **unit price contract,** the schedule of values is *not* a catalog of contract unit prices. Some contracts may expressly include language to the effect that the schedule of values is specifically for "partial payment invoicing purposes only," and "is not to be used as any basis of upward or downward adjustment in the contract price." Most contracts, however, are silent with respect to this express provision and leave this idea as an implied condition.

In practice, the schedule of values unit prices, if any, are often used in a negotiation involving a change, when one party discovers that a schedule of values unit price might be to its advantage. In every one of these cases, however (in a lump-sum contract), the other party is not *bound* to accept that particular unit price.

Don't get mesmerized by a schedule of unit prices that looks like it should be used for applications other than those for which it was intended. Don't allow yourself to be stuck with situations that you are otherwise not contractually obligated to. Refer to **unit price contracts** for important related discussion.

Approved "Yesterday"

One final note before we leave the subject: get your schedule of values approved *yesterday*. Any delay in its approval will directly delay your first payment. Delay in your payment will delay payment to your subvendors. Payment delay to your subvendors will slow your project down. All this right at the start gets the project off entirely in the wrong direction.

Instead, get your billing procedures in place, and set your cash flow process up with the most streamlined procedures.

Scheduling

Purpose

Too many people equate the scheduling function with little more than contract compliance; a schedule is just another piece of paper that needs to be submitted at the preconstruction meeting. They think of a schedule more as a document than a concept. The truth is, planning, scheduling, monitoring, and updating the network of construction activities actually constitutes *the* fundamental process through which all others in the organization follow. Sequences affect estimates, schedules become contract and subcontract commitments, and extended delays dramatically affect multiple trades, their relationships, and times of completion.

Company Responsibilities

Missed schedules cause disproportionate costs and interferences, resulting in economic loss and bad reputations that are difficult to shake off. Effective scheduling requires the vision, expertise, and determination of the estimator, project manager, project engineer, superintendent, and the army of specialty contractors if the entire set of objectives has any hope of being met with a minimum of conflict. The scheduler commits the plan to paper, and keeps the information distributed to everyone affected, actually or potentially.

From that standpoint, planning and scheduling remain *everyone's* responsibility. The time status of every component must habitually become the focal point around which all other information is arranged. The potential effect of every issue on the progress schedule must always be a key consideration throughout each issue's resolution.

Duties include:

- Identifying each major construction activity, its relationship with other activities, and all other necessary support.

- Correlating the activity list with the **contract documents** and the **schedule of values**.

- Soliciting and confirming all information from the best combination of sources, incorporating it into the plan, and distributing it in a timely manner.

- Monitoring actual progress relative to planned progress, continually assessing its actual and potential impacts, displaying cause and effect relationships, and determining necessary corrections.

- Monitoring the plan's implementation and maintaining all **documentation** relative to good and bad performances of all parties.

Even basic scheduling efforts can satisfy many specification requirements. The point, however, is that project planning and scheduling must be done by the company correctly and consistently because it is *the* most important function that project personnel can perform for the company's sake. Realize at the outset that from the schedule all else flows. Acknowledge that without an adequate scheduling effort, purchasing, correspondence, submittals and approvals, accounting for changes, and dealing with each day's decisions would become random, uncoordinated, and therefore extremely inefficient—and ineffective.

Subcontractor Responsibilities

The **pass-through clause** ties each subcontractor directly to the complete specification requirements for scheduling as they relate to the work of each respective subcontractor. In this way, the subcontractor is responsible for items such as:

- The timely compliance of all work

- Providing adequate labor

- Performing the work in a manner that will not interfere with or otherwise delay the orderly sequence of work by others

In addition, there is at least an implied responsibility for the subcontractor to meet requirements in a manner that will not cause total contract time to be exceeded.

Beyond these basic considerations, your subcontract form should include some adequate and specific scheduling responsibilities on the part of the subcontractor, conveying ideas such as:

- Time is of the essence to all dates and schedules.

- All schedules change continually. The subcontractor must accordingly be aware of all *current* scheduling requirements as they may have been changed, and comply with them in every respect.

- It is necessary to adjust manpower, equipment, overtime, and Saturday, Sunday, and holiday work as necessary to meet all schedules. Beyond these things, your subcontract should also contain an adequate **acceleration** clause. This clause would give the contractor the right to accelerate the work of any particular subcontractor as specifically directed, whenever it becomes apparent to the contractor that the subcontractor's portion of the work is not likely to be completed on time or as promised. The clause can then go on to state that if the need for acceleration is not the fault of the particular subcontractor, that company may be reimbursed for the difference between the regular costs and the acceleration costs, but if the need is the fault of the subcontractor, the subcontractor will remain responsible for all acceleration costs. The clause should end with a note that clarifies that in either case, the subcontractor *cannot* refuse to accelerate as specifically directed without breaching the contract.

Finally, the subcontract should provide some condition (such as tying that performance directly to a **liquidated damages** provision of the general contract) that can be assigned to the respective subcontract's failure to accelerate when so directed.

Dos and Don'ts

1. *Whenever possible use time-scaled logic diagrams.* Avoid bar charts to the extent that you can. With the inexpensive computer software that is available today, there is very little excuse for not producing schedules that not only include accurate information, but also display it all clearly enough to be able to communicate it to the owner, design professional, and your own people. Make it readable, understandable, and visible.

2. *Make sure that the document is reasonably accurate before you issue it.* This is an item that should be too fundamental to even include on such a list, but too many schedules are issued and distributed that are just plain wrong. The information is put into the computer, printed or plotted, folded up, and mailed. This is the main reason why many people don't take schedules seriously. It's almost a guarantee that a detailed review of the activities, their durations, and their relationships will disclose some error that needs to be fixed before the thing should be issued. This item is included in this list only because the problem is actually rampant.

3. *Update the schedule continually.* Use the schedule as wallpaper, not as file folder stuffing. If you're having a phone conversation about your project, you are by definition discussing some activity that is—or should be—on your schedule. Use your schedule-wallpaper as your notepad to record the effect of your conversation on the particu-

lar activity. Refer to your schedules every day, and use them as your to-do list in communicating with your field staff. The updating process itself should then become little more than cleaning it up and making your notes presentable. If done this way, your schedule will always be up-to-the-minute, and the updating process itself is done only to make it presentable.

4. *Don't lose sight of the original targets.* A huge problem with computer schedules and their updates is that it is too easy to lose track of your original objectives. Once the first update is plotted, the update information ripples through the schedule network and generates an entire new set of project milestones. In such a case, it is all too common for the original targets to be folded up and filed. Attention gets focused on a new set of targets and diverted away from the original set of targets. Instead, have some mechanism for always keeping the original targets painfully evident on every schedule update. In each schedule update, include a specific consideration to explain your "get-well" plan—a plan that you've specifically considered and implemented that will help the project regain its original targets. Make it a habit.

5. *Evaluate your updates comprehensively.* Don't just focus your attention on the immediate update. Understand the long-term, consequential effects of current events on later milestones on the project completion date. Be prepared to take appropriate action, notify the owner, or fire up the necessary efforts that will refocus project objectives.

6. *Be visible in your regular use of schedules.* Don't just leave the document as some abstraction that people receive in the mail periodically. Keep the schedule posted in the job trailer. Use the schedule activity list as a regular agenda in the job meetings. If someone makes a remark in the job meeting, stand up, walk to the schedule, identify the effect of the issue on a schedule, and let everyone at the meeting watch you write the note directly on the document. When you report your schedule status, include clear references to **change order files, job meeting** notes, and other **documentation.** Be obvious in your demonstration that you use your schedules as a legitimate management tool, and the information contained is accurate, clear, and complete. Let the entire project team know that you have all the project information under control and you know what you're doing with it.

7. *Schedule with appropriate detail.* Include useful logic. Understand that *complicated* does not mean *sophisticated*. Sophisticated schedules, in contrast, can be surprising in their *simplicity*. Using "appropriate" detail means nothing more than including the items that reflect the activity of every major player—both inside and

outside of the contract circle—that may have an effect on your performance, and tracing their influences, in order that the true cause-effect can be displayed.

8. *Include outside influences.*   Include owner and design professional activities that may have an effect on your performance. Permits, shop drawing approval, delivery of owner "NIC" equipment, and inspections/testing might be some of the more obvious types of items to consider.

9. *Insert changes accurately.*   Identify the total change duration completely, indicate those activities that are affected by a particular change, and insert each change in its logical place. Demonstrate by way of the new relationships precisely how each change is affecting your operation.

10. *Use a schedule as* **notice.**   If your schedule is prepared and updated correctly, it will include a wealth of project documentation, genuinely reflecting the results of all the outside influences on your activities. You've highlighted each **change order proposal,** you've discussed each in each job meeting, and you've brought effects to the design professionals' attention in your **correspondence.** The schedule now ties it all together, and shows (sometimes painfully) exactly what's going on. Distribute the entire schedule to all of these individuals. Have some document which you regularly include which summarizes the effects, calls attention to the major problems that have delayed your work, and closes with a list of those things that these outside parties must do to keep things from getting worse. Distributing your schedules in this way regularly will keep all of the documentation contemporaneous, and automatically provide notice on almost every project issue regularly. It's one more—but very effective—way of covering all the bases all the time.

Spying

Contents

Related Topics

The Problem

At the risk of appearing paranoid, I think we in business are exposed more to industrial espionage today than ever before. In actuality, industrial spying is on the rise, and has become an industry in its own right. Some even consider the field of industrial espionage to be a growth industry, citing that risks (strangely enough) are low, and the return can be very high.

Basic Types of Industrial Spies

There are basically three types of industrial spies:

- At the lowest level is the *disloyal employee*. Whether or not "justified" in his or her own mind because of low pay, lack of consideration, etc., so many people within the organization are privy to so much sensitive information that the situation cannot be ignored.

- The next group of spies is the *part-timers*. Not just employees with regular access to certain types of information, these may be employees or even outside individuals (with access) who occasionally (or more often) take proactive steps to secure and document information to which they otherwise would not be privy.

- The third category is the *professional spies*. Yes, this category does include private investigators, but can go far beyond this obvious group. These are individuals who base their livelihood on securing and selling information for handsome ransoms.

A Hidden Form

What can be considered to be a type of espionage is simply the stealing of specialist employees from competitive firms. In order to keep or gain leads over a rival, a company may employ an agent to buy out a competitor's key personnel at higher salaries. Although a normal business risk, this turns out to be one against which few firms have found adequate protection. Beyond the obvious, however, this form of espionage can take on a more insidious nature. This can occur when a company recruits an employee from a rival firm, and has that employee remain on the job with the original employer. The employee becomes, for all practical purposes, an inside spy, even though the employee may not actually pass on any information to the new employer until he or she finally leaves for the new position.

Risk in Negotiation

The attractiveness of the varying degrees of industrial espionage in negotiation is huge. The stakes can be very high, and the payoff immediate. Consider, for example, the value to the purchaser of construction services (or the would-be approver of a **change order**) to know the lowest number that will actually settle the deal. In an instant, this information can be worth thousands, tens of thousands, or even hundreds of thousands of dollars, whereas the investment to gain such information may be relatively small.

Need to Respect Security

Security within your organization must be treated with the most profound respect. The company must have a clear and firm security policy that definitely underscores the need to guard information. It might begin with routinely requiring employees to sign statements of confidentiality and using screening procedures for employees who are likely to have access to information at various levels.

Consider allowing access to your company information strictly on a need-to-know basis. Control access to work areas. Take a tough stand against apparent conflicts of interest. Above all, do not be naive to industrial espionage.

Security Tips

The guidelines that follow will help keep the problem in the forefront of your organization's consideration and help minimize the risk of industrial spying. They will not eliminate the problem, but can give you the means to exert at least some degree of control:

1. Have your human resources department provide appropriate forms to be signed by every employee—forms that emphasize the security-sensitive nature of their positions and require confidentiality as a fundamental requirement of each position and as a specific condition of employment.

2. Highlight the attention given to the issue within the organization. Make it very clear to would-be spies that the company is onto the problem, is constantly on the lookout, and will take decisive action if such a problem is discovered.

3. Exclude anyone from information who does not have a need to know. For those who do have a need, share only what is necessary. Do your best to determine any existing or apparent conflicts of interest.

4. Maintain communications and trust among employees at every level. Let your employees know that you give points for information relating to the identification of any party digging into an issue that does not seem to involve him or her, and why.

5. Ensure that all backup and work product information is locked and never left unattended.

6. Meet in your own facility whenever possible. Shift caucus and meeting rooms in which company business is discussed. Any room other than those on your home turf can be bugged.

7. Discipline security violations promptly, and as visibly and to the fullest extent that your human resources department will allow within the limits of the law.

Become cautious about security. Do not be naive to the problem, and do not dismiss the possibility of spying and bugging. Admittedly, this issue is difficult for many people, because they wouldn't dream of doing it themselves. The truth, however, is that industrial spying is a growing reality which unfortunately must be dealt with.

Strange Specifications

Concept

Strange specifications are "specifications" for different components of a project that are lifted from other areas and incorporated into a complete project specification. At first glance, they appear to be complete specifications for a particular item, but their origins by their nature all but guarantee problems with the rest of the complete specifications for the project.

Origins

Strange specifications are related to **cut-and-paste** in that strange specs originate in other areas and are dumped into your complete project specifications. They can come from many sources, but the more common examples include:

1. *Product requirements lifted from manufacturers' brochures.* Product manufacturers' brochures often contain facsimiles of specifications sections that are specifically designed to make it easy for the design professional to lift as is and include essentially unmodified within the manufacturer list as "acceptable," and the words "or equal" are included. The "equal" manufacturers will have different specifications. If the differences are slight, they are ignored. If they are significant, you might be entitled to a change order if forced to provide the specified item at an increase in cost. Refer to **impossibility and impracticability** and **implied warranty** for related discussion.

2. *Specifications written by manufacturers' representatives.* Because the specification preparation effort is often so unpleasant (refer to **cut-and paste**), design professionals are often receptive to a manufacturer's representative's offer to prepare those specification sections for the manufacturer's product. Proprietary cautions aside, the product representative may do an excellent job of specification preparation but for one consideration: it's done in a vacuum. The rep-

resentative comes off the street and completes the specification section without considering the project as a whole. Similarly lacking is the benefit of familiarity with the design development process experienced for *that* job.

3. *Specifications written without a specific product in mind.* On occasion, a specification might be written without a specific product in mind. Desirable qualities or requirements might be listed without ever confirming whether they are actually available in a single product. If this becomes a problem, it is usually because in reality some qualities will be found in one product and some qualities in others.

Subcontractor Bids

General Contractor Reliance

General contractors regularly rely on subcontractors' bids and quotations in preparation of the bids and proposals that they in turn submit to the owners. The general contractor often commits its price to the owner through the incorporation of a bid bond, but most often has no similar protection against the flurry of subcontractor quotations at the time of bid. The problem is further compounded with the variety of formats in which subcontractors submit their sub bids to general contractors. A complete written proposal that incorporates everything up front is rare. Oversimplified faxes and telephone quotes are much more common.

Whether or not a general contractor can ultimately compel a subcontractor to enter into a contract for the price used in the general contractor's estimate may depend on the information that was given to the subcontractor before the subcontractor submitted its price, the manner in which the price was accepted by the general contractor, and the "reasonableness" of the subcontract later tendered to the subcontractor.

Promissory Estoppel

In order to hold subcontractors to the bid prices, general contractors have relied on the doctrine of *promissory estoppel* for years. This doctrine is a recognition by the law that in some instances, fairness simply requires holding people to promises that they make, even though they have not technically entered into a contract. Such a condition arises when the person making the promise does so knowing or having reason to know that someone else is likely to act or not act on the basis of that promise, and that action or inaction in fact occurs. The **remedies** granted for failure to keep the promise, however, may be limited.

The general contractor who uses a subcontract's quote in the preparation of its own bid is not generally required to enter into a subcontract with that company. Unless some specific restriction applies, the general contractor may negotiate with the subcontractor in an effort to obtain better price and time considerations. Most courts dealing with this issue have held that under the doctrine of promissory estoppel, the subcontractor is bound to its quote even though the general contractor is not bound to accept it.

Off the Hook

Certain actions by a general contractor can almost certainly let a subcontractor off the hook, and remove any obligation on the part of the sub to honor its quote. These can include the following:

1. *Counteroffer.* In order to bind a sub to its quoted price, the general contractor *must accept the sub's quoted price as it is submitted.* This is usually accomplished by tendering a subcontract to the subcontractor for its execution. If a general contractor *asks* a subcontractor to change its quoted price, the general contractor may have released the sub from its quote even if the sub refuses to change its price. Similarly, if the general contractor attempts to impose any conditions on the acceptance of the sub's quote, the subcontractor may be released from an obligation to honor the quoted price. The law considers, generally, that the general contractor must treat the subcontractor's quote as the complete and final offer in order to require the subcontractor to enter into a contract. A general contractor's response that deviates from the "reasonably implied" terms of the subcontractor's quote can be viewed as a counteroffer which may effectively terminate the general contractor's ability to accept or enforce the subcontractor's quoted price.

2. *Acceptance time.* A subcontractor can put limits on the time available to the general contractor to accept the subcontractor's quote. If the general contractor then does not accept the quote within the specified time, the offer lapses and the sub's bid cannot be enforced. If the sub does not put a specific time limit on the acceptance of its quote, the quote can usually be accepted within a "reasonable time." The answer as to the limit of "reasonable" will vary, of course, from project to project, and may well depend on price fluctuations or other events that might alter the conditions of a subcontractor's bid. Generally it may therefore be proven to be reasonable for a general contractor to either accept the subcontractor's quote within 30 days of receipt, or have the subcontractor execute an extension of its bid to some time that the general contractor might specify.

3. *Subcontract terms.* If a general contractor requests a sub bid,

or a subcontractor submits its quote without having seen any proposed form of subcontract, the sub's quote may be viewed ultimately as an offer to enter into a "reasonable" subcontract. Again, the "reasonable" issue varies from job to job and condition to condition. In such cases, the courts have reasoned that the subcontractor's quote did not necessarily operate as a promise to enter into a one-sided contract, and that the general contractor could not reasonably foresee or rely on the subcontractor's agreeing to enter into a one-sided owner's subcontract. This situation can be avoided as a technical matter if the general contractor provides the subcontractor with a complete copy of its subcontract form before bidding. If a subcontract form has been offered prior to the sub bid, the general contractor should maintain the right to the promissory estoppel doctrine. If, however, the general contractor has not provided the sub a copy of its subcontract before bidding, the general contractor may be limited to the use of some standard form subcontract, such as those provided by the American Institute of Architects, Construction Specification Institute, and Associated General Contractors of America.

Maximizing Enforceability

As a practical matter, several things can be done by a general contractor to maximize the possibility that it will be able to force the subcontractor to hold to the quotes that the general contractor has used to prepare its bid. These suggestions include:

1. Providing a complete copy of all subcontract documents to the subcontractor before it submits its bid (see **contract documents**).

2. Notifying the potential subcontractor in writing that the general contractor will rely on the lowest quotes by a subcontractor in preparing its bids to the owner.

3. Not attempting to negotiate the price or other terms to the subcontractor's bid, unless you are prepared to lose the ability to enforce that bid.

4. Sending the subcontract to the subcontractor for execution as soon as possible after receiving the general contract. The general contractor might even consider including a provision in its subcontract form that allows it to submit its subcontract to the subcontractor before actually receiving the general contract (in anticipation of the general contract) but specifies that the subcontract is contingent on the execution of the contract between the owner and the general contractor.

The subcontractor similarly should understand the gravity of the promise that it is making to a general contractor by submitting its bid and take certain precautions to avoid being obligated to a one-sided subcontract. These might include:

- Placing a time limit on the acceptance of all quotes.

- Providing written qualifications that specifically state the conditions anticipated in the preparation of its bid.

- Providing written objections to any contract terms that it does not agree to prior to or simultaneous with the submission of its bid.

Phone and Fax Bids

The issues discussed in this section are given a twist with the telephone and the fax machine. Faxes are not the problem they once were thought to be by not providing an original signature with the document, largely because the accuracy of the time/date stamp is generally accepted, and the entire world has come to rely on faxes as a regular part of the business effort. Telephone quotes, however, continue on as a regular part of the bid process, and are more dangerous now than ever. If a general contractor receives a telephone quote from a subcontractor that is not confirmed promptly by fax or otherwise in writing, the general contractor should have a form in its office that outlines the price and time considerations to be requested from the sub during the phone conversation.

There should be a standard phrase included on the form which prompts the telephone interviewer to notify the subcontractor on the phone that the subcontractor's bid is being accepted with the expectation:

- That the subcontractor will enter into an agreement with the general contractor on its own standard form of subcontract in an unmodified condition

- That the sub price is good for some reasonable period of time (say 60 days)

- That the general contractor is relying on the telephone quote in preparation of its general bid

At a minimum, the telephone quotation form recording the information from the subcontractor should be immediately faxed to the subcontractor as a confirmation of those terms, with a confirmation copy placed in the mail.

Subcontractor Schedule of Values

Practical Requirement

The conditions regarding a subcontractor schedule of values are the same as those for any **schedule of values.** Each subcontractor should be required to provide its general contractor with a schedule of values for its work, broken down into appropriate **detail** so that the general contractor can properly evaluate each component of the work as it occurs.

Problems

Problems with subcontractor schedules of values fall into just a few, but significant, categories:

1. *Timely submission.* Even when they are required to be attached to a particular subcontract form, or required to be submitted to the general contractor within some reasonable time period after execution of the subcontract, somehow invoice after invoice comes in from subs to general contractors without a schedule of values. It is with the first invoice that a general contractor gets its first opportunity to evaluate the pricing breakdown of the subcontractor for the entire project. If no schedule of values is submitted with the invoice, the general contractor is left on its own to somehow evaluate the invoice for accuracy relative to the balance of work remaining on the subcontract.

In such a situation, the subcontractor will be expecting payment for a lump sum invoice, and will be indignant when the general contractor criticizes the value of that invoice relative to the amount (estimated by the general contractor) that remains for the performance of the balance of the subcontract. This process kicks the general contractor–subcontractor relationship over the cliff at the outset of the relationship. Even with the best of intentions, two businesspeople who are trying to conduct themselves legitimately will push themselves far apart through genuine misunderstanding. Refer to **agreements versus understandings** for important related discussions.

2. *Inadequate detail.* If allowed, subcontractors on balance have a tendency to provide schedules of values and payment invoicing in

inadequately oversimplified formats. This makes it difficult at best for anyone to perform any meaningful evaluation, and breeds continuing disagreement. Instead, the greater the level of detail provided in a subcontractor's schedule of values, the greater the chances of a complete, proper, meaningful evaluation of the invoice, and a reduced probability of disagreements and misunderstandings. Refer to **detail** for important related discussions.

3. *Missing administrative scope.*   The general contractor's subcontract form will invariably require a subcontractor to provide all kinds of administrative support to the subcontract, often as an express condition of payment. Month after month then goes by without the certified **as-built documents** being submitted, without the maintenance manuals being provided, without the system walk-throughs and onsite training being performed, without guarantees and warranties being provided, without the minutes of safety meetings being delivered, and on and on and on.

Look for opportunities to express these types of problems as cost items in the contractor's schedule of values. Have the subcontractor, for example, assign a value to maintenance manuals. Similarly, assign a value to as-built documents. Even consider my favorite: including a separate item for the punchlist (if you want to guarantee completion of a punchlist item, assign a tangible value to it).

Include an express requirement in your own subcontracts that the subcontractor schedule of values must be *attached* to the subcontract form. Don't give your own people the opportunity to procrastinate on this important function. Resolve the schedule of values at the time of subcontract preparation. Include a condition in your own subcontract that, if the subcontractor schedule of values has not been provided with the subcontract or submitted and approved prior to the start of work for any reason, or otherwise contains detail insufficient to allow proper evaluation of the subcontractor's completed work, then the value of work completed in any payment period will be determined by you at your sole discretion, but in good faith. Even though it is implicit these days in most construction agreements, note in your own subcontract form that the subcontractor schedule of values and invoice amounts are subject to approval by the owner, engineer, or architect.

4. *Prime contract acknowledgment.*   Be clear in your own subcontract that the subcontractor should acknowledge that the prime contract schedule of values may be different from the subcontractor schedule of values, and as a result may require the exercise of judgment in order to determine appropriate payment values to the subcontractor. Note that you will have the discretion to make this judgment, which will be accepted by your subcontractor unless shown to be abusive. Refer to **pay-when-paid** for important related discussion.

Subsurface Site Conditions

Bidder's Obligation

Different courts have held that a contractor having knowledge from previous work in an area of subsurface conditions differing from those indicated by the **contract documents** is not obligated to bring this information to the attention of the owner.

In numerous cases where actual conditions under the surface have differed materially from those indicated or inferred from information in the contract documents, owners have sought to shift the practical obligation to provide accurate information with respect to subsurface conditions to the bidder if that bidder has had extensive experience in the general area where the contract was performed. In other words, there is an attempt to incorporate a provision in the owner-contractor agreement that in effect has the owner directing the contractor "Stop me before I hurt myself."

Implicit in a contractor's bid, unless information in the contract documents is provided to the contrary, is the simple idea of fairness: that the contractor based its bid on the boring logs, plans, specifications, and other information on the conditions provided in the contract. (Of course, it's much better if the contractor explicitly represents this idea in the bid.) In the absence of any **exculpatory clause** that would otherwise make the contractor completely responsible for any **unforeseen conditions** under the surface, a bidder is entitled to rely on the accuracy of owner-issued information in computing its bid.

Actual Knowledge

In such cases, the contractor's general experience should have nothing to do with the determination of this outcome. However, if the contractor can be shown to have had *specific actual knowledge* that conditions in the site did in fact differ materially from those represented in the contract, the bidder would have had an absolute duty to disclose the superior **knowledge** to the owner. Refer to **patent errors** and **knowledge** for related discussion.

Conclusion

Without the demonstration of the bidder's actual knowledge of differing conditions, and without the presence of an enforceable **exculpatory clause** which would otherwise require the contractor to be entirely responsible for conditions under the surface which differ materially from those indicated in the contract, a bidder's *general knowledge* of the area with respect to subsurface conditions should have no bearing on the responsibility for a changed condition.

Refer to **exculpatory clauses** and **unforeseen conditions** for important related discussion.

Surprise

Overrated Tactic

There are definitely a certain number of people out there who believe that surprise is a good way to keep an opponent off balance, to negotiate, and to keep the pressure on. We have all been caught by surprise many times, and it absolutely does antagonize, intimidate, and upset us all—at least for a short period of time.

We were surprised at Pearl Harbor. Initially, we were scared, but then we got mad—fast. Anger turned into determination, which solidified an intense purpose. That driven purpose resulted in the sound defeat of Japan.

On balance, surprise may be an effective tactic for an immediate, short-term gain. While it may be a useful tactic in certain circumstances as part of an overall program, as a general strategy, it might be very overrated. If you are the one initiating the surprise, you will stand a greater chance of angering and then galvanizing your opponent against you than in bringing any negotiation or problem resolution to any cooperative level.

Types of Surprises

Before you can effectively respond to a surprise, consider the various types of surprises that you may find yourself subjected to:

1. **Authority** and lack-of-authority surprises

2. **Detail** or lack-of detail surprises

3. **Expert** surprises, such as the appearance of prominent specialists

4. Information surprises, such as new data, statistics, new rules, strange answers, and new sources of information or authority

5. Issue surprises, such as new demands, position changes, risk changes, argument changes, and position reversals

6. Action surprises, such as delays, recesses, walkouts, emotional outbursts, interruptions, and power displays

7. One-upsmanship surprises, such as "disbelief," personal attacks on **integrity** and intelligence, and displays of distrust

8. **Time** surprises, such as changes, new **deadlines,** and the need to work all night or through the weekend

Result

Surprises create distress and antagonism. They block communication, and force people into competitive, galvanized positions, as opposed to moving people closer to cooperative attitudes. Surprises invariably cause one person to look unprepared.

If you are ready for the potentially unpleasant responses to your surprises, you may find yourself having won a battle. If this happens, do not be complacent. Don't expect it to happen again soon. In fact, prepare yourself to then deal with an entire organization that has become determined to not allow you to do it again.

When you find yourself being the target of a surprise, look for ways to turn the events around. Give yourself time to think. Listen, and offer as little new information as possible, at least initially. Train yourself to avoid responding to issues until you are thoroughly prepared. If you are presented with a surprise, consider calling foul. Let the surpriser know that the new information has created other issues which must now be considered. Look for ways to interrupt the negotiation, and dilute the surprise.

Telephone Negotiations

Best Use

Telephone negotiations will work for the party who is prepared and will most often place the unprepared party at a decided disadvantage. Negotiate over the phone only if you have to, if circumstances lead you to believe it would be advantageous, and if you are certain that you are entirely prepared.

Characteristics

Certain characteristics of a telephone negotiation that you should be aware of include:

1. The caller has the advantage of surprise.

2. The person called is usually disorganized. He or she has to find a pen, calculator, file, and notes.

3. Phone calls usually come when the person being called is busy and is preoccupied with other things.

4. Some categories of information can't be given as proof, or otherwise verified. Fax machines have altered this dramatically, but the effect is still there in varying degrees.

5. Callers cannot see each other's reactions.

6. It is more difficult to gain complete understanding.

7. Presentation materials generally cannot be used, or cannot be used effectively. While it is possible to distribute copies that you can go over, there will be a definite communication gap.

8. There is usually less time to think. Phone conversations are usually hurried along.

9. It's less difficult for the other party to say no if he or she doesn't have to look at your face.

10. There is no way of determining who is really privy to your conversation. Not only can you not tell who is standing next to your

caller, but with the improvements in telephone technology, it's even becoming difficult to be aware of when you are actually on a speakerphone.

Dos and Don'ts

Follow the suggestions below in order to keep yourself at maximum advantage in a telephone negotiation situation:

1. If you are called, get the full story. Then call back.

2. The less you talk, the more the other person will.

3. Take detailed notes.

4. Confirm agreements promptly in your own words.

5. Confirm all agreements and significant statements with a written letter, memorandum, or fax.

6. Have an excuse handy to end the call.

7. Make a checklist to avoid omissions.

8. Do not conclude a telephone conversation unless you completely understand it and you have prepared and confirmed your position.

9. If, after thinking about an agreed deal, it begins to look bad, or you have discovered an error, immediately call back.

10. If necessary, qualify your conclusion. Advise the other party at the conclusion of your negotiation that you believe you understand in total, but if anything occurs to you further, you will call back. Leave the conversation with the understanding that you expect the opportunity to reopen the issue after further consideration.

Termination by Contractor

Contract Provision

This section is a reciprocal of, and very closely related to, **termination by owner**; refer there for important related discussion.

Government contracts will incorporate not only a termination by owner provision, but also one that allows termination of the contract by the contractor for various specific circumstances. Private construction agreements, however, may be another matter entirely. In this category, most will go on to include a "termination by owner" provision, but many somehow neglect to include a reciprocal provision providing for the particular circumstances by which the *contractor* may terminate the agreement.

Look for these kinds of inconsistencies in your construction agreements. If you find them, they may not only indicate the lack of treatment of the particular subject, but more important, may also show that a one-sided approach has been taken to drafting the agreement.

Justifications

The common justifications for termination of a contract by a contractor are implicitly reasonable. As such, the reasons—at least in general concept—are most often relatively easy to transcend. The purposes, then, for clarifying the criteria in a contract clause are to define each specific reason, and, more important, to assign specific time limits, dollar limits, or other criteria which narrow the descriptions to clearly unmistakable events. Remove the subjectivity, and reduce each evaluation to arithmetic, and you might leave yourself with a clear catalog of specific triggering events.

Typical reasonable justifications to allow a contractor to terminate an agreement include:

1. The work is stopped for a period of 30 days, through no fault of the contractor.

2. The work is stopped for a period of 14 days because of the presence of hazardous materials not specified in the contract.

3. A court order or public authority having jurisdiction for an act of government, such as declaration of national emergency, makes material unavailable.

4. The design professional has failed to issue a certificate of payment, and has not provided adequate or proper cause.

5. The owner has not made payment on a certificate for payment within the time stated in the **contract documents.**

6. Repeated suspensions, delays, and interruptions constitute in the aggregate more than a certain percentage (say 100 percent of the total number of days scheduled for completion), or some other significant total (say 90 days) in any 365 days.

Beyond these reasons, an often-overlooked justification for termination by the contractor is failure by the owner to provide the contractor reasonable evidence that sufficient financial arrangements have been made to fulfill the owner's continuing obligations under the contract, including provisions for all currently identified changes and even claims. This requirement, perhaps more than the others, is more likely to be a specific contract provision, and not one of the implied variety.

If you can manage to get these written requirements clearly incorporated into your agreement, your termination provision should go on to clarify that if *any* of the above reasons exist, the contractor may terminate within some reasonable period of time (say, three additional days).

Permission by Contractor

By written notice to the owner, citing defects in owner performance or in the contract, as described in the previous subsection, the contractor may, in lieu of termination, suspend the work until the defects are corrected. In such event, if it is conducted properly, the contractor should be entitled to recover from the owner as provided by your **change clause** or **dispute clause.** If the work, however, is suspended or stopped for such justifiable cause, and the contractor follows through with proper termination of the agreement, the contractor should maintain the right to recover from the owner payment for work executed, together with all losses with respect to materials, equipment, tools, and construction equipment provided to the point of termination, including related overhead, profit, and damages.

Increase the Power of the Provision

In your own contracts, try to increase the power of your termination provision by closely coordinating it with other relevant provisions of your contract. Refer to **title to materials** for very important related discussion.

Beyond that, you might consider including a provision in your own agreements specifying that, if the work is suspended or terminated for reasons beyond the control of the person entering the contract, then the contractor maintains the right to enter, at its convenience, the premises on which the subject materials, equipment, supplies, and other components of work are installed or stored, and take immediate possession of and remove all or any part of those items for which payment has not been made by the owner. The provision can then go on to provide that the owner should even reimburse the contractor for all cost and expenses associated with the retaking of the equipment, including rehandling, storage, disposal, freight, legal fees, and any other associated cost.

Adding this kind of punch to a basic termination provision can leave you with significant added ammunition that might work to put you in a better position to either finally work out your differences, or maximize your final position in any eventual litigation or **arbitration.**

Termination by Owner

A Risky Decision

A private owner's decision to terminate a construction contract because of contractor default is a difficult one on both legal and business grounds. It is usually made in the context of disappointment with a project that is not progressing according to certain expectations, however naive or realistic those expectations might be. The owner's disappointment is usually met with corresponding disappointment on the part of the contractor, who might in fact be dealing with a bad design, cost extras, and other effects on the project. Maybe the contractor is being given inadequate attention, or a set of circumstances beyond the contractor's control is somehow being blamed on the contractor.

For sure, an owner's consideration for terminating for default is one of very high stakes. If the project is terminated, the work will be further significantly delayed and disrupted. Final completion costs will run into low orbit. Finally, the situation as it will ultimately be reviewed in litigation or arbitration will be under the most intense scrutiny, with the acknowledgment that the impact on the project was significant, with a potentially devastating effect of a termination on a contractor's entire business. The entire situation will not at all be taken lightly.

Shifting the Balance

Even if an owner believes that it is justified in terminating a construction contract for default, because of a material or substantial breach of the contract on the part of the contractor, certain considerations may tilt the balance against termination—even where such material default on the part of the contractor does exist, and the termination appears to be correct. Questions regarding issues such as whether or not the breach was "material," whether procedures set forth in the contract were explicitly followed, and whether the contractor can document material breaches on the part of the owner all add up to a condition where such a termination action by the owner may not only be invalid, but may actually put the owner itself into a material breach of the contract.

When an arbitration panel or a court considers a case of termination for default, focus on all aspects of the termination is very intense, because the stakes are so high. An owner who improperly terminates a contractor for default breaches the contract itself, and should be liable to the contractor for the significant damages normally attributable to such a significant breach. While it is true that any contractor who is found to have been properly terminated for default will be liable to the owner for damages attributable to the breach, any contractor who has been working hard in good faith, documenting its efforts clearly, and really was dealt a bad hand with a bad contract, bad design, and bad job conditions may be able to paint a very clear picture of unjust and improper actions on the part of the owner.

Effects of a Termination

Correctly viewed, a termination does not terminate the contract, but stops the terminated party's right to proceed with work under the contract. A terminated contractor loses the right to continue with the work and, thereby, the right to any profit on work not completed. The owner disavows any obligation to permit the contractor to continue with the work and to pay the contractor for future work. Beyond this basic idea, most contracts today also permit the owner to withhold payments of amounts otherwise earned, although such earned amounts must be credited to the contractor's account.

Grounds for Contractor Termination

Although contract forms certainly differ, their catalogs of specific grounds for termination of a contractor follow very similar guidelines. The degree to which contracts elaborate on each principle varies, but the basic grounds are summarized as follows:

1. Failure to meet a completion date
2. Failure to pursue some adequate means of progress
3. Failure to pay subcontractors and suppliers
4. Guilty of some other material breach

The federal acquisition process provides certain procedures for the government's contracting officers to follow when they consider a termination for default. The instructions might well be considered by private owners in their own evaluations of any reasonableness of the termination action. The regulations identify the following as "factors in determining whether to terminate a contractor for default":

1. The terms of the contract and applicable laws and regulations
2. The specific failure of the contractor and the excuses for the failure
3. The availability of the supplies or services from other sources
4. The urgency of the need for the supplies or services, and the period of time to obtain them from other sources, as compared with the time delivery that would be compared from the delinquent contractor
5. The degree of essentiality of the contractor in the government acquisition program and the effect of a termination for default on the contractor's ability as a supplier under the other contracts
6. The effect of a termination for default on the ability of the contractor to liquidate guaranteed loans, progress payments, or advance payments
7. Any other pertinent facts and circumstances

The factors above illustrate the degree to which the owner's exercise of its termination option must be tempered by a profound respect for the actual net effects on both the project and the contractor.

Defenses to Termination

There are a number of procedural and substantive defenses that a contractor may use to defend against a termination for default. Like any defense, the validity of any action will depend on the facts of the situation, but the following might be considered:

1. Any notice by the owner regarding default, termination, or cure fails to satisfy the specific terms of the contract.
2. Contractual time limit for notice and cure, time allowed between cure notice and notice of default, or some other significant time limit has not been observed.
3. Delays are justified by changes to the contract, changed conditions, **force majeure** events, constructive actions by the design professionals or the owner, or other causes of delay that will ultimately be recognized under the terms of the contract or at law.
4. Nonpayment by the contractor to subcontractors has in fact been the result of the contractor exercising its legitimate rights pursuant to its subcontract agreements for nonperformance, while it has been taking steps to correct such performance deficiencies.

5. Progress with the work and/or completion of the contract is technically or commercially impractical to a substantial degree.

6. Completion of the contract depends on some specific action (such as submittal approval or timely payment) of the owner or its agents which has not been forthcoming or has otherwise been delayed.

7. Completion of the contract will not result in a product that conforms to the plans and specifications. This defense is very questionable, however. The Court of Claims has stated that "an experienced contractor cannot rely on government prepared specifications where...he knows or should know that the prepared specifications could produce the result...." Refer to **patent errors** for related discussion.

Three Schedules:
As-Planned, As-Built, and Adjusted

Contents

"Adjusted Schedule" Analysis

Simplified Example

Real-World Scenario

Related Topics

Acceleration

Bar Charts

CPM/PDM Schedules

Delay

Logic Diagrams

No Damages for Delay

Scheduling

Weather Delay

"Adjusted Schedule" Analysis

The purpose of making any distinction among the three schedules—as-planned, as-built, and adjusted—is to develop a mechanism that will separate the effects of one party on the performance of a contract from all the other complications of the project record.

The principle is to isolate all those impacts in a project caused by a single party and remove them from the contemporaneous schedule analysis. If accomplished correctly—and as supported by the project record—the result will be a determination of the theoretical date that the project would have been completed by, had the particular effects of the party being considered not been a factor. All other project effects would remain in the analysis.

This analysis is done by a simple but specific procedure. It boils down to:

1. Determining the as-planned schedule: the original, detailed plan to construct the project as it was bid.

2. Developing the as-built schedule: that schedule which accurately represents all the effects on the project by all parties—as they actually occurred.

3. Determining the adjusted schedule: a recalculation of the as-built schedule, with the effects of the offending party *removed*.

Simplified Example

Consider a schedule of 100 days' duration. Throughout each schedule update, you have correctly included the effects of two change orders, a subcontract delay that was known to everyone, and a problem with the delay in your own material for a certain activity. In these cases, the effects of all the circumstances are properly represented on the construction schedule contemporaneously, and distributed as part of the regular schedule update. The project is delayed, through the combined fault of three parties—yourself, your subcontractor, and the owner.

In determining the amount of time attributable to the owner as a consequence of the change, revisit those schedule updates that incorporate the two change orders. Recalculate the schedule updates leaving every other documented effect in the schedule, but *removing the change orders as if they had never existed.* The result would be your "adjusted schedule." It will be a display of the project the way it would have been if the influences of the owner had not been a factor. As such, this very clear demonstration realistically and accurately reassigns the true value of time correctly attributable to a single party.

Real-World Scenario

In a real-world scenario, the process is identical to that described in the simplified example above. With even basic scheduling software, such an analysis is straightforward and fairly easy to complete. The only difference between a real-world scenario and the simplified example above is in the number of activities dealt with. The logic is sound, and the procedure is the same. The degree of success will be rooted only in the degree of accuracy in the individual insertions of the project effects. To the extent that you have been able to maintain this accuracy, and to the extent that you have been fair in representation of all project effects, your final determination of your adjusted schedule will be clear, logical, and accurate.

Time

Owner Warranty

When the time to complete a contract is stipulated in the **contract documents,** the owner implicitly warrants that the project can, in fact, be completed in a logical manner (without extreme measures) within that stated duration. A contractor therefore has the right that, barring an obvious or glaring deficiency (refer to **patent errors** for related discussion), the work can be planned and executed in reasonable sequences and that the company will be off the site by the time that the specified period is up.

Conditions either inherent in the design, or that have changed between the time of bid and the time of contract execution or site start, may, however, create some difficulty with the stated time requirement. If, for example, the contract duration is 60 days, and you subsequently discover after the execution of your contract that the specified boiler will take 90 days for delivery, there is a very good chance that you would not be held responsible for the additional time.

Another example: Although the boiler *is* deliverable within the 60 days, a logical construction sequence dictates that the boiler be installed before some other construction (such as the roof) can logically proceed. It is interesting in this type of situation that, in any other circumstance, you as a contractor would very quickly be held responsible to identify and properly deal with such necessary construction sequences. "You should have known better. ..."

Dealing with Delay

Many times, however, the issue may not be as clear as a single long-lead-item delay. More often, it will involve schedule **logic diagram** sequences and/or activity relationships with effects that could not be apparent to the contractor at the time of bid. Because of the complexity of the real-world scenario, the success of any time-increase application will depend directly on your ability to demonstrate reasonable, competent, and accurate **scheduling** logic, and to provide a mechanism that will incorporate all changed information in a way that will display clearly and definitely a direct cause-effect relationship resulting in the extension of time.

A complicated and confusing **CPM/PDM schedule** and its updates by themselves might not be enough. It may not be clear enough or well enough understood to convince approving authorities that it really is the construction reality, not just a scheduling technician's sophisticated abstraction. Although the CPM schedule may actually be an important basis to support your argument on technical merits, look for other ways to convincingly demonstrate that direct cause-effect. Consider the particular owner's level of sophistication and disposition, and willingness to consider your arguments.

Response Guidelines

Proper response boils down to securing complete **documentation** from the best available sources. From that point, a convincing demonstration of cause-effect is absolutely essential. In order to accomplish these objectives:

1. Be sure that your files are complete, correct, and up-to-date.

2. Confirm all circumstances relating to the contract time, contract award date, contract start date, and any approved extensions in the contract award or start dates.

3. Outline each item interfering with the contract time. Confirm all details for yourself in appropriate detail.

4. Confirm all in-house circumstances. Nail down the facts that:

   - You ordered the time at the earliest possible opportunity
   - The submittals were processed (in both directions) as expeditiously as possible
   - The delivery time required before schedule interruptions has been confirmed from the best source

5. Immediately secure written certifications from the highest authorities possible in the companies whose products and services are creating the interferences. Confirm either that better deliveries are not at all possible, or that there will be additional costs or other circumstances for better delivery, if such better delivery is possible. Be sure to secure the reasons for each case in sufficient detail. Get the information from the highest level possible. The gravity of the situation will help define the organizational level from which such documentation should be secured.

6. Notify the owner and/or design professionals. Concisely describe the problem and the reasons for it. From that point, you might consider either (a) recommending some other product, design, or alternative that may be available that *will* allow you to meet the original time requirement or (b) calculating the resulting increase in time, and advising the owner.

Time and Material (T&M)

Use

Time and material (T&M) is a pricing option for changes that is most often provided for in a contract's **change clause.** From the perspective of the party performing the work, there is reduced opportunity for achieving any wide profit margins through performance, but this potential for higher profit is given up in consideration of the significantly reduced risk in performing the work. From the other party's perspective, T&M is a blank check. Because T&M apparently eliminates the need for the T&M contractor to be as closely concerned with crew composition, productivity, and so on, than would be the case in a hard-dollar, lump-sum situation, sustained production efficiency becomes the major issue as far as the payer is concerned. The amount of supervision, verification, and regular review generally required by the party who is writing the check can accordingly be disproportionate to the amount of work in question if efficiency is to be controlled. But if this kind of effort is not put into reviewing and verifying the T&M work, there can be major questions as to whether the work was actually performed with sufficient levels of efficiency. For these reasons, it is generally far more effective (from the payer's perspective) to resolve all the details of a change beforehand and agree on a final price before allowing changed work to begin.

Improving T&M Control

There are, however, situations in which allowing a contractor to proceed under a T&M arrangement (or if you're a contractor, allowing a subcontractor to proceed under T&M) may be unavoidable. In such cases, there are precautions that can be taken to improve your control over an otherwise potentially unclear situation. The method boils down to ensuring complete record keeping, regular verification, and continual review of productivity.

Verification Procedure

Follow the suggestions below to keep control over a contractor (or subcontractor) from which you've ordered the performance of T&M work:

1. *"Daily" means* daily.   A 2-inch stack of T&M tickets presented near or at the end of T&M work is impossible to decipher with any degree of accuracy. Even if you've kept your own meticulous records, the process would be tedious and error-prone. In contrast, requiring the T&M performer to present T&M tickets *every day* will prompt your own people into doing the reviews and completing the procedures on a current basis. Include a requirement in your own contracts and subcontracts, and notify the T&M performer that T&M tickets that have not been signed off *on the day that the T&M work was performed* will *not* be recognized as an additional expense.

2. *Hourly verification.*   If multiple items are being billed on a T&M basis, or if the same individuals and equipment are being used concurrently on contract work, verify the total number of hours billed for a given person or piece of equipment on a given day. Try to identify those instances where the change plus contract time spent apparently exceeds the total time spent for a given day. Find these mistakes or abuses early, in order to straighten out chronic abusers.

3. *Labor and equipment classification verification.*   Verify that the wage rates and equipment rates included in a T&M billing correspond to the actual verifiable rates that should be charged.

4. *Overhead and profit application.*   Your contracts should specify overhead and profit rates allowed for every type of change. If for some reason they do not, determine if any precedent has been set, or if there is some other way to confirm the reasonably expected amounts. Different rates of overhead and profit might apply to the straight-time and overtime portions of extra work. If so, verify that these rates are being properly applied throughout the T&M billing. Refer to **pass-through clause** for related discussion.

5. *Photographs.*   Film and photos remain the cheapest investment that any company can make, and carry with them the probability of significant returns on such investment. In every situation involving any question whatsoever, develop the habit in your own people to immediately photograph any item *potentially* subject to question. If the particular problem or issue is significant, consider arranging for a professional photographer to document the facts. See **documentation** and **photographs** (**progress** and **special**).

6. *Early evaluation of production rates.*   As soon as is reasonable after the start of T&M work, review the actual production rates against those rates that you can reasonably expect. Small liberties taken by the T&M performer at the start can be put back into perspective quickly. Significant chronic abuse, however, must be dealt with early and decisively. If you feel that the T&M tickets presented for your signature are excessive (or aggressive), try to first resolve the problem at that level. Do not allow any further T&M work to proceed

under any circumstances, unless you are prepared to follow through on the hard work of *continuous* evaluation and verification.

Submission Perspectives

When presenting your own time and material tickets to a client, it is important to be aware that your client has the same concerns about you as those that you have about your own subcontractors. Owners can experience the same feelings of loss of control. T&M tickets are difficult to check, the work has to be watched closely, and the totals always seem to add up to values greatly exceeding those originally expected (or hoped for). Your client may perceive you as operating without any risk at all, and therefore without any motivation to complete the item with any appearance of cost efficiency. The results of all this can range from simple bad feelings about the whole arrangement, to delays in **change order** approval, and an ultimate dispute over the T&M components, procedure, and **unit price contract.**

Consider your long-term relationship with a particular client before moving ahead too quickly with T&M—as opposed to lump sum—for changed work.

T&M as Confirmation Procedure

The T&M procedure can be used in those instances where you are forced into the position to perform work in which either the responsibility for certain work is not clear, or in which you have been directed to proceed at no additional cost with work that you definitely believe is in addition to your contract. If circumstances lead you to determine that it is in your overall best interest to proceed with such work pending a final decision or in anticipation of a later claim, use T&M tickets and the T&M procedure to keep accurate and indisputable records.

Approach your opponent, and advise the individual that you do consider the subject work at this point an addition to your contract. Accordingly, you are now only concerned with accurate **documentation.** Further advise the individual responsible for inspection of the project that you will be keeping your T&M records as a means of accurate verification of work performed, and recognize at this point that your opponent is not considering the subject work to be extra. Under these circumstances, go on to request that your client regularly (daily?) provide a signature on your T&M tickets as a means of verification of work performed only, and not as any authorization at this point of extra work.

If you can actually secure such confirming signatures, you will overcome a major subsequent hurdle in ultimate verification of the facts of performance. If the other party refuses to sign such verifications of actual work performed, consider sending some kind of letter or other written documentation to the client that you have offered such service strictly as a means of verifying the accuracy of information, and that your client refuses to participate. Ultimately, this history of your communication (or efforts to communicate) may go a long way in supporting your own contention that your work has been reasonable and efficient, that you have made every effort to involve your opponent in the verification of work performed, and that the work was in fact performed as efficiently as possible. In an extreme case, you might consider still presenting the T&M tickets each day, then noting on *each ticket* the refusal by your opponent to even consider the performance facts. It should then be clear to whoever will ultimately decide the issue that not only have you nothing to hide, but also your opponent has refused to consider the information that you've regularly tried to bring to its attention for confirmation.

Time Management

Benefits

Time is managed along two lines: (1) increasing efficiency by refining your own management techniques in order to increase output for a given period of time and (2) working smarter by learning to become effective in your movements, delegating, and employing the skills of others in order to increase your own work output. Throughout it all, it is important to allow time for other activities that you enjoy doing. Attention to this area will reduce stress on your system and in turn will improve your total operating efficiency.

Tips and Techniques

Follow the suggestions below to help you squeeze more into your day:

1. Develop observation skills. Observe intently what is going on around you. Improve your ability to get clear, accurate impressions that will increase the odds of correct initial responses.

2. Improve your capacity for observation and quick decision making by increasing your alertness, energy level, knowledge base, and experience. Read, listen to tapes, and attend seminars on topics relevant to your work.

3. Increase your alertness by overcoming any natural tendencies to become preoccupied. Change your routines. Practice daily a relevant skill that interests you. Cultivate new interests centered on observation.

4. Improve your energy levels by eliminating personal criticism, defensiveness, and other negative effects that drain your own energy and attention. Become aware of those times that you lose energy by establishing times during the day to check on your own activities at all levels. Establish and maintain an exercise pro-

gram to improve levels of overall physical fitness and stamina. (Refer to **health** for related discussion.) Use the creative power of sleep; the more demands you make on yourself, the more sleep you will probably need.

5. Give attention every day to expanding your knowledge and experience, and increase your managerial skills.

6. When you can't find an answer, stop. Let the problem cool. Save time by restating the problem and observing it from a different angle.

7. Understand that talking is more than just transmitting words. Speak with your whole body. Using your own words as you explain your problem to another often leads you to flow directly to an answer that you've been searching for in your own mind.

8. Use language with precision. Don't talk in circles. Avoid the possibility of confusion resulting from unnecessary details.

9. Be sure that you understand statements made by others by restating the concept in your own words to get a "yes" response.

10. Take the responsibility to be sure that others completely understand *you* before proceeding to the next step.

11. Draw diagrams and pictures to confirm your own understanding, or to confirm understanding and agreement in the minds of others.

12. Remember that one appropriate analogy is often worth more than hours of discussion.

13. It is not as important to be able to read rapidly as it is to be able to decide what not to read.

14. Set priorities. Decide what are the most important activities, and arrange your efforts specifically around them.

15. Organize your day. Have a definite game plan based on your priorities. Control interruptions. Don't let the "immediate" demands of your day interfere significantly with your plan. Become "now" oriented. Once you decide on an activity, *focus* your energy on it until it is completed or filed for future reference. Refer to **the zone** for important related discussion.

16. Delegate. Develop the skills to train others, and then depend on them. Use **delegation** as much as you possibly can.

17. Start with the tough jobs. Do the most important or challenging work early, when your energy levels are at their highest. Save busy work and errands for later, lower-energy periods.

18. Reduce meetings. Resolve as much as you can by phone. Send subordinates whenever possible. Schedule meetings to run up against the noon hour or the day's end in order to cut rambling. (Refer to **job meetings** for important related discussion.)

19. Avoid procrastination. The pressure of **deadlines** can create inefficiency, ineffectiveness, and rework if work is put off until near the end, but can also create a clear focus if the work is planned and done early.

Title to Materials

Contents

The Conventional Agreement

Returning Equity to the Relationship

Related Topics

"Conspicuous" Contracts

Lien Rights

Pay-When-Paid

Remedies

The Conventional Agreement

Most standard form owner-contractor agreements provide that the title for materials provided by the contractor pursuant to the agreement passes from the contractor to the owner at some point prior to final completion of the project. Some agreements may provide for such a transfer of title on delivery to the jobsite, and others stipulate that such a title transfer will occur on payment by the owner of the gross amount of the item as defined in the **schedule of values**—even though retainage will continue to be withheld. Beyond these basic criteria, the specific language of the written agreement may be entirely consistent with or may be subject to further modification by state statutes or other laws which may affect some detail of the title transfer. Even with such modifications, the situation is still not likely to differ significantly from that described here.

What all this means is that, if you as a contractor have furnished and installed materials pursuant to your construction agreement, and there is some significant problem that is either preventing you from completing the agreement or otherwise resulting in the nonpayment to you, your right to retake materials pursuant to your contract—even those items that have not been paid for—may not at all be clear. Worse yet, it might in fact be clear that you have no right to such an action, and if you pursue such retaking you might find yourself on the wrong end of criminal charges. As unfair as it may be, this type of situation can occur even where the contract is subject to termination, or in fact has been terminated, by the contractor for valid cause. Refer to the **power of the standard form** and **"conspicuous" contracts** for important related discussion.

Returning Equity to the Relationship

Whatever the language in your standard form contract, this title issue is one of those which seems to be glossed over in almost every contract negotiation. Instead of letting this happen, use the opportunity during the negotiation of a new contract, and certainly in the preparation of your own standard form of owner-contractor agreement, to ensure that you as a contractor will retain title of all materials provided until your receipt of payment in full—including retainage. Such a condition will usually place title transfer at final completion of the project, if that will be associated with retainage release. The major reason for providing for the proper title transfer only on full payment is to allow the contractor the right to legally retake the materials and equipment provided under the agreement if the work has been stopped for reasons not the fault of the contractor, or for other conditions that exist that clearly justify a contractor's termination for cause. Your owner-contractor agreement should therefore have its title clause include a clear right to the contractor to retake such equipment upon work stoppage or justification for contractor termination, and, in such event, also entitle the contractor to recover all its costs and expenses associated with such retaking of the material. These costs should include remobilizing, retaking, handling, storage, disposal, freight, legal fees, and all other associated costs.

Keep control over your materials and equipment, and you might have one more avenue that will help keep your final outcome as equitable as it can be under the circumstances.

Trade Practice

Contents

Definition

Application

Related Topics

Boilerplate

Contract versus Contact

Impossibility and Impracticability

Quality

Definition

Trade practice, sometimes referred to as *trade custom,* is defined by the Uniform Commercial Code as:

> ... any practice or method of dealing having such regularity of observance in place, vocation, or trade as to justify an expectation that it will be observed with respect to the transaction in question. (*UCC Sec. 1-205 2*)

Read the definition very carefully. The operative words are "having such regularity ... to justify an *expectation* that it *will be observed* ...."

The phrase is not ambiguous. Nowhere does it use language like "It is done that way most of the time," or "They usually do it that way around here." In practice, then, the test is simple: If trade practice is to be used as an argument, it must be demonstrated that the item is performed that way—*in every case.*

As anyone who has ever worked with lumber knows, a 2×4 stud is not 2 in $\times$ 4 in, but $1\frac{1}{2}$ in $\times$ $3\frac{1}{2}$ in. An 8-in concrete block is really $7\frac{5}{8}$ in, and so on. Practices and customs might seem unusual at first, but most often things eventually start to make sense. It is therefore necessary to clearly understand how items are discussed and what people really mean before a contract is interpreted in its literal condition.

Application

In applying trade practice to an issue, a contractor must demonstrate that the practice is followed with *absolute regularity*. It is not enough that it is "usually" done in a certain way.

The problem of absolute regularity is often compounded, and the issue is one of work responsibility, not one of work design. In almost every instance where a category of work is "unusually" incorporated into a certain specification section, trade practice alone is not likely to be an effective argument against the responsibility to perform the work as part of the specification section.

Finally, it is very important to realize that trade practice cannot be relied on to excuse a contractor from the performance of a requirement if that requirement is clear and subject to one **interpretation.** The idea of trade practice cannot be used to turn an interpretation into one that is unreasonable, illogical, or inconsistent.

Unforeseen Conditions

Right to Recovery

Historically, there is no inherent *right* for a contractor to recover costs and damages associated with extra work resulting from conditions that are either below the surface of the site or within some existing structure that was unexpected, and that could not be reasonably anticipated—that is, unforeseen conditions.

Beginning with the federal government, owners have theorized that the owner can avoid paying for unnecessary contingencies that become necessary on the part of a responsible bidder, by assuming at least a certain amount of risk associated with such unforeseen conditions. They have reasoned that a responsible contractor that understands that it is assuming the complete and total risk of all conditions that are unforeseen would have to provide enormous contingency estimates in its bid to cover such risks. If a contractor does not include such contingency, it risks losing the project—and the entire company—if significant unforeseen conditions are discovered. On the other hand, if the unforeseen conditions provided for by contingency do not occur, the owner is *not* uncomfortable with the resulting windfall to the contractor. And so most public and private contracts now contain specific clauses that provide for the right of the contractor to recover additional time and money for extra work resulting from the discovery of unexpected conditions. These clauses are often identified in title by "unforeseen conditions," "changed conditions," "concealed conditions," or "differing site conditions" clauses.

Type I and Type II Conditions

"Unforeseen conditions" clauses have evolved into fairly consistent language which addresses the two most common types of changed or unforeseen circumstances:

- Type I conditions are those which differ materially from those conditions that are specifically represented in the **contract documents.**

- Type II conditions are those which are unusual and unexpected; they would not normally be anticipated under the particular circumstances.

Contract Clauses and Components

The American Institute of Architects *General Conditions of the Contract for Construction* (document A201, 1976 and 1987 editions), the federal government's Standard Form 23-A, every state government form, and most municipal contract forms patterned after one or more of these documents contain similar language regarding unforeseen conditions.

The components of each clause typically include:

1. *Identification* of the subject: Conditions that are encountered at the site which are either subsurface or otherwise concealed.

2. *Nature* of the conditions. They must be of either the type I or the type II variety. They must be conditions which differ materially from those indicated in the contract documents, or which differ materially from those ordinarily found to exist and generally recognized as inherent in the "character" of the work. Under such conditions the contractor is entitled to additional compensation.

3. *A requirement* for the observing party to provide notice to the other party, usually before conditions are disturbed, and within some specifically restated time requirement.

4. A *procedure* for the owner or its representatives to investigate the conditions, confirm the situation, and determine appropriate action. If, after such investigation, the owner or its representatives does not agree with the contractor's contention that the conditions at the site are materially different, the contractor is entitled to a written conclusion, along with specific reasons.

5. A *time requirement* that narrows the contractor's window to submit its claim in opposition to any determination made by the owner or its representatives. Refer to **change clause** and **dispute clause** for important related discussion.

Disclaimers of Subsurface Information

Despite all the theories summarized above, the idea of unforeseen conditions has been approached in recent years from many contradictory angles. Almost no party other than government agencies really wants to consider any liability for risks associated with such conditions. The reasons are that such unforeseen conditions cannot be "blamed" on any party and, probably more important, such conditions can result in effects on the project—and the owner's budget—that are extreme.

Despite the inclusion of an unforeseen conditions or a differing site conditions clause in a contract, it has become increasingly common for the owners—particularly on private projects—to attempt to disclaim all responsibility for information regarding **subsurface site conditions** and **geotechnical information.** Yes, this approach appears at least on the surface to directly contradict the intent of the unforeseen conditions clause, and in the final analysis may be unenforceable, but a contractor must be aware of this practice and understand its effects. Refer to **exculpatory clauses** for important related discussion.

The intention of disclaimer clauses on subsurface information is actually to relieve the owner from any liability associated with information that it provided as part of the bid documents. The enforceability—or lack of it—is the basis for a confusing debate, one that has to date been determined largely in favor of the contractor, but perhaps not for long.

Dangers of Missing Clauses

Yes, it is true that contractors have recovered costs associated with differing site conditions even though there was no differing or unforeseen site conditions clause present in the contract. However, this situation is risky, the law is inconsistently applied, and the decision subject to many other arguments in the final analysis.

Without specific presence of such a clause, courts have decided cases more or less this way: "By the provisions of the contract, the plaintiff was required and *expected* to examine the site, and to investigate the site itself as to the subsurface conditions to be encountered. Also, it is required to estimate correctly the difficulties involved with the performance of the work. Whether or not the investigation made by the plaintiff was adequate, *it assumed all the risks and hazards of the project when it submitted its bid.* The owner should not be placed in a position of encouraging careless bids by contractors who might anticipate that, should conditions differ from optimistic expectations reflected in the bids, the owner would bear the cost of the bidder's error."

This type of attitude is in huge contrast with the original theories that form the basis of the intention of the unforeseen conditions or differing site conditions clause in the first place. Add to this the **exculpatory clauses,** specifically the disclaimers of subsurface information, and you might have a potential mix for a disaster if unforeseen conditions are encountered.

Unit Price Contracts

Unit Prices

Unit prices can be included in the prime contract, or the general contractor can incorporate them into the subcontract agreements. They can be put there to remove at least a portion of the uncertainty attached to an item's definition, the method of calculation, and the price itself for a unit of completed work. The objective in including unit prices is to add certainty to the consideration of possible additions and/or corrections that have a good probability to come up. Having such prices established at the time of the original bid (if you are the contractor), or in the preparation of a subcontract, would make it very easy for you to evaluate the cost of potential changes, and to secure final approval of price once the scope of work has been confirmed and approved.

Level of Detail

Refer to **detail** for important related discussion. It is interesting to note that there seems to be an inverse correlation between the final size and complexity of any unit price "substantiation" and the likelihood that any individual component will be objected to. In other words, the greater the level of detail in representing the individual components that will result in a particular unit price, the greater the probability that you will be able to make the final unit price appear "reasonable." In addition, it is usually easier to secure approval for a large number of small items than it is for a small number of large ones. All psychology aside, these correlations have been proved in the final test over and over again. Realize right at the start that no one but you can visualize the true complicated sequence of events in all its excruciating detail, with all its interferences and inconveniences. Take the time to describe that detail, and you will improve the odds of maximizing your ultimate price.

Unit Prices and Unit Price Contracts

The unit prices provided in a lump-sum contract as a basis of arriving at the lump sum may be there as a convenient description, or as a billing mechanism (refer to **schedule of values**). As a very practical matter, it may be desirable for you to use them to substantiate changes to the contract. As a technical matter, however, you are under no *obligation* to use those unit prices. In contrast, a *unit price contract* is specifically designed so that the unit prices *will* specifically be used as a basis to adjust the contract. The final component for such adjustment will be a confirmed field measurement of the particular units in place. Refer to **as-built documents** for important related discussion.

Changing the Unit Price

And so the unit price contract "clearly" specifies that the particular unit prices will be in effect for the duration of the project, and will be specifically used as *the* basis for adjusting the contract for changes involving the respective items of work. As clear as this language may appear to be on the surface, in the words of New York attorney Max Greenberg: "It ain't necessarily so."

Understand at the outset that the unit prices included in your bid and in the contract were provided by your company through a particular understanding of the requirements of the items of work. If the conditions of the changed work are different from those anticipated in the preparation of the unit prices, and are different than those that could be reasonably inferred or anticipated in the preparation of such unit prices for changed work, you may very likely have a legitimate basis for revisiting those unit prices. You may be able to demonstrate that because the conditions are materially different from those actually used in the preparation of your unit price, the particular unit price is not applicable for this specific circumstance. Use the concept described in **detail** to describe those components of the new unit price that were not considered in the original price.

Don't get mesmerized by your schedule of values in a lump sum contract, or even by the unit prices in your unit price contract. Consider the specific issue with the current set of circumstances. Determine whether the particular issue is or is not within the realm of the original contemplation of your unit price. Don't be satisfied accepting unit prices that no longer apply.

Value of Work—Actual Cost

Contents

Value of Work Performed

Actual Costs

Related Topics

Change Clause

Dispute Clause

Schedule of Values

Time and Material (T&M)

Unit Price Contracts

Value of Work Performed

The courts in a number of locations have rendered decisions regarding the value of work performed. In repeated instances, the principle seems to hold that, although it might be true that someone else could possibly perform the work for less money and that your own forces are not fully efficient, it is still you who performed the work in good faith, and it is therefore your costs that will establish the value.

In other situations, the cost of the work itself may not be the only measure of the value of the work. If, however, a contractor realizes a special benefit to the performance of the work, the contractor should be entitled to retain that benefit.

Actual Costs

In both litigation and arbitration, rulings and awards have consistently concluded that if conditions of the change are materially different than those in existence or reasonably anticipated in the preparation of unit prices incorporated into the contract, a contractor should be compensated on the basis of actual cost, and not on the original unit prices established in the contract.

In construction contracts, the **change clause,** the **dispute clause,** a differing site conditions clause, or some other provision may provide the owner with the option of compensating a contractor for changes at: (1) the bid unit prices, (2) an agreed lump sum, (3) the actual cost of performance, or (4) on a **time and material (T&M)** basis.

Such clauses are normally enforceable. In cases, however, where the extent of the changed conditions is so extreme that it could not have been contemplated by the contractor at the time of executing the agreement, it has been consistently held that in theory it is unconscionable to limit a contractor's recovery to those bid unit prices. In such cases, the equitable value would be based on the contractor's actual cost.

As is too often the case, the theory is easy, but the practical reality a bit more difficult. Reasonable people can easily understand the idea. A contractor's ability to prevail on the basis of the theory, however, depends on the facts of the situation, the ability to provide **documentation** for those facts, and the ability to clearly demonstrate why those conditions are so materially different from those that could have been anticipated under any circumstances.

Video, Preconstruction

Need

It's becoming increasingly desirable to supplement the preconstruction photo survey with a preconstruction video. Even if your company does not own a video camera, they are so readily available from individuals or by rental there is no excuse not to use one.

The preconstruction video is *not* a substitute for the preconstruction photographs. It is a supplement. Difficulties with the video lie principally in the limited ability to select and reproduce specific photographs for review and/or demonstration. A further difficulty is the difficulty of reviewing the video file to select a particular photo record. Conventional photographs allow one to flip through an album that's very closely correlated with field reports and the general project record. Videos, on the other hand, need to be reviewed sequentially.

The major advantage of the video is that the record picks up so much more on the tape than the photographer is actually observing at the time. It ties the photo survey together to clearly demonstrate the relationship of each area.

Procedure

Follow the guidelines of the section **photographs, preconstruction** to organize your approach and take the video as you would still photos. Additional recommendations to help produce an acceptable video include:

1. Walk slowly and hold the camera *steady*.

2. Proceed along a planned route. Pan the camera very slowly.

3. Narrate:
   - Start the tape with the complete project identification, date, photographer's name, and any other relevant information.
   - Identify the video as a preconstruction video produced specifically for the purpose of recording actual conditions of the site prior to commencement of physical work.

- Describe each view. Try to do so in a way that would allow a person unfamiliar with the site to locate the area, identify the point of view, and understand what the video screen shows. To this end, be aware of the background of the subject of the video: street signs and directions, curb lines, unique site features (ponds, hills, etc.), building or other structure locations, and any other items that would allow a viewer to locate on a drawing the photographer's location and direction of view.

4. Return the completed video to the home office for filing, to supplement the regular preconstruction photographs record file.

Contents

Definition

A *weather delay* is the delay experienced on the jobsite as a direct cause of rain, snow, or heavy wind. Simply the presence of the inclement weather does not by itself constitute a weather delay. If, however, the inclement weather affects activities on the project's critical path, the weather can justifiably be considered to have the delayed the project.

Whose Fault?

Most construction agreements place weather-related delays in the **force majeure** category. Weather is considered an act of God and is therefore the "fault" of neither party. With this consideration, most construction agreements go on to dutifully include the idea that such weather delays, being the fault of neither party, would justify an extension of time, but will not justify any compensation for that time extension—a noncompensible extension of time.

It's important at this point, however, to note that if the project is in an as-planned stage or, for reasons strictly the fault of the contractor, is in a delayed stage, then such straightforward, almost naive application of weather delay may in fact be appropriate.

If, however, the project has been delayed for reasons not the fault of the contractor, and so is in a condition that exposes the critical path activities of the project to such weather delays for reasons *not the fault of the contractor,* then the weather delays might be considered to be a consequential delay. In other words, if a prior delay to the project is the reason why the roof is not yet complete, the resulting effect of a weather delay on the building because the roof is not complete is actually part of the damages resulting from the delay in the roof. Such a cause-effect relationship can lift a weather delay out of the **force majeure** category, and put it into the *damages* category.

Quantification

The actual total delay to a project caused by weather impact can significantly exceed the original absolute value of the actual time of inclement weather. For example, if it rains for 4 hours in 1 day, the site can be left in the same condition as if it had rained for 14 hours. If the 4-hour rain leaves the site in an unworkable condition that interferes with the work, the entire day may be chargeable as a weather delay.

The effect may, however, be compounded. In certain climates and in certain site conditions, such a 4-hour rain may leave the site unusable and unworkable for several days before the work can continue. In such cases, the 4 hours of rain may in fact cause a net delay of the project of 2, 3, or even more days. These effects must be tracked and clearly documented if you are to realize them in your subsequent analysis, but the effects are real. Focus on the activities that have in fact been interrupted, and catalog the true effect of their inability to resume.

Contract Clarifications

Use any opportunity that you find during your contract negotiating stage to clarify how weather delays will be defined and applied to the contract. For example, a "rain delay" can be defined as the duration of rain on the site or the duration of the work delay on site as a result of rain occurring for 4 hours or more during a work day plus each day necessary for adequate drying of the site to allow work to proceed. Similar considerations can be given to snow or wind damage. If you have the opportunity, think it through and define the condition with clarity.

"What Do You Want to Do?"

The Best of Intentions

In doing their best to progress with the work as expeditiously as possible, contractors regularly encounter conditions at the site which are not represented in the documents, could not have been anticipated during the bidding process, and may or may not be the fault of a party to the contract. With the best of intentions, too many contractors are inclined to take action in varying degrees, ranging from determining a redesign (and assuming the liability for it); to performing changed work or added work at their own immediate expense, with questionable ability to recover an equitable value within some reasonable time frame; to performing the work while knowingly writing off the extra cost or having to deal with **surprise** that it did the work for free—at a later date.

In most such cases, it is not a situation where an opportunist contractor jumps on an extra item to put the owner into a corner with respect to increased payment. Instead, it is often a situation where the contractor—who is at the immediate point of impact—takes the initiative to move the work along, thereby minimizing the immediate interference and actually minimizing the ultimate net effect on the owner.

The "Opportunistic" Perspective

Even though the contractor in such cases can be said to have been operating in the utmost good faith, with the best intentions, and with only the benefit of the project in mind, the site, the contract, or the **contract documents** may be in a condition where these situations are occurring a bit more frequently than any party to the contract is comfortable with.

And so, in the interest of keeping its costs under control, the contractor "responsibly" finds itself regularly bringing these issues to the attention of the design professionals and the owner. Finally, in the interest of moving the thing along, the contractor is likely to end its presentation of the issue with a natural conclusion: the price for the extra work.

Even though this approach is equitable, responsible, and expeditious, the reality is that some owners begin to look at the contractor as opportunistic in its approach. Every time a contractor opens its mouth, it seems, it's "asking for an extra." Although probably unfair, it's a perspective that a contractor should be aware of.

The Six Magic Words

A better approach that a contractor should consider is really no different from the scenario described above, but involves a very subtle twist in the final outcome. The idea is simply that rather than immediately (aggressively?) following up on a problem identification with an immediate price, follow the procedure that you normally would as a responsible contractor, but then stop. Rather than follow up with an immediate price, impact analysis, or whatever, *stop*.

Once the item is identified, and clearly explained, use these magic words: "What do you want to do?" You might be amazed at the results. The owner might consider the issue with you in detail, or consider the issue in detail with its design professionals, or some combination. Throughout the process, the situation is transformed from a competitive one to a cooperative one. The situation moves from an owner-against-the-contractor one to an us-against-the-problem one. At the conclusion of the cooperative process, the owner may anxiously turn to you and *ask* you for a price for the optional scenarios developed in the cooperative analysis.

The difference is very subtle, but very powerful. You have transformed a relationship from one in which you would have been considered the antagonist/opportunist, to one where you are a member of the problem-solving team—in fact, the only member who can actually *solve* the problem to the ultimate benefit of the owner.

Zero-Defect Construction

Contents

Performance Criteria

Do It Right the First Time

Impossible Performance

Responsibility = Problems

Related Topics

Leadership

Never Say These Things

Quality

Performance Criteria

The *zero-defect* standard is a concept born in the defense industry. In a contract for the production of a ship-defense missile, the government imposed the zero-defect performance criterion. Eight thousand missiles were to be produced under the contract and delivered in 11 production lots. For a lot to pass, 31 randomly selected missiles had to be tested. If there was a single defect, the entire lot failed.

As a technical matter, this concept may ultimately have no place in the cryptic and confusing world of construction, but it can be useful in underscoring a general principle which we might apply as a practical matter for achieving certain performance standards within our organizations.

Do It Right the First Time

At every level of project management and site supervision within the construction company, it can often be demonstrated that any given individual might have responsibility to complete some workload that is simply beyond the number of hours in a day. We are all spread fairly thin.

The time pressure routinely steals from the complete treatment of too many issues. Too often, we just don't have the time to do it right the first time. We don't have enough time to perform the assignment properly and completely.

Somehow, however, we do find the time within the organization to do it again (in a reactive, corrective way) and even do it a third time. We involve higher levels of management to resolve problems created directly by the failure to bring closure to the issue at the original management level. We don't have enough time to do it once, but we do manage to have enough time to do it three times.

This is not a cliché in an effective project management class, but a serious reminder that, if a company is to remain profitable and control its liabilities, it must regularly approach assignments with the zero-defect performance standard as an ideal.

Impossible Performance

Given the things that certainly will go wrong with the construction contract—**defective specifications,** subcontract problems, **patent errors, subsurface site conditions,** and so on, it is clear to all of us as professionals that the odds are squarely stacked against a true achievement of a zero-defect performance to any measure. As a technical matter, then, I agree that, if we approach our jobs with the naive hope that we might actually achieve a zero-defect result, we are probably setting ourselves up for a serious disappointment. The point here, however, is that, although we can approach our jobs with the understanding that the odds are against us, it is no excuse to approach our jobs with resignation and an *expectation* that the projects will not be completed acceptably. We must understand the concept of "do it right the first time," accept the idea that failures in its application will be inevitable, and remember that the failures themselves are *unacceptable.* Be professional. Persist. Pick yourself up from the last performance failure, and approach the next assignment with a renewed anticipation for the zero-defect objective.

Responsibility = Problems

Finally, it is important to acknowledge the idea that the higher you move up a company ladder, the greater percentage of your job will be applied to dealing with exceptions to procedure and resolving problems. Presumably, you are moving up the ladder because you have judgment and capabilities above those of your subordinates. If this were not the case, business at every level would be reduced to simply following a routine, clearly established procedure for every business situation. To the degree that this is possible, each successive level of judgment would be removed from the performance.

Procedures never have and never will accommodate every situation. Procedures are established to deal with most situations in a given category, with the understanding that some level of authority will be present to deal with the inevitable exception to the procedure.

If you accept this fact of business management, accept the fact that as you rise up the ladder your job will be increasingly focused on solving the problems that all those below you cannot solve, and approach your job each day with this philosophy in mind, your stress level should reduce significantly, and your effectiveness in your position will increase exponentially.

The Zone

Contents

Related Topics

The Here and Now

Push the clock back to the 1989 Superbowl in Miami. The San Francisco 49ers are trailing the Cincinnati Bengals 16 to 13. With just over 3 minutes remaining in the game, the 49ers are sitting on their own 8-yard line, with nothing but real estate in front of them, and a very unfriendly clock. The chances for a winning touchdown or even a field goal don't look good.

But the main factor that is keeping the entire Cincinnati bench from even thinking about relaxing, even under these circumstances, is the fact that the San Francisco quarterback is Joe Montana.

Joe Montana is thought of as an individual with the ability to get in the "zone"—an ability that guarantees a championship performance no matter how intense the pressure, how poor the odds, or how great the challenge.

Performance in the Present

The zone is that state of mind in which the only time period of genuine concern is the *present*; there is no past, and there is no future. The zone is being able to maintain that state of focus in which you are able to perform at or above the maximum expectation that you've placed on yourself under the pressure of the moment.

Those rare individuals who truly understand the zone calmly rise to the occasion over and over again, and make it look easy. The relaxed but intense focus generates an intense concentration that efficiently keeps targeted on the necessary outcome. Details have a way of becoming less important. Problems are not looked at as major setbacks, but as temporary inconveniences.

I try to enter the zone when I am focusing on a business situation that needs an intelligent and insightful response. My wife enters the zone when she is shopping, another business situation that requires the same.

Not Reserved for Superstars

Let's go for a moment back to that night in Miami. Joe Montana is in the zone. Like a meticulous surgeon he calmly executes play after play marching his team toward the end zone. There is a penalty. Joe remains completely calm, focused, and in control. He completes a short pass for the touchdown, and San Francisco wins the Superbowl.

The zone might be easiest to recognize as we watch the performances of world-class athletes, but the zone is not reserved for these superstars. The zone is actually a state of mind that we have all been in at different points in our lives, whether we've realized it or not. The zone is a heightened mental state that we *can* achieve in business.

Getting in the Zone

Resist the first misconception about peak performance: that you must try your hardest and bear down in order to win. Instead, train yourself to settle down. Call for a time out. Refocus. Relax. Sometimes simply trying too hard will cause you to miss a cue, miss a point, and misdirect your energy. Anxiety will cause you to choke and fold.

Resist the second misconception about performance: that your reaction must be spontaneous. Don't confuse a rapid response with a hurried, poorly coordinated, and partially thought-out reaction. Don't mistake spontaneity for a reflexive action. When high-achieving and peak-performing individuals appear to be performing spontaneously, it's because of the training and practice that has gone on before to prepare for the situation at hand. At such a time, the individual is pushing his or her version of a playback button, collecting and repeating actions that have been developed and practiced with success in the past.

Work on your relaxed focus. This is not to be confused with any lack of intensity, but means that you've been able to clear your mind of distractions, and center your attention only on what is important *now*.